Imperium Press was founded in 2018 to supply students and laymen with works in the history of rightist thought. If these works are available at all in modern editions, they are rarely ever available in editions that place them where they belong: outside the liberal weltanschauung. Imperium Press' mission is to provide right thinkers with authoritative editions of the works that make up their own canon. These editions include introductions and commentary which place these canonical works squarely within the context of tradition, reaction, and counter-Enlightenment thought—the only context in which they can be properly understood.

IMPERIUM ANTHOLOGY OF ENGLISH VERSE

Introduction by
BENJAMIN AFER

PERTH
IMPERIUM PRESS
2023

Published by Imperium Press

www.imperiumpress.org

Introduction © Benjamin Afer, 2022
Used under license to Imperium Press

All rights are reserved. No part of this publication may be reproduced, stored in a retrieval system, or transmitted in any form or by any means, electronic, mechanical, photocopying, recording, or otherwise, without prior permission of Imperium Press. Enquiries concerning reproduction outside the scope of the above should be directed to Imperium Press.

FIRST EDITION

A catalogue record for this
book is available from the
National Library of Australia

ISBN 978-1-922602-70-1 Paperback
ISBN 978-1-922602-71-8 Hardcover
ISBN 978-1-922602-72-5 E-book

Imperium Press has no responsibility for the persistence or accuracy of URLs for external or third-party Internet websites referred to in this publication and does not guarantee that any content on such websites is, or will remain, accurate or appropriate.

CONTENTS

Introduction: The Majesty of Effect	xiii
Beowulf	3
From Sir Gawain and the Green Knight	6
WILLIAM LANGLAND	
From Piers Plowman	11
GEOFFREY CHAUCER	
From the General Prologue to the Canterbury Tales	21
ANONYMOUS BALLADS	
Robin Hood and the Monk	27
The Ballad of Sir Patrick Spens	38
The Twa Corbies	40
Edward, Edward	41
The Corpus Christi Carol	43
EDMUND SPENSER	
From The Faerie Queene	44
WALTER RALEIGH	
A Farewell to False Love	58
A Farewell to the Vanities of the World	59
A Vision upon the Fairy Queen	61
PHILIP SIDNEY	
Astrophil and Stella	61
Ye Goatherd Gods	63
WILLIAM SHAKESPEARE	
Sonnets	66
JOHN DONNE	
Death, Be Not Proud	68
No Man Is an Island	68

Ben Jonson
- A Fit of Rhyme Against Rhyme — 69
- An Ode to Himself — 70
- On Gut — 72
- On my First Son — 72
- The Sun Rising — 72

Robert Herrick
- To the Virgins, to Make Much of Time — 73

George Herbert
- Love (III) — 74
- Virtue — 75

John Milton
- Lycidas — 75
- On His Blindness — 81
- On the Late Massacre in Piedmont — 81
- *From* Paradise Lost — 82

Richard Lovelace
- La Bella Bona Roba — 104
- To Althea, from Prison — 105
- To Lucasta, Going to the Wars — 106

Andrew Marvell
- The Garden — 106
- To His Coy Mistress — 108

Alexander Pope
- *From* The Rape of the Lock — 110

Samuel Johnson
- London: A Poem — 118
- The Vanity of Human Wishes — 126

Thomas Gray
- Elegy Written in a Country Churchyard — 137
- The Bard: A Pindaric Ode — 141

William Blake
- Auguries of Innocence — 145
- Jerusalem — 149
- Mock on, Mock on, Voltaire, Rousseau — 150
- The Clod and the Pebble — 150

The Tyger	151

ROBERT BURNS
Comin Thro' the Rye	152
Tam o' Shanter	153
To a Mouse	159

WILLIAM WORDSWORTH
She Was a Phantom of Delight	161
The Solitary Reaper	162
The World Is Too Much with Us	163
Lines Composed a Few Miles above Tintern Abbey	164

SAMUEL TAYLOR COLERIDGE
Dejection: An Ode	169
Kubla Khan	173
The Rime of the Ancient Mariner	175

LORD BYRON
Darkness	195
From Don Juan	197
She Walks in Beauty	223

PERCY BYSSHE SHELLEY
Ode to the West Wind	224
Ozymandias	226
From Prometheus Unbound	227
To a Skylark	229

JOHN CLARE
Autumn	232
First Love	233

JOHN KEATS
La Belle Dame sans Merci	234
Ode on a Grecian Urn	235
Ode to a Nightingale	237
On First Looking into Chapman's Homer	239

THOMAS BABINGTON MACAULAY
Horatius at the Bridge	240

Henry Wadsworth Longfellow
- A Psalm of Life — 261
- *From* Evangeline, A Tale of Acadie — 263
- The Landlord's Tale: Paul Revere's Ride — 270

Edgar Allen Poe
- Annabel Lee — 274
- Eldorado — 275
- The Raven — 276

Alfred, Lord Tennyson
- Break, Break, Break — 281
- *From* In Memoriam A. H. H. — 281
- The Charge of the Light Brigade — 284
- The Lady of Shalott — 286
- Ulysses — 291

Robert Browning
- Childe Roland to the Dark Tower Came — 293
- My Last Duchess — 302

Walt Whitman
- O Captain! My Captain! — 303
- The Dalliance of the Eagles — 304

Emily Dickinson
- Because I could not stop for Death — 305
- Tell all the truth but tell it slant — 306
- There's a certain Slant of light — 306

Lewis Carroll
- Jabberwocky — 307
- The Walrus and the Carpenter — 308

Thomas Hardy
- A Broken Appointment — 311
- In Time of 'The Breaking of Nations' — 312
- The Darkling Thrush — 312
- Wessex Heights — 313

Gerard Manley Hopkins
- Binsey Poplars — 315
- God's Grandeur — 316
- Pied Beauty — 316

The Windhover	317
Wreck of the Deutschland	317

WILLIAM ERNEST HENLEY
Invictus	326

A. E. HOUSMAN
A Shropshire Lad, VIII	327
A Shropshire Lad, XL	328

RUDYARD KIPLING
Gunga Din	328
If—	331
The Beginnings	332
The Gods of the Copybook Headings	333

W. B. YEATS
An Irish Airman Foresees His Death	335
Leda and the Swan	336
Sailing to Byzantium	336
The Lake Isle of Innisfree	337

HILAIRE BELLOC
The Rebel	338

STEPHEN CRANE
A Man Said to the Universe	339
In the Desert	339

G. K. CHESTERTON
Elegy in a Country Churchyard	340
From The Ballad of the White Horse	340
The Donkey	358
The Rolling English Road	359

ROBERT FROST
Stopping by Woods on a Snowy Evening	360
The Road Not Taken	360

EDWARD THOMAS
Adlestrop	361
Gone, Gone Again	362
The Child on the Cliffs	363

WALLACE STEVENS
   Sunday Morning 364
   The Snow Man 368

ALFRED NOYES
   The Barrel-Organ 368
   The Highwayman 374

JAMES ELROY FLECKER
   The Golden Journey to Samarkand 378

EZRA POUND
   Canto I 382
   Canto XLV 384
   In a Station of the Metro 385
   The Seafarer 386

RUPERT BROOKE
   The Soldier 389

ROBERT E. HOWARD
   A Song of the Naked Lands 389

THE MAJESTY OF EFFECT

Introduction to the 2023 Imperium Press Anthology of English Verse

By Benjamin Afer (Panama Hat)

> Poetry should surprise by a fine excess and not by singularity, it should strike the reader as a wording of his own highest thoughts, and appear almost a remembrance.
>
> KEATS

Two years ago, a friend approached me and asked if there would be any value in putting out a book of "right-wing" poetry. This struck me as a rather daft thing to want, because such a sentiment misunderstands firstly what art and poetry is, secondly the problem of the term "right-wing," and thus its apparent antithesis, the "left-wing." I have argued endlessly that "right-wing" is a poor descriptor of what we in dissident circles actually are. The term implies, by way of its origins in the French Revolution, that we are satisfied with the doings of the radicals thus far, and only wish to delay future change. This is obviously untrue. Our task is the continuation or resurrection of those great immaterial values that make an individual, a people, a civilisation, flourish; what Evola called his capital-T Tradition. There is that famous anecdote about Bakunin, as related by Jonathan Bowden in his speech about T. S. Eliot, in which the thundering anarchist once passed a gang of rascals and ruffians who were destroying a house and were burning it to the ground. It is said that Bakunin, himself a noble well-accustomed to luxury and fine manners, got out of his coach and joined in the destruction. "He raced about putting his cane through things," Bowden relates, "stamping on pictures and throwing things out of windows with the other ruffians, who just accepted that he was one of them because he joined in. When the conflagration had ensued, and most of the house had gone up, Bakunin was asked why he'd done it and he said, 'Because it's there.' That's an ontological prerequisite, a very extreme Left-wing attitude. You want to destroy things because they are there." Consider that—then consider how almost every poem contained in this anthology, and more to the point every poem worth remembering in English, is the complete opposite to that candid illustration of the leftist, or revolutionary mindset. These poems are all dedicated to the consummate experiences of man, God, and the world. If you want to smear them with a term from the political pickle barrel, then they are in that sense "right-wing." More accurately, they stand for a set of immaterial values that scorch the slack wasteland of modernity like a cleansing fire. Most if not all of these poems suppose hierarchies.[1] Most burn with a religious passion stemming from pre-assumed, richly brocaded metaphysical systems. They display the sheer power contained within the cadences of the English language when wielded by a master.

Nowadays, we are painfully aware of what has happened to the academies and institutions that once hosted and nurtured the names within this book—they are are full of doctrinaire drones; they are overrun by mid-wit intelligences that talk and talk without ever producing anything of any value whatsoever. They can barely read the poems contained within this book, let alone draw any vitality from them, because that's exactly what they've been trained not to do. Unless any given text is personalistic, deconstructive and scorns any kind of positive European cultural or ethnic identity (bar philosemitism), they crush it. Unless a text is subversive of any kind of hierarchy or metaphysics beyond the neuroses and narcissism of the individual, they stamp it out. They are a vicious and ill-tempered board of pharisees, driven solely by false conviction. Faced with the richest and most nourishing of feasts, their indoctrination forces them to retch and turn away to consume dirt.

With that situation in mind, when the gentlemen of Imperium Press first approached me with the offer to edit

---

[1] For a subtly reactionary body of work written with incredible skill that related to this thinking, see the late Sir Geoffrey Hill's collected works, published as *Broken Hierarchies: Poems 1952-2012*.

this book, I excitedly set about compiling lists of great verse, taking care to insert even "lesser" works by notable authors that are of strong personal appeal to me. But I realised, as I envisaged the inevitably cumbersome result, that one of poetry's best aspects is *portability*. It very quickly dawned on the editor and I that this book needed to be truly portable, as opposed to the smug convention among publishers of calling a book "portable" when it is in fact a few pounds short of immobile. We imagine that every man among the ruins might keep a copy on him like a lucky talisman, as I so often did and still do with so many treasured, tiny volumes. Novels often pride themselves on being dictionary-sized doorstoppers, which is fine, since we shouldn't criticize a dreadnought for its tonnage *vis-à-vis* its guns, but what makes poetry poetic, by contrast, is that you can send forth little lines and stanzas at immediate notice, to colossal effect. To torture the analogy further, if the weighty novel is a lumbering dreadnought, then verse is like a devilish U-boat. A poem's concealed but highly efficacious armaments can go forth whenever the occasion or mood requires it (in my case, often when the occasion or mood does not). This is helped by the fact that good poems stick fast in the mind. Taking the time to actually learn a poem by heart is something I encourage everyone to do, but when a poem punches you in the right way, the effort is unnecessary—the lines embed themselves whilst you're still reeling from the impact.

As I thought about it further, I realised that all my favourite individual editions of poetry have been small, shockingly small, considering the powers contained within. I was especially fond of small volumes as a boy because they could fit, often invisibly and without discomfort, into a trouser or blazer pocket. Thus, just as the best lines could be recalled instantaneously from the brain, entire libraries of any kind of poetry could be produced and consumed at will. I explicitly remember a miniscule, seemingly ancient (probably 1920s) *Pocket Kipling* containing poems and short stories. This spindrift anodyne, plus a sufficiently dozy teacher, kept me sane through the difficult years in which I was cruelly forced to study chemistry. (Talk about a man amongst the ruins.) The books I had in my childhood and early teens were mostly decrepit second handers dating back as far as the 1910s, with portentous titles like *"A Cambridge Child's Young Boy's Oxford Treasury Companion Garden of Late Early Period Modern English Verse (third ed.)."* I poke fun only out of love.[2] What was fascinating about those books was that you could see the definitions of terms like "modern" develop as the years plugged on. I quite seriously remember some of them that seemed to consider "modern" to mean everything between Milton and Joyce. Often, the bias of the editors made it all the more interesting to read, and it was obvious whether they adhered to strict academic traditionalism, or perhaps begrudgingly squeezed in the likes of Lawrence, Pound, Eliot *et al* after their usual stopping-point of Hopkins. Others were the faddish Imagism-lovers of 1914, Apollinaire-mad letter-jumblers, or Jazz Age Auden-worshippers. Remember, none of this was specified when you bought the book—it was all tented under "modern verse."

What this meant for me was that the slightly schizophrenic nature of the reading, as opposed to simply going by individual authors or eras (for whatever they're worth), had an enormous breadth. I wasn't prejudiced to one particular method or style. I think I was able, via that reading, to appreciate, independent of form, period, and everything else, the merits of a good poem, which is a tricker thing than it sounds. Hence why the breadth of this volume is a point of pride. I hope that by our careful selection, we have provided that same benefit to taste, as opposed to trying to cultivate an ideological devotion to, say, traditional formalism or radical modernism.

This ability to spot a good poem is essential because poetry, perhaps moreso than other arts, suffers from what we might call the modernist, or rather "academic" disease. The problem is that even though many modern and contemporary poets ought to be capable of putting together a good poem, the academic and critical waters often burst their banks and flood the craft to the point of total submersion. The basic fact is

---

[2] "Indifference to art is betrayed by the pompous solemnity of the homage often rendered it. True love remains silent or mocks." — Nicolás Gómez Dávila. *Escolios a un Texto Implícito: Selección*, p. 111

that a weak poem remains a weak poem even if it holds some other significance to the academics. This, incidentally, is why a proper education in poetry begins with the simple, pretension-free nursery rhymes that teach an infant the simple joys of metre and wordplay. As simple and apparently meaningless as they can be, the fact that we often remember them for the rest of our lives indicates an enormous strength to such simple things. Chesterton said it best:

> Stand up and keep your childishness:
> Read all the pedants' screeds and strictures.
> But don't believe in anything
> That can't be told in coloured pictures.

Philip Larkin, a favourite of mine whose poems we unfortunately cannot include due to copyright restrictions, summed the academic-modernist problem up brilliantly in one of his weekly jazz-review columns for the *Daily Telegraph*.[3]

> The danger, therefore, of assuming that everything played today in jazz has a seed of solid worth stems from the fact that so much of it is tentative, experimental, private [...] And for this reason one has to fall back on the old dictum that a critic is only as good as his ear. His ear will tell him instantly whether a piece of music is vital, musical, exciting, or cerebral, mock-academic, dead, long before he can read Don DeMichael on the subject, or learn that it is written in inverted nineteenths, or in the Stygian mode, or recorded at the NAACP Festival at Little Rock. He must hold on to the principle that the only reason for praising a work is that it pleases, and the way to develop his critical sense is to be more acutely aware of whether he is being pleased or not.

I was going to summarise contemporary poetry, especially that which emanates from the American universities (pretty much all of it) with that phrase of Larkin's: "tentative, experimental, private." In fact, poetry being written now isn't

---

[3] Those columns have been collected into a book—*All What Jazz*—and consist essentially of a sustained attack on modernist pretension. Like all Larkin, it is essential reading.

at all tentative—it's extremely arrogant and lacking and kind of subtlety or humility. It isn't experimental—it doesn't do anything creative with form or technique, it doesn't bother with those very much at all. It is however, private. So private, that no one outside of the author, or perhaps the author's immediate circle of equally self-important loons should bother reading it. The unjustified lewdness, uncensored narcissism, over-educated dullness, and sheer, plain, torturous dear-diary banality of contemporary verse reaches a level so astounding it defies all critical niceties. Most of it isn't worthy of being called bad poetry. There have been some fantastic bad poets in our language.[4] Rather, it doesn't come close to achieving anything within a reasonable definition of "poetry." The bulk of contemporary poetry should also provide an interesting case study into whether certain types of people should be taught to read or write at all.

But the problem of quality and artistic standard applies to our own circles too. I would argue, perhaps to some raised eyebrows from fellow dissidents, that Ezra Pound's greatest contribution to English verse was as a Great Cham (i.e. khan—a title given to Dr. Johnson) rather than a working poet; an overseer that decided who needed promoting and who needed immediate improvement or assistance. His type of renegade, outer-party bar-raising power is what we so sorely need in dissident spheres. Perhaps those men are still finding their way to us. Perhaps they are here but have not yet got the knowledge or the confidence. This collection, I hope, will give just as much confidence to our future critics as it will to our future poets. Young men aspiring to the arts need an iron hand of guidance, one that is not afraid to strike as well as caress. The only thing worse than not producing any art would be to produce poor, under-developed art. Remember, once upon a time, the great institutions that provided guidance to so many in need of it would have been open to us. Now they

---

4 My first recommendation in this category would be William Topaz McGonagall—a Scotch poet known as the worst in the English language, but whose work is, in my opinion, extremely entertaining and quite instructive in 'comedic' metres, even if this was not his intention.

are not. We need to build a wall for our vines to cling to, so to speak, in the wasteland outside of the academies. In labouring over this book, I have prayed that it gives the aspiring poets among us a chance not only to read and cherish a selection of great verse, but also to disassemble and really understand what makes these poems roar. That is the only way to learn how to write quality verse. Too many in our ranks know what a traditional (and thus in their mind good) poem looks and sounds like, but nothing else, and so end up producing a rather sad mockery—a stillborn bird cursed never to fly.

To that end, for as much as the names in this book are role models, the aspiring poet should copy the sense of order that they bring to their work, and not the adventure, chaos, and disrepute with which they might have lived their life. Don't fall into that infantile rightist trap for forever worshipping the "great men" without ever emulating the values that drove them. There is little to learn from Coleridge's opium-eating, or Pound's rather affected mania. Try to copy Poe's intense talent for lyrical rhythm, but don't think that his alcoholism helped him do it. He knew that. Lord Byron's death in the Greek War for Independence didn't make him a great poet, just as Edward Thomas' death in The Great War didn't make him Lord Byron.

When Sir Walter Raleigh wrote his final, epic farewell, he did so as if his life had started over again. *A Farewell to the Vanities of the World* is a poem that often draws a tear from me—it is as though the great captain had never fought the Spanish Armada, or voyaged to the Americas, or been so close to Queen Elizabeth. All that matters is the poem, and that someone remembers a line or two of it. Any glory outside that is, truthfully, vanity. T. S. Eliot beavering away at Lloyd's Bank and A. E. Housman fulminating in his Classics study were both very consciously teaching us lessons. Even if the heat of poetic fame descends upon us, we must always remember that our status or "personality" as poets is a side issue. Nothing matters except your commitment to writing verse. More curtly, one doesn't have to be Sir Walter Raleigh to be a great poet. To make an extreme comparison, Philip Larkin made just as many, if not more penetrating observations about the world, and he hardly ever left Hull. If physical intensity is what you seek, try the S.A.S.

"Who ought to write?" is part of a tricky paradox when it comes to poetry. Very few people stand before the masterpieces in the National Gallery and suppose they could produce something alike in any way. Yet fewer hear *Mass in B Minor* and rush home to take up the composition paper with the intent of matching it. But all too many hear the deceptive simplicity of a good poem, comprehendible to anyone with a working eye or ear, and imagine that because the enjoyment is a universal thing, so must be the composition. For the reactionary, this is especially interesting, because on the one hand, poetry is perhaps the most plebeian art. Before most other art forms had emerged, humans would compose and recite verse, often because it was the only way to record the history, cultural memory, and myth of a particular group. Popular poems were being belted out as song by the poor in pubs long before mass-schooling was around to teach the poor to read (I wonder if oral culture will return now that they no longer do?) Anyone and everyone can appreciate the bardic wit and Brittonic bawdiness of *The Canterbury Tales*, or the cantering, doom-laden majesty of *The Charge of the Light Brigade*, or the tragicomic theatricality of *Gunga Din*, but it takes a Chaucer, a Tennyson, and a Kipling, respectively, to write them. There, at last, is the other hand. You don't need genius to write something witty, admirable or memorable—you do need a clear, unclouded vision or feeling for what you depict, and the spirit of a craftsman, which means the ability to not only spend years of one's life toiling over the desk to get every syllable right (I've never believed that story about Coleridge doing *Kubla Khan* in one sitting) but to encapsulate the spirit contained in these lines by Vita Sackville-West:

> All craftsmen share a knowledge. They have held
> Reality down fluttering to a bench;
> Cut wood to their own purposes; compelled
> The growth of pattern with the patient shuttle;
> Drained acres to a trench.[5]

Naturally, there have been limitations to this book that are

---

[5] From *The Land* (1926)

bound to cause anger. Copyright cut-off is one, and aforementioned considerations of length another. I fully expect a barrage of "but how could you leave out such and such a poem?" or "why did you choose this over that" and so on. I maintain, however, that despite whatever arguable flaws this book might have, it is a worthy companion to the wider depths of English literature. That aforementioned portability is only achievable by way of careful selection, after all. Perhaps older and apparently better-read men among us will take the opportunity to pass this book off as a cram-sheet anthology of greatest hits for the kiddies to get up to speed, but more to fool them for their arrogance. I don't believe it is possible to read any of these poems too many times in one's life. Even when simply leafing through my rough copy, I was constantly snagged by wonderful phrases and elegant lines that compelled yet another full reading. But I won't pretend that having to leave out so many cherished poems was ever going to be easy, or that I would get away with it complaint-free. All I ask is that nobody scans through the table of contents, notes the absence of a personal favourite, and slides the book back towards me with a smug smile. What has made editing the list so painful is that practically every poem included in the original, hopelessly long first draft was in some way a masterpiece. It will forever haunt me that I had to make a zero-sum decision between, say, *Daffodils* and *Tintern Abbey*, but I do not regret what I eventually chose to include.

It's easy for a more casual enjoyer of poetry to guffaw at this squeamishness, but the practising poet, who knows how much blood and toil goes into even a comparatively third-rate poem, must be permitted his tearful cheek. Admiring a sublime carving is a very different matter when your own hands have tried, probably in vain, to achieve something similar.

Another feature bound to cause consternation is the use of excerpts from longer poems. At first, I was resolutely opposed to this. How can you go about chopping up *Paradise Lost* or *The Ballad of the White Horse* to lay them out like choicest cuts in a butcher's window? But my fire was dampened by the editor's counterargument. How could we claim to be introducing our young men to English verse *without* providing something from those longer works? So, with considerable trepidation, I took up the axe. I want to assure you that the work was anything but easy, and if it were up to me to spoil what I'm sure will be a beautiful design, there would be one of those stark health warnings like you get on tobacco packaging on the front of the book, advising the reader to seek out the full poem if a particular excerpt happened to excite them, lest editorial overreach permanently damage their palate.

Something else which worries me is that the butcher's cuts might be a little too succulent. An enrapturing climax heard by itself too often can dull the music meant to accompany it. For example, in a poem by Amy Clampitt which I cannot quote due to some truly rotten copyright restrictions, there is a line about a cheetah whose coat turns from a petalled garden into a sandstorm as she runs. The line is marvellous, but the poem as a whole is forgettable. (It's called *The Stone Face of Emily Dickinson,* for those interested.) After his death, a line was discovered in one of Philip Larkin's manuscript books—"Dead leaves desert in thousands." There was a poem written to host it, but it is evident to any practising poet that Larkin held it back from print because that grand line made all the others seem hopelessly weak. What these concerns mean for the book is that there are far fewer excerpts than there might have been, and those that appear are from poems which lend themselves better to being quoted from. Once more, I can only pray that I have, circumstances considered, put together an anthology destined to last in popularity.

This is, of course, an anthology of specifically English poetry, and that perhaps is the most important thing about it. The editors, when pitching this project to me, made it clear that it should only include poems originally written in English. My output in these circles so far has concerned itself mainly with western civilisation, or rather a kind of Europeanism, since it is ridiculous to suppose that each of our now crumbling cultures and peoples developed in a vacuum. But this book has given me the chance to take a much-needed step back from the grand notions of "The West," and instead back to the specific culture and language that has given me everything I have, even if my claim to truly be a part of it will always be marred by a particular circumstance of birth. I am not a linguist, nor am I familiar with any academic theory of language. I have enough Spanish grammar to read some of it, small Latin and less Greek, but in a realistic sense I do not understand any other language. It might seem then that what I am about to say is unqualified, but I insist on it nevertheless.

English is a very beautiful language. I am told by multilingual friends that there is something about English, a curious, paradoxical mixture of grammatical freedom and grammatical entanglement, a simultaneous wealth and poverty of synonyms, the way the vowels curve around each other, that gives it a beauty of its own. Without a shred of irony, or the worry that what he said might be considered ludicrous and chauvinistic, a venerable fellow who speaks (to my knowledge) Bengali, French, Arabic, and English fluently told me that there's something about the way Shakespeare says

> But, look, the morn, in russet mantle clad,
> Walks o'er the dew of yon high eastward hill.

That can't be done to quite the same delicious effect in other tongues. Like all sublime things, the beauty lies in a fundamental paradox—that English is at once so earthy and so noble, and once I realised that, I could go on to get to the heart of English poetry. I had been introduced to Tennyson's *The Charge of the Light Brigade* at the age of ten, which sparked off my ever-increasing obsession with the power of the poem. (The reason I use the word "punch" to describe the effectiveness of a poem is because when I first read *The Charge of the Light Brigade*, I could easily have tumbled as far as The Crimea.) But it was another work entirely that brought my fumbling mind to realise the absolute sublimity of English. For about three hundred years my old school has run an annual King James Essay Prize. Open to all boys, it requires 2,500 words on some topic related to the King James Bible. I can't remember why I entered it—I wasn't particularly interested in religion back then, and being such a feckless student, I didn't often bother to enter the kinds of competitions only the "swots" (try-hards) cared about and won, but for whatever reason, that year, I did. I dug out the yet-unopened, purple-bound, gold-edged bible which I had been sent to school with as a kit-list requirement and started to read. I had been subjected to countless excerpts and psalms from the KJV since birth, but for the first time in my life, I paid attention, as I did with the poetry I had by then grown to love. I wasn't quite grown-up enough yet to take in the Word of God, but I was entranced by the craftsmanship and musicality of the words, the phrasing, the way each sentence was carefully weighted to ring against those around it. I had my topic. Over the next few weeks I devoured the KJV and scribbled an over-boiled missive on The Beauty of the Language of the King James Bible. I don't doubt that someone writes a similar essay every year, but that year, quite unexpectedly, I won. As a young man, this told me not that I had anything to show off, but that my argument that the KJV was ultimately some of the greatest poetry ever written was vindicated. The King James style contains the formula that powers all great English poetry—*a simplicity of style combined with majesty of effect*: "Ask, and it shall be given you; seek, and ye shall find; knock and it shall be opened unto you. For every one that asketh receiveth; and he that seeketh findeth; and to him that knoweth it shall be opened" (Luke 11:9-10). The vocabulary of that passage is simple, but the elaborate rhetorical patterns of repetition elevate it above everyday conversation. When I think of the King James Bible now, I am taken back to a time when English was spoken by a tiny percentage of the world, regions of Britain still had their own tongues, and some dialects were so complex they sounded like a different language. Both Lord Dunsany and Walt Whitman claimed that their respective styles were influenced solely by the KJV.

At the mention of Whitman, I will add that despite my cold remarks about contemporary American and American-derived poetry, working on this book has very much re-invigorated my respect for the Anglo-American tradition. After all, that is what "English poetry" means—the Anglo-American, and to a lesser extent "commonwealth" poets. I have often attacked contemporary Americanism on the grounds that it is not sufficiently European, but in doing so I have forgotten that the original American literary canon, particularly that derived from the aristocracy of New England, is as integral to our tradition as anything from the old world. There is perhaps no better exemplar of this tradition than T. S. Eliot, who said, "I'm American in my mind and British in my heart." And he was very much a part of that Anglo-American generation that viewed the two ends of the Atlantic as one country: New England was Old England; Old England was New England. Second to Eliot would perhaps be the novelist Henry James; there's a long tradition of patrician Anglo-Americana that thinks of itself in this way. Of course, some Americans take this Anglo-patricianism a little too far, themselves forgetting the influence of Celts and other such groups upon the usage of language. H. P. Lovecraft was so immensely proud of his pure English stock that he went into a manic depression upon learning that he was in fact partly Welsh. I wonder what he would have made of the unique, bardic melodies of someone like Dylan Thomas?

It's important to remember this tradition when we look upon the deformed and inhuman cauldron of the modern United States. Terrible changes have occurred at every level of that country which have more-or-less destroyed the seamless brotherhood of English souls that T. S. Eliot so admired. As we know, there has been an engineered demographic catastrophe, the same kind that is happening here in Europe and Britain. And this is why a book like this is so important to us. It contains a kind of cultural codex as to what English writing is, or at any rate what it can be. It's a powerful antidote to the forces of modernity that want to desperately to wash us and our traditions away.

How painful it is to witness the utilitarian crimes now being committed against English. It is, as Tolkien lamented, the most spoken language in the world, and that does it no favours. In a now-famous letter to his son Christopher he said:

> Hump, well! I wonder (if we survive this war) if there will be any niche, even of sufferance, left for reactionary back numbers like me (and you). The bigger things get the smaller and duller or flatter the globe gets. It is getting to be all one blasted little provincial suburb. When they have introduced American sanitation, moral pep, feminism, and mass production throughout the Near East, Middle East, Far East, U.S.S.R., Hither Further and Inner Mumbo-land, Gondhwanaland, Lhasa, and the villages of the darkest Berkshire, how happy we shall be. At any rate it ought to cut down on travel. There

will be nowhere to go. So people will (I opine) go all the faster. Collie Knox says 1/8 of the world's population speaks 'English', and that is the biggest language group. if true, damn shame__ say I. May the curse of Babel strike at all their tongues till they can only say 'baa baa'. It would mean much the same. I think I shall have to refuse to speak anything but Old Mercian.

The *escolios* of Nicolás Gómez Dávila (I had to mention him at least once) were described by the German Catholic writer Martin Mosebach as "a highly compact emergency kit for a stay in the Arctic for an indefinite period of time," and in editing this book that line has been a constant presence. The Grand Old Man of Colombia also remarked that each of his little aphorisms were like hand grenades tossed by a guerrilla onto the marching columns of progressive thought—I will reiterate that what these poems stand for other than beauty for its own sake is a collection of immaterial values, the very thing that we must resurrect if we want to secure our own future. Progressives don't ever ignore these poems. If you go into an English literature class in any university today, they'll be teaching all the poems included here, especially the more traditional ones. But it's really just one long exercise in subversion—they'll tell you why the despicable Wife of Bath was in fact a smooth-operating feminist 800 years before her time, why Byron and Shelley were either woke proto-Marxists or evil examples of toxic masculinity, why Shakespeare needs ethnic "correction," why Tennyson was a moody reactionary and Kipling a genocidal colonialist. None of these travesties hold any merit, and those at the top of the academies know that. They have to constantly douse the canon with their slime because if they stop, even briefly, this material will self-revive and go on to influence the minds of capable young men, which is what it should do, and that's why we have such great hopes for this volume and what it stands for in the hands of the dissident communities.

Delve into this anthology and be proud of your language without a shred of trepidation. To be born to the English tongue is surely one of the greatest privileges of birth there is. To say so is deeply unfashionable today, but as you clutch this "little" book, remember the immense treasures contained

THE MAJESTY OF EFFECT

within it. Remember the towering greatness that your tongue connects you to, and the unique beauty and power to which it grants you access. In an age when our identities and traditions are under siege by a corrosive, alien, and satanic force, here you have the words that will invigorate the soul.

> Let knowledge grow from more to more,
> > But more of reverence in us dwell;
> > That mind and soul, according well,
> May make one music as before,
>
> TENNYSON

BENJAMIN AFER.

JUNE 2022.

IMPERIUM ANTHOLOGY OF ENGLISH VERSE

BEOWULF

XXXVI

Ða ic æt þearfe gefrægn þeodcyninges
andlongne eorl ellen cyðan,
cræft ond cenðu, swa him gecynde wæs.
Ne hedde he þæs heafolan, ac sio hand gebarn
modiges mannes, þær he his mæges healp,
þæt he þone niðgæst nioðor hwene sloh,
secg on searwum, þæt ðæt sweord gedeaf,
fah ond fæted, þæt ðæt fyr ongon
sweðrian syððan. þa gen sylf cyning
geweold his gewitte, wællseaxe gebræd
biter ond beaduscearp, þæt he on byrnan wæg;
forwrat Wedra helm wyrm on middan.
Feond gefyldan (ferh ellen wræc),
ond hi hyne þa begen abroten hæfdon,
sibæðelingas. Swylc sceolde secg wesan,
þegn æt ðearfe! þæt ðam þeodne wæs
siðast sigehwila sylfes dædum,
worlde geweorces. ða sio wund ongon,
þe him se eorðdraca ær geworhte,
swelan ond swellan; he þæt sona onfand,
þæt him on breostum bealoniðe weoll
attor on innan. ða se æðeling giong
þæt he bi wealle wishycgende
gesæt on sesse; seah on enta geweorc,
hu ða stanbogan stapulum fæste
ece eorðreced innan healde.
Hyne þa mid handa heorodreorigne,
þeoden mærne, þegn ungemete till
winedryhten his wætere gelafede,
hilde sædne, ond his helm onspeon.
Biowulf maþelode (he ofer benne spræc,

wunde wælbleate; wisse he gearwe
þæt he dæghwila gedrogen hæfde,
eorðan wynne; ða wæs eall sceacen
dogorgerimes, deað ungemete neah):
'Nu ic suna minum syllan wolde
guðgewædu, þær me gifeðe swa
ænig yrfeweard æfter wurde
lice gelenge. Ic ðas leode heold
fiftig wintra; næs se folccyning,
ymbesittendra ænig ðara,
þe mec guðwinum gretan dorste,
egesan ðeon. Ic on earde bad
mælgesceafta, heold min tela,
ne sohte searoniðas, ne me swor fela
aða on unriht. Ic ðæs ealles mæg
feorhbennum seoc gefean habban;
for ðam me witan ne ðearf waldend fira
morðorbealo maga, þonne min sceaceð
lif of lice. Nu ðu lungre geong
hord sceawian under harne stan,
Wiglaf leofa, nu se wyrm ligeð,
swefeð sare wund, since bereafod.
Bio nu on ofoste, þæt ic ærwelan,
goldæht ongite, gearo sceawige
swegle searogimmas, þæt ic ðy seft mæge
æfter maððumwelan min alætan
lif ond leodscipe, þone ic longe heold.'

'TWAS NOW, men say, in his sovereign's need
That the earl made known his noble strain,
Craft and keenness and courage enduring.
Heedless of harm, though his hand was burned,
Hardy-hearted, he helped his kinsman.
A little lower the loathsome beast
He smote with sword; his steel drove in
Bright and burnished; that blaze began

To lose and lessen. At last the king
Wielded his wits again, war-knife drew,
A biting blade by his breastplate hanging,
And the Weders'-helm smote that worm asunder,
Felled the foe, flung forth its life.
So had they killed it, kinsmen both,
Athelings twain: thus an earl should be
In danger's day!—Of deeds of valor
This conqueror's-hour of the king was last,
Of his work in the world. The wound began,
Which that dragon-of-earth had erst inflicted,
To swell and smart; and soon he found
In his breast was boiling, baleful and deep,
Pain of poison. The prince walked on,
Wise in his thought, to the wall of rock;
Then sat, and stared at the structure of giants,
Where arch of stone and steadfast column
Upheld forever that hall in earth.
Yet here must the hand of the henchman peerless
Lave with water his winsome lord,
The king and conqueror covered with blood,
With struggle spent, and unspan his helmet.
Beowulf spake in spite of his hurt,
His mortal wound; full well he knew
His portion now was past and gone
Of earthly bliss, and all had fled
Of his file of days, and death was near:
"I would fain bestow on son of mine
This gear of war, were given me now
That any heir should after me come
Of my proper blood. This people I ruled
Fifty winters. No folk-king was there,
None at all, of the neighboring clans
Who war would wage me with 'warriors'-friends'
And threat me with horrors. At home I bided
What fate might come, and I cared for mine own;
Feuds I sought not, nor falsely swore

Ever on oath. For all these things,
Though fatally wounded, fain am I!
From the Ruler-of-Man no wrath shall seize me,
When life from my frame must flee away,
For killing of kinsmen! Now quickly go
And gaze on that hoard 'neath the hoary rock,
Wiglaf loved, now the worm lies low,
Sleeps, heart-sore, of his spoil bereaved.
And fare in haste. I would fain behold
The gorgeous heirlooms, golden store,
Have joy in the jewels and gems, lay down
Softlier for sight of this splendid hoard
My life and the lordship I long have held."

From SIR GAWAIN AND THE GREEN KNIGHT

Fytte the First

I

SIÞEN Þe sege & þe assaut watʒ sesed at Troye,
Þe borʒ brittened & breut to brondeʒ & askeʒ,
Þe tulk þat þe trammes of treasoun þer wroʒt,
Watʒ tried for his tricherie, þe trewest on erthe;
Hit watʒ Ennias þe athel, & his highe kynde,
Þat siþen depreced prouinces, & patrounes bicome
Welneʒe of al þe wele in þe west iles,
Fro riche Romulus to Rome ricchis hym swy þe,
With gret bobbaunce þat burʒe he biges vpon first,
& neuenes hit his aune nome, as hit now hat;
Ticius (turnes) to Tuskan, & teldes bigynnes;
Langaberde in Lumbardie lyftes vp homes;
& fer ouer þe French flod Felix Brutus
On mony bonkkes ful brode Bretayn he setteʒ,
      with wynne;
  Where were, & wranke, & wonder,

Bi syþeȝ hatȝ wont þer-inne,
& oft boþe blysse & blunder
Ful skete hatȝ skyfted synne.

II

Ande quen þis Bretayn watȝ bigged bi þis burn rych,
Belde bredden þer-inne, baret þat lofden,
In mony turned tyme tene þat wroȝten;
Mo ferlyes on þis folde han fallen here oft
Þen in any oþer þat I wot, syn þat ilk tyme.
Bot of alle þat here bult of Bretaygne kynges
Ay watȝ Arthur þe hendest, as I haf herde telle;
For-þi an aunter in erde I attle to schawe,
Þat a selly in siȝt summe men hit holfen,
& an outrage awenture of Arthureȝ wondereȝ,
If ȝe wyl lysten þis laye bot on little quile,
I schal telle hit, as-tit, as I in toun herde,
   with tonge;
 As hit is stad & stoken,
 In stori stif & stronge,
 With lel letteres loken
 In londe so hatȝ ben longe.

III

Þis kyng lay at Camylot vpon kryst-masse,
With mony luflych lorde, ledeȝ of þe best,
Rekenly of þe rounde table alle þo rich breþer,
With rych reuel oryȝt, & rechnles merþes;
Þer tourneyed tulkes bi-tyme ȝ ful mony,
Justed ful Jolilé þyse gyntyle kniȝtes,
Syþen kayred to þe court, carols to make.
For þer þe fest watȝ ilyche ful fifteen days
With alle þe mete & þe mirþe þat men couþe a vyse;
Such glaumande gle glorious to here,
Dere dyn vp-on day, daunsyng on nyȝtes,

Al watȝ hap vpon heȝe in halleȝ & chambreȝ,
Wirth lordeȝ & ladies, as leuest him þoȝt;
With all þe wele of þe worlde þay woned þer samen,
Þe most kyd knyȝtes vnder krystes seluen,
& þe louelokkest ladies þat euer lif haden,
& he þe comlokest king þat þe court haldes;
For al watȝ þis fayre folk in her first age,
    on sille;
 Ie hapnest vnder heuen,
 Kyng hyȝest mon of wylle,
 Hit were now grey nye to neuen
 So hardly a here on hille.

IV

Wyle nw ȝer watȝ so ȝep þat hit wat new cummen,
Þat day double on þe dece watȝ þe douth serued,
Fro þe king watȝ cummen with knȝtes in to þe halle,
Þe chauntre of þe chapel cheued to an ende;
Loude crye watȝ þer kest of clerkeȝ & oþer,
Nowel nayted o-newe, neuend ful ofte;
& syþen riche forth runnen to reche honed-selle,
Ȝeȝed ȝeres ȝiftes on hiȝ, ȝelde hem bi hond,
Debated busyly aboute þo giftes;
Ladies laȝed ful loude, þo þay lost haden,
& he þat wan watȝ not worth, þat may ȝe wel trawe.
Alle þis wirþe þay maden to þe mete tyme;
When þay had wachsen, worþyly þay wenten to sete,
Þe best burne ay abof, as hit best semed;
Whene Guenore ful gay, grayþed in þe myddes,
Dressed on þe dere des, dubbed al aboute,
Smal sendal besides, a selure hir ouer
Of tryed Tolouse, of Tars tapites in-noghe,
Þat were anbrawded & beten with þe best gemmes:
Þat myȝt be preued of prys with penyes to buy,
    in daye;
 Þe comlokest to discrye,

Þer glent with y3em gray;
A semloker þat euer he sy3e,
Soth mo3t no mon say.

AFTER THE siege and the assault had ceased at Troy,
The city been destroyed and burned to brands and ashes,
The warrior who wrought there the trains of treason
Was tried for his treachery, the truest on earth.
This was Aeneas the noble; he and his high kindred
Afterwards conquered provinces, and became patrons
Of well nigh all the wealth in the West Isles.
As soon as rich Romulus turns him to Rome,
With great pride he at once builds that city,
And names it with his own name, which it now has;
Ticius turns to Tuscany and founds dwellings;
Longobard raises homes in Lombardy;
And, far over the French flood, Felix Brutus
Establishes Britain joyfully on many broad banks,
Where war and waste and wonders
By turns have since dwelt,
And many a swift interchange of bliss and woe.
And when this Britain was founded by this great hero,
Bold men loving strife bred therein,
And many a time they wrought destruction.
More strange things have happened in this land
Since these days than in any other that I know;
But of all the British kings that built here,
Arthur was ever the most courteous, as I have heard tell.
Therefore, I mean to tell of an adventure in the world,
Which some count strange and extraordinary
Even among the wonders of Arthur.
If ye will listen to this lay but a little while,
I will tell it forthright as I heard it told in town,
As it is set down in story
That cannot be changed,
Long written in the land in true words.

This King lay royally at Camelot at Christmas tide
With many fine lords, the best of men,
All the rich brethren of the Round Table,
With right rich revel and careless mirth.
There full many heroes tourneyed betimes,
Jousted full gaily; then returned these gentle knights
To the court to make carols.
For there the feast was held full fifteen days
Alike with all the meat and the mirth that men could devise.
Such a merry tumult, glorious to hear;
Joyful din by day, dancing at night.
All was high joy in halls and chambers
With lords and ladies as pleased them best.
With all the weal in the world they dwelt there together,
The most famous knights save only Christ,
The loveliest ladies that ever had life,
And he, the comeliest of kings, who holds the court.
For all this fair company were in their prime in the hall,
The happiest troop under heaven
With the proudest of kings.
Truly it would be hard to name anywhere so brave a band.
When New Year was fresh and but newly come,
The court was served double on the dais.
As soon as the king with his knights was come into the hall,
The chanting in the chapel came to an end;
Loud was the cry there of clerks and others.
Noel was celebrated anew, shouted full often;
And afterwards the great ones ran about to take handsel;
Called aloud for New Year's gifts, paid them out briskly,
Busily discussed the gifts;
Ladies laughed full loud, though they had lost;
And be that won was not wroth, that may ye well trow.
All this mirth they made till the meat time;
When they had washed, worthily they went to their seats,
The best man ever above, as it best behoved.
Queen Guinevere full beauteous was set in the midst,
Placed on the rich dais adorned all about.

Fine silk at the sides, a canopy over her of precious cloth
Of Toulouse, and tapestries of Tars,
That were embroidered and set with the best gems
That money could buy.
Truly no man could say
That he ever beheld a comelier lady than she,
With her dancing gray eyes.

William Langland

From PIERS PLOWMAN

IN A somer seson, whan softe was the sonne,	
I shoop me into shroudes as I a sheep were,	*clothed : cloak*
In habite as an heremite unholy of werkes,	
Wente wide in this world wondres to here.	
Ac on a May morwenynge on Malverne hilles	*morning*
Me bifel a ferly, of Fairye me thoghte.	*marvel*
I was wery forwandred and wente me to reste	*weary wandering*
Under a brood bank by a bourne syde;	*stream's side*
And as I lay and lenede and loked on the watres,	
I slombred into a slepyng, it sweyed so murye.	*sounded so merry*
Thanne gan I meten a merveillous swevene—	*began to dream*
That I was in a wildernesse, wiste I nevere where.	*I knew not where*
A[c] as I biheeld into the eest an heigh to the sonne,	*But*
I seigh a tour on a toft trieliche ymaked,	*tower : finely*
A deep dale bynethe, a dongeon therinne,	
With depe diches and derke and dredfulle of sighte.	*dark*
A fair feeld ful of folk fond I ther bitwene—	
Of alle manere of men, the meene and the riche,	

Werchynge and wandrynge as the world asketh.	
Somme putten hem to the plough, pleiden ful selde,	*themselves : played*
In settynge and sowynge swonken ful harde,	*sweating*
And wonnen that thise wastours with glotonye destruyeth	*won : wasters*
And somme putten hem to pride, apparailed hem therafter,	*themselves*
In contenaunce of clothynge comen disgised-	
In preieres and penaunce putten hem manye,	
Al for the love of Oure Lord lyveden ful streyte	*living hard lives*
In hope to have heveneriche blisse—	*heavenly*
As ancres and heremites that holden hem in hire selles,	*anchorites*
Coveiten noght in contree to cairen aboute	*Coveted : roam*
For no likerous liflode hire likame to plese.	*luxurious living : body*
And somme chosen chaffare; they cheveden the bettre—	*trade : fared*
As it semeth to oure sight that swiche men thryveth;	*such : thrive*
And somme murthes to make as mynstralles konne,	*mirth : know*
And geten gold with hire glee— [gilt]lees, I leeve-	*their : guiltless*
Ac japeres and jangeleres, Judas children,	*But jesters*
Feynen hem fantasies, and fooles hem maketh—	*Feigning*
And han wit at wille to werken if they wolde.	*have*
That Poul precheth of hem I wol nat preve it here:	*Paul : prove*
Qui loquitur turpiloquium is Luciferes hyne-	*hind*
Bidderes and beggeres faste aboute yede	*Tramps : went*
[Til] hire bely and hire bagge [were] bredful ycrammed,	*their*
Faiteden for hire foode, foughten at the ale.	*Scrounging*

In glotonye, God woot, go thei to bedde,	*God knows*
And risen with ribaudie, tho Roberdes knaves;	*thieving knaves*
Sleep and sory sleuthe seweth hem evere.	*pursue them*
Pilgrymes and palmeres plighten hem togidere	*pledge : together*
For to seken Seint Jame and seintes at Rome;	
Wenten forth in hire wey with many wise tales,	*their*
And hadden leve to lyen al hire lif after.	*lie*
I seigh somme that seiden thei hadde ysought seintes:	
To ech a tale that thei tolde hire tonge was tempred to lye	
Moore than to seye sooth, it semed bi hire speche.	*tell truth : by*
Heremytes on an heep with hoked staves,	*a heap of them*
Wenten to Walsyngham—and hire wenches after:	
Grete lobies and longe that lothe were to swynke	*loafers : tall : work*
Clothed hem in copes to ben knowen from othere,	*themselves : capes*
And shopen hem heremytes hire ese to have.	*clad : ease*
I fond there freres, alle the foure ordres,	*friars*
Prechynge the peple for profit of [the wombe]:	
Glosed the gospel as hem good liked;	*Explained*
For coveitise of copes construwed it as thei wolde.	*to get clothing*
Manye of thise maistres mowe clothen hem at likyng	*may dress*
For hire moneie and hire marchaundise marchen togideres.	
Sith charite hath ben chapman and chief to shryve lordes	*shrive*
Manye ferlies han fallen in a fewe yeres.	*marvels*
But Holy Chirche and hii holde bettre togidres	*agree*

The mooste meschief on molde is mountynge up faste.	*great : earth*
Ther preched a pardoner as he a preest were:	
Broughte forth a bulle with bisshopes seles,	
And seide that hymself myghte assoillen hem alle	*a brief absolve*
Of falshede of fastynge, of avowes ybroken. —	
Lewed men leved hym wel and liked hise wordes,	*Laymen believed*
Comen up knelynge to kissen his bulle.	*kneeling : seal*
He bonched hem with his brevet and blered hire eighen,	*their eyes*
And raughte with his rageman rynges and broches.	*parchment*
—Thus ye gyven youre gold glotons to helpe,	*gluttons*
And leneth it losels that leccherie haunten	*to louts : follow*
Were the bisshop yblessed and worth bothe his eris,	*ears*
His seel sholde noght be sent to deceyve the peple.	
Ac it is noght by the bisshop that the boy precheth—	*But*
For the parisshe preest and the pardoner parten the silver	*share*
That the povere [peple] of the parissche sholde have if they ne were.	*poor*
Persons and parisshe preestes pleyned hem to the bisshop	*complained*
That hire parisshes weren povere sith the pestilence tyme,	*their*
To have a licence and leve at London to dwelle,	
And syngen ther for symonie, for silver is swete.	*stipends*
Bisshopes and bachelers, bothe maistres and doctours—	
That han cure under Crist, and crownynge in tokene	*have charge : tonsure*

And signe that thei sholden shryven hire parisshens,	shrive
Prechen and praye for hem, and the povere fede—	poor
Liggen at Londoun in Lenten and ellis.	Lodge : Lent
Somme serven the King and his silver tellen,	count
In Cheker and in Chauncelrie chalangen his dettes	claiming for
Of wardes and of wardemotes, weyves and streyves.	waifs and strays
And somme serven as servaunts lordes and ladies,	
And in stede of stywardes sitten and demen.	stewards : judge
Hire messe and hire matyns and many of hire houres	Their Mass and Matins
Arn doone undevoutliche; drede is at the laste	Are said : dread
Lest Crist in Consistorie acorse ful manye"	accurse
I parceyved of the power that Peter hadde to kepe—	
To bynden and unbynden, as the Book telleth—	
How he it lefte with love as Oure Lord highte	ordained
Amonges foure vertues, most vertuous of ale vertues,	
That cardinals ben called and closynge yates	gates
There Crist is in kyngdom, to close and to shette,	
And to opene it to hem and hevene blisse shewe.	
Ac of the Cardinals at court that kaughte of that name	But : received
And power presumed in hem a Pope to make	
To han the power that Peter hadde. impugnen I nelle—	have
For in love and in lettrure the eleccion bilongeth;	learning
Forthi I kan and kan naught of court speke moore.	Therefore

Thanne kam ther a Kyng: Knyghthod hym ladde; *before him*
Might of the communes made hym to regne. *commons*
And thanne cam Kynde Wit and clerkes he made, *Mother Wit*
For to counseillen the Kyng and the Commune save.
The Kyng and Knyghthod and Clergie bothe
Casten that the Commune sholde hem [communes] fynde. *Planned : support*
The Commune contreved of Kynde Wit craftes,
And for profit of al the peple plowmen ordeyned
To tilie and to travaille as trewe lif asketh. *true life*
The Kyng and the Commune and Kynde Wit the thridde *too*
Shopen lawe and leaute—eeh lif to knowe his owene. *Cause : loyalty : each man*
Thanne loked up a lunatik, a leene thyng withalle,
And knelynge to the Kyng clergially he seide,
"Crist kepe thee, sire Kyng, and thi kyngryche, *kingdom*
And lene thee lede thi lond so leaute thee lovye, *grant : rule*
And for thi rightful rulyng be rewarded in hevene."
And sithen in the eyr on heigh an aungel of hevene *sitting*
Lowed to speke in Latyn—for lewed men ne koude *Stooped : simple*
Jangle ne jugge that justifie hem sholde, *Discuss nor judge*
But suffren and serven—forthi seide the aungel: *thus*
"*Sum Rex, sum Princeps: neutrum fortasse deinceps;*
O qui iura regis Christi specialia regis,

Hoc quod agas melius—iustus es, esto pius!
Nudum ius a te vestiri vult pietate;
Qualia vis metere, talia grand sere.
Si ius nudatur, nudo de iure metatur;
Si seritur pietas, de pietate metas."

Thanne greved hym a goliardeis, a gloton of wordes,   *buffoon*
And to the aungel an heigh answerde after:
"Dum rex a regere dicatur nomen habere,
Nomen habet sine re nisi studet iura tenere."
Thanne [c]an al the commune crye in vers of Latyn   *began*
To the Kynges counseil—construe whoso wolde—   *howsoever*
"Precepta Regis sunt nobis vincula legis."
With that ran ther a route of ratons at ones   *rats*
And smale mees myd hem: mo than a thousand   *mice with them*
Comen to a counseil for the commune profit;
For a cat of a court cam whan hym liked
And overleep hem lightliche and laughte hem at his wille,   *caught*
And pleide with hem perillousli and possed aboute.   *played : pushed*
"For doute of diverse dredes we dar noght wel loke"   *fear : look about*
And if we grucche of his gamen he wol greven us alle—   *grumble*
Cracchen us or clawen us and in hise clouches holde.   *Scratch*
That us lotheth the lif er he late us passe.   *ere*
Mighte we with any wit his wille withstonde,
We myghte be lordes olofte and lyven at oure ese'.   *above him : ease*
A raton of renoun, moost renable of tonge,   *ready*
Seide for a sovereyn [salve] to hem alle,   *to help himself*
"I have yseyen segges," quod he, "in the Cite of Londoun   *seen men*

Beren beighes ful brighte abouten hire nekkes,	*necklaces*
And somme colers of crafty work; uncoupled they wenden	*collars : wander*
Bothe in wareyne and in waast where hem leve liketh,	*warrens : wastes*
And outher while thei arn elliswhere, as I here telle.	*are*
Were ther a belle on hire beighe, by Jesus, as me thynketh,	*on their collars*
Men myghte witen wher thei wente and awey renne.	*know*
And right so," quod that raton, "reson me sheweth	
To bugge a belle of bras or of bright silver	*buy*
And knytten it on a coler for oure commune profit	
And hangen it upon the cattes hals—thanne here we mowen	*neck : hear*
Wher he ryt or rest or rometh to pleye;	*romp*
And if hym list for to laike, thanne loke we mowen	*to play*
And peeren in his presence the while hym pleye liketh,	*appear*
And if hym wratheth, be war and his wey shonye."	*shun*
Al the route of ratons to this reson assented;	
Ac tho the belle was ybrought and on the beighe hanged	*But*
Ther ne was raton in al the route, for al the reaume of France,	*realm*
That dorste have bounden the belle aboute the cattes nekke,	
Ne hangen it aboute his hals al Engelond to wynne,	*ears*
[Ac] helden hem unhardy and hir counseil feble,	*held themselves*
And leten hire laboure lost and al hire longe studie.	*esteemed*

A mous that muche good kouthe, as me tho thoughte,	*knew*
Strook forth sternely and stood bifore hem alle,	*Ran*
And to the route of ratons rehersed thise wordes:	*rats*
"Though we hadde ykilled the cat, yet sholde ther come another	
To cracchen us and al oure kynde, though we cropen under benches.	*scratch : creep*
Forthi I counseille al the commune to late the cat worthe,	*Thus : alone*
And be we nevere so bolde the belle hym to shewe.	
The while he caccheth conynges he coveiteth noght oure caroyne,	*rabbits : flesh*
But fedeth hym al with venyson; defame we hym nevere.	
For bettre is a litel los than a long sorwe:	
The maze among us alle, theigh we mysse a sherewe!	*fear : villain*
For I herde my sire seyn, is seven yeer ypassed,	*say*
"Ther the cat is a kitoun, the court is ful elenge".	*wretched*
That witnesseth Holy Writ, whoso wole it rede—	
Vae terra ubi puer rex est, &c.	
For may no renk ther reste have for ratons by nyghte.	*man*
For many mennes malt we mees wolde destruye,	
And also ye route of ratons rende mennes clothes,	
Nere the cat of the court that kan you overlepe;	*Were it not for*
For hadde ye rattes youre [raik] ye kouthe noght rule yowselve.	*will : could*

"I seye for me', quod the mous, " I se so muchel after, — *As for me*
Shal nevere the cat ne the kiton by my counseil be greved,
Ne carpynge of this coler that costed me nevere. — *carping*
And though it costned me catel, biknowen it I nolde, — *dearly*
But suffren as hymself wolde [s]o doon as hym liketh—
Coupled and uncoupled to cacche what thei mowe. — *what they can*
Forthi ech a wis wight I warne—wite wel his owene!' — *Thus : watch*
(What this metels bymeneth, ye men that ben murye, — *dream means*
Devyne ye—for I ne dar, by deere God in hevene)! — *Divine*
Yet hoved ther an hundred in howves of selk— — *hovered : caps*
Sergeants, it semed, that serveden at the Barre,
Pleteden for penyes and pounded the lawe, — *Pleading*
And noght for love of Oure Lord unlose hire lippes ones. — *their*
Thow myghtest bettre meete myst on Malverne Hilles — *measure*
Than get a mom of hire mouth til moneie be shewed! — *peep*
Barins and burgeises and bondemen als — *Barons*
I seigh in this assemblee, as ye shul here after;
Baksteres and brewesteres and bochiers manye, — *butchers*
Wollen webbesters and weveres of lynnen,
Taillours and tynkers and tollers in markettes,
Masons and mynours and many othere craftes:
Of alle kynne lybbynge laborers lopen forth somme- — *living : stood*
As dykeres and delveres that doon hire dedes ille — *diggers : do their work badly*

And dryveth forth the longe day with "Dieu sauve Dame Emme!"	*spend all day*
Cokes and hire knaves cryden, " Hote pies, hote!	*crying*
Goode gees and grys! Go we dyne, go we!'	*pork and goose*
Taverners until hem tolden the same:	
"Whit wyn of Oseye and wyn of Gascoigne,	*wine of Alsace*
Of the Ryn and of the Rochel, the roost to defie!'	*Rhine*
—Al this I seigh slepyng, and sevene sythes more.	*seven times*

Geoffrey Chaucer

From THE GENERAL PROLOGUE TO THE CANTERBURY TALES

Here bygynneth the Book of the tales of Caunterbury.

WHAN THAT Aprille with his shoures soote,	*showers sweet*
The droghte of March hath perced to the roote,	*drought*
And bathed every veyne in swich licóur	*sweet liquor*
Of which vertú engendred is the flour;	*virtue*
Whan Zephirus eek with his swete breeth	*also*
Inspired hath in every holt and heeth	*grove and heath*
The tendre croppes, and the yonge sonne	*tender shoots*
Hath in the Ram his halfe cours y-ronne,	*run*
And smale foweles maken melodye,	
That slepen al the nyght with open ye,	*eye*
So priketh hem Natúre in hir corages,	*stirs their heart*
Thanne longen folk to goon on pilgrimages,	*to go*
And palmeres for to seken straunge strondes,	*long : beaches*
To ferne halwes, kowthe in sondry londes;	*far away saints : known*

And specially, from every shires ende
Of Engelond, to Caunterbury they wende, *go*
The hooly blisful martir for to seke,
That hem hath holpen whan that they were seeke. *sick*
    Bifil that in that seson on a day, *It befell : one day*
In Southwerk at *The Tabard* as I lay,
Redy to wenden on my pilgrymage *to go*
To Caunterbury with ful devout corage, *heart*
At nyght were come into that hostelrye
Wel nyne and twenty in a compaignye
Of sondry folk, by áventure y-falle *perchance to fall*
In felaweshipe, and pilgrimes were they alle, *fellowship*
That toward Caunterbury wolden ryde. *they wished to*
The chambres and the stables weren wyde, *were*
And wel we weren esed atte beste. *we were eased*
And shortly, whan the sonne was to reste,
So hadde I spoken with hem everychon,
That I was of hir felaweshipe anon, *their : at once*
And made forward erly for to ryse, *And I pledged*
To take oure wey, ther as I yow devyse. *as I said before*
    But nathelees, whil I have tyme and space, *nonetheless*
Er that I ferther in this tale pace, *Before : proceed*
Me thynketh it acordaunt to resoun
To telle yow al the condicioun
Of ech of hem, so as it semed me,
And whiche they weren and of what degree,
And eek in what array that they were inne; *also*
And at a Knyght than wol I first bigynne.

    A K NYGHT ther was, and that a worthy man,
That fro the tyme that he first bigan
To riden out, he loved chivalrie,
Trouthe and honóur, fredom and curteisie.
Ful worthy was he in his lordes werre, *war*

And thereto hadde he riden, no man ferre, *further*
As wel in cristendom as in hethenesse, *heathen lands*
And evere honóured for his worthynesse.

    At Alisaundre he was whan it was wonne; *Alexandria*
Ful ofte tyme he hadde the bord bigonne *sat at the head of the table*

Aboven alle nacions in Pruce. *Prussia*
In Lettow hadde he reysed and in Ruce,— *Lithuania : Russia*

No cristen man so ofte of his degree.
In Gernade at the seege eek hadde he be *Granada : also*
Of Algezir, and riden in Belmarye. *Algeciras : Benamarin*

At Lyeys was he, and at Satalye, *Ayas : Attalia*
Whan they were wonne; and in the Grete See *Mediterranean*
At many a noble armee hadde he be. *expedition*
At mortal batailles hadde he been fiftene,
And foughten for oure feith at Tramyssene *Tremessen*
In lyste thries, and ay slayn his foo. *three tourneys : always*

This ilke worthy knyght hadde been also *same*
Somtyme with the lord of Palatye *Palathia*
Agayn another hethen in Turkye; *Against*
And evermoore he hadde a sovereyn prys. *superior fame*
And though that he were worthy, he was wys,
And of his port as meeke as is a mayde. *disposition*
He nevere yet no vileynye ne sayde, *coarseness*
In al his lyf, unto no maner wight. *no manner of man*

He was a verray, parfit, gentil knyght. *perfect*
But for to tellen yow of his array, *dress*
His hors weren goode, but he was nat gay; *gaudy*
Of fustian he wered a gypon *wore a tunic*
Al bismótered with his habergeon; *marked : hauberk*
For he was late y-come from his viage, *campaign*
And wente for to doon his pilgrymage.

A Good Wif was ther of biside Bathe, *from near Bath*
But she was som-del deef, and that was scathe. *somewhat deaf :*
a pity
Of clooth-makyng she hadde swich an haunt *such a talent*
She passed hem of Ypres and of Gaunt.
In al the parisshe wif ne was ther noon
That to the offrynge bifore hire sholde goon; *offering : go*
And if ther dide, certeyn so wrooth was she
That she was out of alle charitee.
Hir coverchiefs ful fyne weren of ground; *kerchiefs : texture*
I dorste swere they weyeden ten pound
That on a Sonday weren upon hir heed.
Hir hosen weren of fyn scarlet reed,
Ful streite y-teyd, and shoes ful moyste and *tightly tied*
  newe.
Boold was hir face, and fair, and reed of hewe.
She was a worthy wommman al hir lyve;
Housbondes at chirche dore she hadde fyve,
Withouten oother compaignye in youthe;
But ther-of nedeth nat to speke as nowthe. *for now*
And thries hadde she been at Jérusalem; *thrice*
She hadde passed many a straunge strem;
At Rome she hadde been, and at Boloigne,
In Galice at Seint Jame, and at Coloigne. *Galicia : St.*
James
She koude muchel of wandrynge by the weye. *knew*
Gat-tothed was she, soothly for to seye. *Gap-toothed :*
truly
Upon an amblere esily she sat, *ambling horse*
Y-wympled wel, and on hir heed an hat *Wimpled*
As brood as is a bokeler or a targe; *buckler : shield*
A foot-mantel aboute hir hipes large, *foot-cloth : hips*
And on hire feet a paire of spores sharpe. *spurs*
In felaweshipe wel koude she laughe and *knew how to :*
  carpe; *talk*
Of remedies of love she knew *per chauncé*, *no doubt*

For she koude of that art the olde daunce.

    Ther was also a Reve and a Millere,
A Somnour and a Pardoner also,   *summoner*
A Maunciple, and myself,—ther were namo.   *no more*
    The Millere was a stout carl for the nones;   *freeman : suitably*
Ful byg he was of brawn and eek of bones.   *also*
That proved wel, for over-al, ther he cam,
At wrastlynge he wolde have alwey the ram.   *win the ram*
He was short-sholdred, brood, a thikke knarre;   *thick-set*
Ther nas no dore that he nolde heve of harre,   *off its hinges*
Or breke it at a rennyng with his heed.
His berd as any sowe or fox was reed,
And therto brood, as though it were a spade.   *broad*
Upon the cop right of his nose he hade   *the very tip*
A werte, and thereon stood a toft of herys,   *wart : tuft of hair*
Reed as the brustles of a sowes erys;   *ears*
His nosethirles blake were and wyde.   *nostrils : black*
A swerd and a bokeler bar he by his syde.   *buckler*
His mouth as greet was as a greet forneys;   *furnace*
He was a janglere and a goliardeys,   *gossip : buffoon*
And that was moost of synne and harlotries.
Wel koude he stelen corn and tollen thries;   *steal thrice*
And yet he hadde a thombe of gold, pardee.   *by God*
A whit cote and a blew hood wered he.
A baggepipe wel koude he blowe and sowne,
And therwithal he broghte us out of towne.

    The Reve was a sclendre colerik man.   *choleric*
His berd was shave as ny as ever he kan;   *close-shaven*
His heer was by his erys round y-shorn;   *ears*
His top was dokked lyk a preest biforn.   *in the front*
Ful longe were his legges and ful lene,
Y-lyk a staf, ther was no calf y-sene.   *like a stick : seen*
Wel koude he kepe a gerner and a bynne;   *garner : bin*

Ther was noon auditour koude on him wynne. *could gain a point on him*
Wel wiste he, by the droghte and by the reyn, *knew : drought*
The yeldynge of his seed and of his greyn.
His lordes sheep, his neet, his dayerye, *dairy*
His swyn, his hors, his stoor, and his pultrye, *swine : store*
Was hoolly in this reves governyng;
And by his covenant yaf the rekenyng
Syn that his lord was twenty yeer of age;
There koude no man brynge hym in arrerage. *arrears*
There nas baillif, ne hierde, nor oother hyne, *herdsman : serf*
That he ne knew his sleighte and his covyne; *deceit*
They were adrad of hym as of the deeth. *afraid*
His wonyng was ful fair upon an heeth; *dwelling*
With grene trees shadwed was his place.
He koude bettre than his lord purchace; *bargain*
Ful riche he was a-stored pryvely. *in secret*
His lord wel koude he plesen subtilly,
To yeve and lene hym of his owene good, *give : loan*
And have a thank, and yet a cote and hood. *earn thanks*
In youthe he hadde lerned a good myster; *trade*
He was a wel good wrighte, a carpenter.
This Reve sat upon a ful good stot, *horse*
That was al pomely grey, and highte Scot. *dappled : named*
A long surcote of pers upon he hade, *overcoat : blue*
And by his syde he baar a rusty blade.
Of Northfolk was this Reve of which I telle,
Biside a toun men clepen Baldeswelle. *town : called*
Tukked he was as is a frere, aboute. *Tucked*
And evere he rood the hyndreste of oure route. *hindmost : company*

Anonymous Ballads

ROBIN HOOD AND THE MONK

In somer, when the shawes be sheyne,	*woods shine*
And leves be large and long,	
Hit is full mery in feyre foreste	*fair*
To here the foulys song,	*hear : birds*

To se the dere draw to the dale,	*deer*
And leve the hilles hee,	*high*
And shadow hem in the leves grene,	*hide themselves*
Under the grene wode tre.	

Hit befel on Whitson
Erly in a May mornyng,
The son up feyre can shyne, *did*
And the briddis mery can syng.

"This is a mery mornyng," seid Litull John,	
"Be Hym that dyed on tre;	*By Christ : cross*
A more mery man then I am one	*than*
Lyves not in Cristianté.	*Christendom*

"Pluk up thi hert, my dere mayster,"
Litull John can sey,
"And thynk hit is a full fayre tyme
In a mornyng of May."

"Ye, on thyng greves me," seid Robyn,	*one*
"And does my hert mych woo:	*woe*
That I may not no solem day	
To mas nor matyns goo.	*Mass nor Matins*

"Hit is a fourtnet and more," seid he,	*fortnight*
"Syn I my Savyour see;	*Since I've been*
To day wil I to Notyngham," seid Robyn,	*to mass*
"With the myght of mylde Marye."	*Virgin Mary*

Than spake Moche, the mylner sun, — *miller's son*
Ever more wel hym betyde! — *go well with him*
"Take twelve of thi wyght yemen, — *strong yeomen*
Well weppynd, be thi side. — *well armed*
Such on wolde thi selfe slon, — *would kill you*
That twelve dar not abyde." — *dare not face*

"Of all my mery men," seid Robyn,
"Be my feith I wil non have, — *By*
But Litull John shall beyre my bow, — *bear*
Til that me list to drawe." — *choose to shoot*

"Thou shall beyre thin own," seid Litull Jon,
"Maister, and I wyl beyre myne,
And we well shete a peny," seid Litull Jon, — *shoot for a penny*
Under the grene wode lyne." — *linden trees*

"I wil not shete a peny," seyd Robyn Hode,
"In feith, Litull John, with the,
But ever for on as thou shetis," seide Robyn,
"In feith I holde the thre." — *bet you three*

Thus shet thei forth, these yemen too, — *two*
Bothe at buske and brome, — *bush and shrub*
Til Litull John wan of his maister — *for socks and shoes*
Five shillings to hose and shone.

A ferly strife fel them betwene, — *great quarrel*
As they went bi the wey;
Litull John seid he had won five shillings,
And Robyn Hode seid schortly nay. — *abruptly*

With that Robyn Hode lyed Litul Jon, — *accused*
And smote hym with his hande;
Litul Jon waxed wroth therwith,
And pulled out his bright bronde. — *sword*

"Were thou not my maister," seid Litull John,
"Thou shuldis by hit ful sore; — *pay for it dearly*
Get the a man wher thou wille,

ROBIN HOOD AND THE MONK

For thou getis me no more."

Then Robyn goes to Notyngham,
Hym selfe mornyng allone, *mourning*
And Litull John to mery Scherwode,
The pathes he knew ilkone. *every one*

Whan Robyn came to Notyngham,
Sertenly withouten layn, *Certainly : lie*
He prayed to God and myld Mary
To bryng hym out save agayn. *safe*

He gos in to Seynt Mary chirch,
And knelyd down before the rode; *cross*
Alle that ever were the church within
Beheld wel Robyn Hode.

Beside hym stod a gret-hedid munke, *large-headed*
I pray to God woo he be! *woe*
Ful sone he knew gode Robyn,
As sone as he hym se.

Out at the durre he ran, *door*
Ful sone and anon; *At once*
Alle the gatis of Notyngham *gates*
He made to be sparred everychon. *barred*

"Rise up," he seid, "thou prowde schereff,
Buske the and make the bowne; *Hurry and ready*
I have spyed the kynggis felon, *yourself*
For sothe he is in this town. *truly*

"I have spyed the false felon,
As he stondis at his masse;
Hit is long of the," seide the munke, *It's your fault*
"And ever he fro us passe. *If : escapes*

"This traytur name is Robyn Hode,
Under the grene wode lynde; *linden trees*
He robbyt me onys of a hundred pound, *once*
Hit shalle never out of my mynde."

Up then rose this prowde schereff,
And radly made hym yare;   *quickly : ready*
Many was the moder son
To the kyrk with hym can fare.   *church : did go*

In at the durres thei throly thrast,   *doors : thrust*
With staves ful gode wone;   *many staves*
"Alas, alas!" seid Robyn Hode,
"Now mysse I Litull John."

But Robyn toke out a too-hond sworde,   *two-handed*
That hangit down be his kne;   *sword*
Ther as the schereff and his men stode thyckust   *thickest*
Thedurwarde wolde he.   *Thitherward*

Thryes thorow at them he ran then,   *Thrice through*
For sothe as I yow sey,   *Truly*
And woundyt mony a moder son,
And twelve he slew that day.

His sworde upon the schireff hed   *sherrif's head*
Sertanly he brake in too;   *two*
"The smyth that the made," seid Robyn,   *made the sword*
"I pray to God wyrke hym woo!   *woe*

"For now am I weppynlesse," seid Robyn,   *weaponless*
"Alasse! agayn my wyll;
But if I may fle these traytors fro,   *Unless*
I wot thei wil me kyll."   *know*

Robyn in to her churche ran,   *their*
Thro out hem everilkon,   *each one*

. . .

Sum fel in swonyng as thei were dede,   *swooning*
And lay stil as any stone;
Non of theym were in her mynde   *kept their heads*
But only Litull Jon.

"Let be your rule," seid Litull Jon,

ROBIN HOOD AND THE MONK

"For His luf that dyed on tre,	*died on the cross*
Ye that shulde be dughty men;	*doughty*
Het is gret shame to se.	

"Oure maister has bene hard bystode	*beset*
And yet scapyd away;	*escaped*
Pluk up your hertis, and leve this mone,	*hearts : moan*
And harkyn what I shal say.	

"He has servyd Oure Lady many a day,	
And yet wil, securly;	*surely*
Therfor I trust in hir specialy	
No wyckud deth shal he dye.	

"Therfor be glad," seid Litul John,	
"And let this mournyng be;	
And I shal be the munkis gyde,	*monk's guardian*
With the myght of mylde Mary,	
And I mete hym," seid Litul John	*If*
"We will go but we too.	

"Loke that ye kepe wel owre tristil-tre,	*meeting tree*
Under the levys smale,	
And spare non of this venyson,	
That gose in thys vale."	

Forthe then went these yemen too,	*two*
Litul John and Moche on fere,	*together*
And lokid on Moch emys hows;	*Much's uncle's*
The hye way lay full nere.	*house*

Litul John stode at a wyndow in the mornyng,	
And lokid forth at a stage;	*from an upper room*

He was war wher the munke came ridyng,	
And with hym a litul page.	

"Be my feith," seid Litul John to Moch,	
"I can the tel tithyngus gode;	*good tidings*
I se wher the munke cumys rydyng,	

I know hym be his wyde hode."

They went in to the way, these yemen bothe,
As curtes men and hende;   *civil : gracious*
Thei spyrred tithyngus at the munke,   *asked news*
As they hade bene his frende.

"Fro whens come ye?" seid Litull Jon,
"Tel us tithyngus, I yow pray,
Of a false owtlay,
Was takyn yisterday.

"He robbyt me and my felowes bothe
Of twenti marke in serten;
If that false owtlay be takyn,
For sothe we wolde be fayn."   *truly : glad*

"So did he me," seid the munke,
Of a hundred pound and more;
I layde furst hande hym apon,
Ye may thonke me therfore."

"I pray God thanke you," seid Litull John,
"And we wil when we may;
We wil go with you, with your leve,
And bryng yow on your way.

"For Robyn Hode hase many a wilde felow,
I tell you in certen;
If thei wist ye rode this way,   *knew*
In feith ye shulde be slayn."

As thei went talking be the way,
The munke and Litull John,
John toke the munkis horse be the hede,
Ful sone and anon.   *At once*

Johne toke the munkis horse be the hed,
For sothe as I yow say;
So did Much the litull page,
For he shulde not scape away.   *escape*

ROBIN HOOD AND THE MONK

Be the golett of the hode   *throat-piece*
John pulled the munke down;
John was nothyng of hym agast,   *afraid*
He lete hym falle on his crown.

Litull John was so agrevyd,
And drew owt his swerde in hye;   *in haste*
The munke saw he shulde be ded,
Lowd mercy can he crye.

"He was my maister," seid Litull John,
"That thou hase browght in bale;   *harm*
Shalle thou never cum at oure kyng,
For to telle hym tale."

John smote of the munkis hed,   *smote off*
No longer wolde he dwell;   *wait*
So did Moch the litull page,
For ferd lest he wolde tell.   *fear*

Ther thei beryed hem bothe,   *buried*
In nouther mosse nor lyng,   *bog nor heath*
And Litull John and Much in fere   *together*
Bare the letturs to oure kyng.

Litull John cam in unto the kyng
He knelid down upon his kne:
"God yow save, my lege lorde,
Jhesus yow save and se!   *watch over*

"God yow save, my lege kyng!"   *liege*
To speke John was full bolde;
He gaf hym the letturs in his hand,
The kyng did hit unfold.

The kyng red the letturs anon,
And seid, "So mot I the,   *that I may thrive*
Ther was never yoman in mery Inglond
I longut so sore to se.   *longed*

"Wher is the munke that these shuld have
  brought?"
Oure kyng can say.
"Be my trouth," seid Litull John,
"He dyed after the way."   *along*

The kyng gaf Moch and Litul Jon
Twenti pound in sertan,
And made theim yemen of the crown,
And bade theim go agayn.

He gaf John the seel in hand,
The scheref for to bere,
To bryng Robyn hym to,
And no man do hym dere.   *harm*

John toke his leve at oure kyng,
The sothe as I yow say;
The next way to Notyngham   *nearest*
To take he yede the way.   *went*

Whan John came to Notyngham
The gatis were sparred ychon;   *each barred*
John callid up the porter,
He answerid sone anon.   *straight away*

"What is the cause," seid Litul Jon,
"Thou sparris the gates so fast?"
"Because of Robyn Hode," seid porter,
"In depe prison is cast.

"John and Moch and Wyll Scathlok,
For sothe as I yow say,
Thei slew oure men upon oure wallis,
And sawten us every day."   *assault*

Litull John spyrred after the schereff,   *asked*
And sone he hym fonde;
He oppyned the kyngus privé seell,   *king's privy seal*
And gaf hym in his honde.

ROBIN HOOD AND THE MONK

Whan the scheref saw the kyngus seell,
He did of his hode anon: *took off*
"Wher is the munke that bare the letturs?"
He seid to Litull John.

"He is so fayn of hym," seid Litul John,   *so pleased*
"For sothe as I yow say,
He has made hym abot of Westmynster,
A lorde of that abbay."

The scheref made John gode chere,
And gaf hym wyne of the best;
At nyght thei went to her bedde,   *their*
And every man to his rest.

When the scheref was on slepe,
Dronken of wyne and ale,
Litul John and Moch for sothe
Toke the way unto the gale.   *jail*

Litul John callid up the jayler,
And bade hym rise anon;
He seyd Robyn Hode had brokyn the prison,
And out of hit was gon.

The porter rose anon sertan,
As sone as he herd John calle;
Litul John was redy with a swerd,
And bare hym throw to the walle.   *stabbed*

"Now wil I be jayler," seid Litul John,
And toke the keyes in honde;
He toke the way to Robyn Hode,
And sone he hym unbonde.

He gaf hym a gode swerd in his hond,
His hed ther with to kepe,   *protect*
And ther as the wallis were lowyst
Anon down can thei lepe.   *did*

Be that the cok began to crow,

The day began to spryng;
The scheref fond the jaylier ded,
The comyn bell made he ryng.   *town bell*

He made a crye thoroout al the town,
Wheder he be yoman or knave,
That cowthe bryng hym Robyn Hode,   *could*
His warison he shuld have.   *reward*

"For I dar never," seid the scheref,
"Cum before oure kyng;
For if I do, I wot serten   *I know certainly*
For sothe he wil me heng."   *hang*

The scheref made to seke Notyngham,   *search*
Bothe be strete and styne,   *alleyways*
And Robyn was in mery Scherwode,
As light as lef on lynde.   *carefree : tree*

Then bespake gode Litull John,
To Robyn Hode can he say,
"I have done the a gode turne for an ill,
Quit me whan thou may.   *Repay*

"I have done the a gode turne," seid Litull John,
"For sothe as I the say;
I have brought the under the grene-wode lyne;
Fare wel, and have gode day."

"Nay, be my trouth," seid Robyn,
"So shall hit never be;
I make the maister," seid Robyn,
"Of alle my men and me."

"Nay, be my trouth," seid Litull John,
"So shalle hit never be;
But lat me be a felow," seid Litull John,

ROBIN HOOD AND THE MONK

"No noder kepe I be."	*Nor else do I care to be*

Thus John gate Robyn Hod out of prison,
Sertan withoutyn layn;   *lie*
Whan his men saw hym hol and sounde,
For sothe they were full fayne.   *glad*

They filled in wyne and made hem glad,
Under the levys smale,
And yete pastes of venyson,   *ate pasties*
That gode was with ale.

Than worde came to oure kyng
How Robyn Hode was gon,
And how the scheref of Notyngham
Durst never loke hym upon.

Then bespake oure cumly kyng,   *comely*
In an angur hye:
"Litull John hase begyled the schereff,
In faith so hase he me.

"Litul John has begyled us bothe,
And that full wel I se;
Or ellis the schereff of Notyngham
Hye hongut shulde he be.   *High hanged*

"I made hem yemen of the crowne,
And gaf hem fee with my hond;   *money*
I gaf hem grith," seid oure kyng,   *pardon*
"Thorowout all mery Inglond.

"I gaf theym grith," then seid oure kyng;
"I say, so mot I the,   *that I may thrive*
For sothe soch a yeman as he is on
In all Inglond ar not thre.

"He is trew to his maister," seid oure kyng;
"I sey, be swete Seynt John,
He lovys better Robyn Hode

Then he dose us ychon. *Than : each of us*

"Robyn Hode is ever bond to hym, *bound*
Bothe in strete and stalle; *stable*
Speke no more of this mater," seid oure kyng,
"But John has begyled us alle."

Thus endys the talkyng of the munke
And Robyn Hode I wysse; *to be sure*
God, that is ever a crowned kyng,
Bryng us alle to His blisse!

THE BALLAD OF SIR PATRICK SPENS

The King sits in Dunferline toun, *town*
Drinkin the blude-reid wine *blood-red*
'O whaur will A get a skeely skipper *skilful*
Tae sail this new ship o mine?'

O up and spak an eldern knight, *spake*
Sat at the king's richt knee; *right*
'Sir Patrick Spens is the best sailor
That ever sailt the sea.'

Our king has written a braid letter *broad*
And sealed it wi his hand,
And sent it to Sir Patrick Spens,
Wis walkin on the strand. *beach*

'Tae Noroway, to Noroway, *Norway*
Tae Noroway ower the faem; *foam*
The King's dauchter o Noroway,
Tis thou maun bring her hame.' *must*

The first word that Sir Partick read
Sae loud, loud laucht he; *laughed*
The neist word that Sir Patrick read
The tear blindit his ee. *blinded : eye*

SIR PATRICK SPENS

'O wha is this has duin this deed
An tauld the king o me,
Tae send us out, at this time o year,
Tae sail abuin the sea?   *upon*

'Be it wind, be it weet, be it hail, be it sleet,
Our ship maun sail the faem;   *must*
The King's dauchter o Noroway,
Tis we maun fetch her hame.'

They hoystit their sails on Monenday morn,
Wi aw the speed they may;
They hae landit in Noroway
Upon a Wodensday.

'Mak ready, mak ready, my merry men aw!
Our gude ship sails the morn.'
'Nou eer alack, ma maister dear,   *Alas*
I fear a deadly storm.'

'A saw the new muin late yestreen   *moon : last eve*
Wi the auld muin in her airm   *old : arm*
And gif we gang tae sea, maister,   *if we go*
A fear we'll cam tae hairm.'

They hadnae sailt a league, a league,
A league but barely three,
When the lift grew dark, an the wind blew loud
An gurly grew the sea.   *fierce*

The ankers brak, an the topmaist lap,
It was sic a deadly storm.   *such*
An the waves cam ower the broken ship
Til aw her sides were torn.

'Go fetch a web o silken claith,
Anither o the twine,
An wap them into our ship's side,   *bind*
An let nae the sea cam in.'

They fetcht a web o the silken claith,
Anither O the twine,
An they wappp'd them roun that gude ship's side,   *bound*
But still the sea cam in.

O laith, laith were our gude Scots lords   *loath*
Tae weet their cork-heelt shuin;   *shoes*
But lang or aw the play wis playd   *however they plied*
They wat their hats abuin.   *above*

And mony wis the feather bed   *many*
That flattert on the faem;   *fluttered*
And mony wis the gude lord's son
That never mair cam hame.   *more : home*

O lang, lang may the ladies sit,
Wi their fans intae their hand,
Afore they see Sir Patrick Spens
Come sailin tae the strand!   *beach*

And lang, lang may the maidens sit
Wi their gowd kames in their hair,   *combs*
A-waitin for their ane dear loes!   *own*
For them they'll see nae mair.   *no more*

Half-ower, half-ower to Aberdour,   *halfway over*
Tis fifty fathoms deep;
An there lies gude Sir Patrick Spens,
Wi the Scots lords at his feet!

THE TWA CORBIES

As I was walking all alane,
I heard twa corbies making a mane;   *ravens : moan*
The tane unto the t'other say,   *that one*
"Where sail we gang and dine to-day?"—

"In behint yon auld fail-dyke,

I wot there lies a new-slain knight;
And naebody kens that he lies there,
But his hawk, his hound, and lady fair.

"His hound is to the hunting gane,
His hawk to fetch the wild-fowl hame,
His lady's ta'en anither mate,
So we may mak' our dinner sweet.

"Ye'll sit on his white hause-bane,   *collar-bone*
And I'll pike out his bonny blue een;   *pick*
Wi' ae lock o' his gowden hair
We'll theek our nest when it grows bare.   *thatch*

"Mony a one for him makes mane,
But nane sall ken where he is gane;   *shall*
O'er his white banes, when they are bare,
The wind sall blaw for evermair."

EDWARD, EDWARD

"Why does your brand sae drap wi' blude,   *sword*
  Edward, Edward?
Why does your brand sae drap wi' blude?
  And why sae sad gang ye, O?"—
"O, I hae kill'd my hawk sae gude,
  Mither, mither:
O, I hae kill'd my hawk sae gude,
  And I hae nae mair but he, O."

"Your hawk's blude was never sae red,
  Edward, Edward:
Your hawk's blude was never sae red,
  My dear son, I tell thee, O."—
"O, I hae kill'd my red-roan steed,
  Mither, mither:
O, I hae kill'd my red-roan steed,
  That was sae fair and free, O."—

"Your steed was auld, and ye hae gat mair,
Edward, Edward:
Your steed was auld, and ye hae gat mair,
Some ither dule ye dree, O."—   *sorrow: endure*
"O, I hae kill'd my father dear,
Mither, mither:
O, I hae kill'd my father dear,
Alas! and wae is me, O."—

"And whatten penance will ye dree for that,
Edward, Edward?
And whatten penance will ye dree for that?
My dear son, now tell me, O."—
"I'll set my feet in yonder boat,
Mither, mither:
I'll set my feet in yonder boat,
And I'll fare o'er the sea, O."—

"And what will ye do wi' your towers and ha,
Edward, Edward?
And what will ye do wi' your towers and ha',
That were sae fair to see, O?"—
"I'll let them stand till they down fa',
Mither, mither:
I'll let them stand till they down fa',
For here never mair maun I be, O."—

"And what will ye leave to your bairns and wife,
Edward, Edward?
And what will ye leave to your bairns and wife,
When ye gang o'er the sea, O?"—
"The warld's room; let them beg through life,
Mither, mither:
The warld's room; let them beg through life,
For them never mair will I see, O."—

"And what will ye leave to your mither dear,

Edward, Edward?
And what will ye leave to your mither dear?
My dear son, now tell me, O."—
"The curse of hell frae me sall ye bear,　　　　　　　　　*shall*
Mither, mither:
The curse of hell frae me sall ye bear,
Sic counsels ye gied to me, O."

THE CORPUS CHRISTI CAROL

Lully, lulley! Lully, lulley!
The falcon hath borne my make away!　　　　　　　　　*mate*

He bare him up, he bare him down,
He bare him into an orchard brown.

In that orchard there was an halle,
That was hanged with purple and pall.

And in that hall there was a bed,
And it was hanged with gold so red.

And in that bed there li'th a knight　　　　　　　　　*lies*
His woundes bleeding day and night.

At that bed's foot there li'eth a hound,
Licking the blood as it runs down.

By that bed-side kneeleth a may,　　　　　　　　　*maid*
And she weepeth both night and day.

And at that bed's head standeth a stone,
Corpus Christi written thereon.

Lully, lulley! Lully, lulley!
The falcon hath borne my make away!

Edmund Spenser

From THE FAERIE QUEENE

The Patrone of true Holinesse,
  Foule Errour doth defeate:
Hypocrisie him to entrappe,
  Doth to his home entreate.

A GENTLE Knight was pricking on the plaine,
  Y cladd in mightie armes and silver shielde,
  Wherein old dints of deepe wounds did remaine,
  The cruell markes of many a bloudy fielde;
  Yet armes till that time did he never wield:
  His angry steede did chide his foming bitt,
  As much disdayning to the curbe to yield:
  Full jolly knight he seemd, and faire did sitt,
As one for knightly giusts and fierce encounters fitt.

But on his brest a bloudie Crosse he bore,
  The deare remembrance of his dying Lord,
  For whose sweete sake that glorious badge he wore,
  And dead as living ever him ador'd:
  Upon his shield the like was also scor'd,
  For soveraine hope, which in his helpe he had:
  Right faithfull true he was in deede and word,
  But of his cheere did seeme too solemne sad;
Yet nothing did he dread, but ever was ydrad.

Upon a great adventure he was bond,
  That greatest *Gloriana* to him gave,
  That greatest Glorious Queene of *Faerie* lond,
  To winne him worship, and her grace to have,
  Which of all earthly things he most did crave;
  And ever as he rode, his hart did earne
  To prove his puissance in battell brave
  Upon his foe, and his new force to learne;
Upon his foe, a Dragon horrible and stearne.

A lovely Ladie rode him faire beside,
   Upon a lowly Asse more white then snow,
   Yet she much whiter, but the same did hide
   Under a vele, that wimpled was full low,
   And over all a blacke stole she did throw,
   As one that inly mournd: so was she sad,
   And heavie sat upon her palfrey slow;
   Seemed in heart some hidden care she had,
And by her in a line a milke white lambe she lad.

So pure and innocent, as that same lambe,
   She was in life and every vertuous lore,
   And by descent from Royall lynage came
   Of ancient Kings and Queenes, that had of yore
   Their scepters stretcht from East to Westerne shore,
   And all the world in their subjection held;
   Till that infernall feend with foule uprore
   Forwasted all their land, and them expeld:
Whom to avenge, she had this Knight from far compeld.

Behind her farre away a Dwarfe did lag,
   That lasie seemd in being ever last,
   Or wearied with bearing of her bag
   Of needments at his backe. Thus as they past,
   The day with cloudes was suddeine overcast,
   And angry *Jove* an hideous storme of raine
   Did poure into his Lemans lap so fast,
   That every wight to shrowd it did constrain,
And this faire couple eke to shrowd themselves were fain.

Enforst to seeke some covert nigh at hand,
   A shadie grove not far away they spide,
   That promist ayde the tempest to withstand:
   Whose loftie trees yclad with sommers pride,
   Did spred so broad, that heavens light did hide,
   Not perceable with power of any starre:
   And all within were pathes and alleies wide,
   With footing worne, and leading inward farre:

Faire harbour that them seemes; so in they entred arre.

And foorth they passe, with pleasure forward led,
   Joying to heare the birdes sweete harmony,
   Which therein shrouded from the tempest dred,
   Seemd in their song to scorne the cruell sky.
   Much can they prayse the trees so straight and hy,
   The sayling Pine, the Cedar proud and tall,
   The vine-prop Elme, the Poplar never dry,
   The builder Oake, sole king of forrests all,
The Aspine good for staves, the Cypresse funerall.

The Laurell, meed of mightie Conquerours
   And Poets sage, the Firre that weepeth still,
   The Willow worne of forlorne Paramours,
   The Eugh obedient to the benders will,
   The Birch for shaftes, the Sallow for the mill,
   The Mirrhe sweete bleeding in the bitter wound,
   The warlike Beech, the Ash for nothing ill,
   The fruitfull Olive, and the Platane round,
The carver Holme, the Maple seeldom inward sound.

Led with delight, they thus beguile the way,
   Untill the blustring storme is overblowne;
   When weening to returne, whence they did stray,
   They cannot find that path, which first was showne,
   But wander too and fro in wayes unknowne,
   Furthest from end then, when they neerest weene,
   That makes them doubt, their wits be not their owne:
   So many pathes, so many turnings seene,
That which of them to take, in diverse doubt they been.

At last resolving forward still to fare,
   Till that some end they finde or in or out,
   That path they take, that beaten seemd most bare,
   And like to lead the labyrinth about;
   Which when by tract they hunted had throughout,
   At length it brought them to a hollow cave,
   Amid the thickest woods. The Champion stout

Eftsoones dismounted from his courser brave,
And to the Dwarfe a while his needlesse spere he gave.
"Be well aware," quoth then that Ladie milde,
   "Least suddaine mischiefe ye too rash provoke:
The danger hid, the place unknowne and wilde,
Breeds dreadfull doubts: Oft fire is without smoke,
And perill without show: therefore your stroke
Sir knight with-hold, till further triall made."
"Ah Ladie" (said he) "shame were to revoke
The forward footing for an hidden shade:
Vertue gives her selfe light, through darkenesse for to wade."

"Yea but" (quoth she) "the perill of this place
   I better wot then you, though now too late
To wish you backe returne with foule disgrace,
Yet wisedome warnes, whilest foot is in the gate,
To stay the steppe, ere forced to retrate.
This is the wandring wood, this *Errours den*,
A monster vile, whom God and man does hate:
Therefore I read beware." "Fly fly" (quoth then
The fearefull Dwarfe:) "this is no place for living men."

But full of fire and greedy hardiment,
   The youthfull knight could not for ought be staide,
But forth unto the darksome hole he went,
And looked in: his glistring armor made
A litle glooming light, much like a shade,
By which he saw the ugly monster plaine,
Halfe like a serpent horribly displaide,
But th'other halfe did womans shape retaine,
Most lothsom, filthie, foule, and full of vile disdaine.

And as she lay upon the durtie ground,
   Her huge long taile her den all overspred,
Yet was in knots and many boughtes upwound,
Pointed with mortall sting. Of her there bred
A thousand yong ones, which she dayly fed,
Sucking upon her poisonous dugs, eachone

Of sundry shapes, yet all ill favored:
Soone as that uncouth light upon them shone,
Into her mouth they crept, and suddain all were gone.

Their dam upstart, out of her den effraide,
    And rushed forth, hurling her hideous taile
    About her cursed head, whose folds displaid
    Were stretcht now forth at length without entraile.
    She lookt about, and seeing one in mayle
    Armed to point, sought backe to turne againe;
    For light she hated as the deadly bale,
    Ay wont in desert darknesse to remaine,
Where plaine none might her see, nor she see any plaine.

Which when the valiant Elfe perceiv'd, he lept
    As Lyon fierce upon the flying pray,
    And with his trenchand blade her boldly kept
    From turning backe, and forced her to stay:
    Therewith enrag'd she loudly gan to bray,
    And turning fierce, her speckled taile advaunst,
    Threatning her angry sting, him to dismay:
    Who nought aghast, his mightie hand enhaunst:
The stroke down from her head unto her shoulder glaunst.

Much daunted with that dint, her sence was dazd,
    Yet kindling rage, her selfe she gathered round,
    And all attonce her beastly body raizd
    With doubled forces high above the ground:
    Tho wrapping up her wrethed sterne arownd,
    Lept fierce upon his shield, and her huge traine
    All suddenly about his body wound,
    That hand or foot to stirre he strove in vaine:
God helpe the man so wrapt in *Errours* endlesse traine.

His Lady sad to see his sore constraint,
    Cride out, Now now Sir knight, shew what ye bee,
    Add faith unto your force, and be not faint:
    Strangle her, else she sure will strangle thee.
    That when he heard, in great perplexitie,

His gall did grate for griefe and high disdaine,
  And knitting all his force got one hand free,
  Wherewith he grypt her gorge with so great paine,
That soone to loose her wicked bands did her constraine.

Therewith she spewd out of her filthy maw
  A floud of poyson horrible and blacke,
  Full of great lumpes of flesh and gobbets raw,
  Which stunck so vildly, that it forst him slacke
  His grasping hold, and from her turne him backe:
  Her vomit full of bookes and papers was,
  With loathly frogs and toades, which eyes did lacke,
  And creeping sought way in the weedy gras:
Her filthy parbreake all the place defiled has.

As when old father *Nilus* gins to swell
  With timely pride above the *Aegyptian* vale,
  His fattie waves do fertile slime outwell,
  And overflow each plaine and lowly dale:
  But when his later spring gins to avale,
  Huge heapes of mudd he leaves, wherein there breed
  Ten thousand kindes of creatures, partly male
  And partly female of his fruitfull seed;
Such ugly monstrous shapes elsewhere may no man reed.

The same so sore annoyed has the knight,
  That welnigh choked with the deadly stinke,
  His forces faile, ne can no longer fight.
  Whose corage when the feend perceiv'd to shrinke,
  She poured forth out of her hellish sinke
  Her fruitfull cursed spawne of serpents small,
  Deformed monsters, fowle, and blacke as inke,
  Which swarming all about his legs did crall,
And him encombred sore, but could not hurt at all.

As gentle Shepheard in sweete even-tide,
  When ruddy *Phebus* gins to welke in west,
  High on an hill, his flocke to vewen wide,
  Markes which do byte their hasty supper best;

A cloud of combrous gnattes do him molest,
   All striving to infixe their feeble stings,
   That from their noyance he no where can rest,
   But with his clownish hands their tender wings
He brusheth oft, and oft doth mar their murmurings.

Thus ill bestedd, and fearefull more of shame,
   Then of the certaine perill he stood in,
   Halfe furious unto his foe he came,
   Resolv'd in minde all suddenly to win,
   Or soone to lose, before he once would lin;
   And strooke at her with more then manly force,
   That from her body full of filthie sin
   He raft her hatefull head without remorse;
A streame of cole black bloud forth gushed from her corse.

Her scattred brood, soone as their Parent deare
   They saw so rudely falling to the ground,
   Groning full deadly, all with troublous feare,
   Gathred themselves about her body round,
   Weening their wonted entrance to have found
   At her wide mouth: but being there withstood
   They flocked all about her bleeding wound,
   And sucked up their dying mothers bloud,
Making her death their life, and eke her hurt their good.

That detestable sight him much amazde,
   To see th'unkindly Impes of heaven accurst,
   Devoure their dam; on whom while so he gazd,
   Having all satisfide their bloudy thurst,
   Their bellies swolne he saw with fulnesse burst,
   And bowels gushing forth: well worthy end
   Of such as drunke her life, the which them nurst;
   Now needeth him no lenger labour spend,
His foes have slaine themselves, with whom he should contend.

His Ladie seeing all, that chaunst, from farre
   Approcht in hast to greet his victorie,

And said, "Faire knight, borne under happy starre,
  Who see your vanquisht foes before you lye:
  Well worthy be you of that Armorie,
  Wherein ye have great glory wonne this day,
  And proov'd your strength on a strong enimie,
  Your first adventure: many such I pray,
And henceforth ever wish, that like succeed it may."

Then mounted he upon his Steede againe,
  And with the Lady backward sought to wend;
  That path he kept, which beaten was most plame,
  Ne ever would to any by-way bend,
  But still did follow one unto the end,
  The which at last out of the wood them brought.
  So forward on his way (with God to frend)
  He passed forth, and new adventure sought,
Long way he travelled, before he heard of ought.

At length they chaunst to meet upon the way
  An aged Sire, in long blacke weedes yclad,
  His feete all bare, his beard all hoarie gray,
  And by his belt his booke he hanging had;
  Sober he seemde, and very sagely sad,
  And to the ground his eyes were lowly bent,
  Simple in shew, and voyde of malice bad,
  And all the way he prayed, as he went,
And often knockt his brest, as one that did repent.

He faire the knight saluted, louting low,
  Who faire him quited, as that courteous was:
  And after asked him, if he did know
  Of straunge adventures, which abroad did pas.
  "Ah my deare Sonne" (quoth he) "how should, alas,
  Silly old man, that lives in hidden cell,
  Bidding his beades all day for his trespas,
  Tydings of warre and worldly trouble tell?
With holy father sits not with such things to mell.

But if of daunger which hereby doth dwell,

And homebred evill ye desire to heare,
Of a straunge man I can you tidings tell,
That wasteth all this countrey farre and neare."
"Of such" (saide he) "I chiefly do inquere,
And shall you well reward to shew the place,
In which that wicked wight his dayes doth weare:
For to all knighthood it is foule disgrace,
That such a cursed creature lives so long a space."

"Far hence" (quoth he) "in wastfull wildernesse
His dwelling is, by which no living wight
May ever passe, but thorough great distresse."
"Now" (sayd the Lady) draweth toward night,
And well I wote, that of your later fight
Ye all forwearied be: for what so strong,
But wanting rest will also want of might?
The Sunne that measures heaven all day long,
At night doth baite his steedes the *Ocean* waves emong.

"Then with the Sunne take Sir, your timely rest,
And with new day new worke at once begin:
Untroubled night they say gives counsell best."
"Right well Sir knight ye have advised bin,"
Quoth then that aged man; "the way to win
Is wisely to advise: now day is spent;
Therefore with me ye may take up your In
For this same night." The knight was well content:
So with that godly father to his home they went.

A little lowly Hermitage it was,
Downe in a dale, hard by a forests side,
Far from resort of people, that did pas
In travell to and froe: a little wyde
There was an holy Chappell edifyde,
Wherein the Hermite dewly wont to say
His holy things each morne and eventyde:
Thereby a Christall streame did gently play,
Which from a sacred fountaine welled forth alway.

Arrived there, the little house they fill,
   Ne looke for entertainment, where none was:
   Rest is their feast, and all things at their will;
   The noblest mind the best contentment has.
   With faire discourse the evening so they pas:
   For that old man of pleasing wordes had store,
   And well could file his tongue as smooth as glas;
   He told of Saintes and Popes, and evermore
He strowd an *Ave-Mary* after and before.

The drouping Night thus creepeth on them fast,
   And the sad humour loading their eye liddes,
   As messenger of *Morpheus* on them cast
   Sweet slombring deaw, the which to sleepe them biddes.
   Unto their lodgings then his guestes he riddes:
   Where when all drownd in deadly sleepe he findes,
   He to his study goes, and there amiddes
   His Magick bookes and artes of sundry kindes,
He seekes out mighty charmes, to trouble sleepy mindes.

Then choosing out few wordes most horrible,
   (Let none them read) thereof did verses frame,
   With which and other spelles like terrible,
   He bad awake blacke *Plutoes* griesly Dame,
   And cursed heaven, and spake reprochfull shame
   Of highest God, the Lord of life and light;
   A bold bad man, that dar'd to call by name
   Great *Gorgon*, Prince of darknesse and dead night,
At which *Cocytus* quakes, and *Styx* is put to flight.

And forth he cald out of deepe darknesse dred
   Legions of Sprights, the which like little flyes
   Fluttring about his ever damned hed,
   A-waite whereto their service he applyes,
   To aide his friends, or fray his enimies:
   Of those he chose out two, the falsest twoo,
   And fittest for to forge true-seeming lyes;
   The one of them he gave a message too,

The other by him selfe staide other worke to doo.

He making speedy way through spersed ayre,
    And through the world of waters wide and peepe,
    To *Morpheus* house doth hastily repaire.
    Amid the bowels of the earth full steepe,
    And low, where dawning day doth never peepe,
    His dwelling is; there *Tethys* his wet bed
    Doth ever wash, and *Cynthia* still doth steepe
    In silver deaw his ever-drouping hed,
Whiles sad Night over him her mantle black doth spred.

Whose double gates he findeth locked fast,
    The one faire fram'd of burnisht Yvory,
    The other all with silver overcast;
    And wakefull dogges before them farre do lye
    Watching to banish Care their enimy,
    Who oft is wont to trouble gentle Sleepe.
    By them the Sprite doth passe in quietly,
    And unto *Morpheus* comes, whom drowned deepe
In drowsie fit he findes: of nothing he takes keepe.

And more, to lulle him in his slumber soft,
    A trickling streame from high rocke tumbling downe
    And ever-drizling raine upon the loft,
    Mixt with a murmuring winde, much like the sowne
    Of swarming Bees, did cast him in a swowne:
    No other noyse, nor peoples troublous cryes,
    As still are wont t'annoy the walled towne,
    Might there be heard: but carelesse Quiet lyes,
Wrapt in eternall silence farre from enemyes.

The messenger approching to him spake,
    But his wast wordes returnd to him in vaine:
    So sound he slept, that nought mought him awake.
    Then rudely he him thrust, and pusht with paine,
    Whereat he gan to stretch: but he againe
    Shooke him so hard, that forced him to speake.
    As one then in a dreame, whose dryer braine

In tost with troubled sights and fancies weake,
He mumbled soft, but would not all his silence breake.

The Sprite then gan more boldly him to wake,
   And threatned unto him the dreaded name
   Of *Hecate*: whereat he gan to quake,
   And lifting up his lumpish head, with blame
   Halfe angry asked him, for what he came.
   Hither (quoth he) me *Archimago* sent,
   He that the stubborne Sprites can wisely tame,
   He bids thee to him send for his intent
A fit false dreame, that can delude the sleepers sent.

The God obayde, and calling forth straight way
   A diverse dreame out of his prison darke,
   Delivered it to him, and downe did lay
   His heavie head, devoide of carefull carke,
   Whose sences all were straight benumbed and starke.
   He backe returning by the Yvorie dore,
   Remounted up as light as chearefull Larke,
   And on his litle winges the dreame he bore
In hast unto his Lord, where he him left afore.

Who all this while with charmes and hidden artes,
   Had made a Lady of that other Spright,
   And fram'd of liquid ayre her tender partes
   So lively, and so like in all mens sight,
   That weaker sence it could have ravisht quight:
   The maker selfe for all his wondrous witt,
   Was nigh beguiled with so goodly sight:
   Her all in white he clad, and over it
Cast a blacke stole, most like to seeme for *Una* fit.

Now when that ydle dreame was to him brought,
   Unto that Elfin knight he bad him fly,
   Where he slept soundly void of evill thought
   And with false shewes abuse his fantasy,
   In sort as he him schooled privily:
   And that new creature borne without her dew,

Full of the makers guile, with usage sly
  He taught to imitate that Lady trew,
Whose semblance she did carrie under feigned hew.

Thus well instructed, to their worke they hast,
  And comming where the knight in slomber lay,
  The one upon his hardy head him plast,
  And made him dreame of loves and lustfull play,
  That nigh his manly hart did melt away,
  Bathed in wanton blis and wicked joy:
  Then seemed him his Lady by him lay,
  And to him playnd, how that false winged boy,
Her chast hart had subdewd, to learne Dame pleasures toy.

And she her selfe of beautie soveraigne Queene,
  Faire *Venus* seemde unto his bed to bring
  Her, whom he waking evermore did weene,
  To be the chastest flowre, that ay did spring
  On earthly braunch, the daughter of a king,
  Now a loose Leman to vile service bound:
  And eke the *Graces* seemed all to sing,
  Hymen iō Hymen, dauncing all around,
While freshest *Flora* her with Yvie girlond crownd.

In this great passion of unwonted lust,
  Or wonted feare of doing ought amis,
  He started up, as seeming to mistrust
  Some secret ill, or hidden foe of his:
  Lo there before his face his Lady is,
  Under blake stole hyding her bayted hooke,
  And as halfe blushing offred him to kis,
  With gentle blandishment and lovely looke,
Most like that virgin true, which for her knight him took.

All cleane dismayd to see so uncouth sight,
  And halfe enraged at her shamelesse guise,
  He thought have slaine her in his fierce despight:
  But hastie heat tempring with sufferance wise,
  He stayde his hand, and gan himselfe advise

To prove his sense, and tempt her faigned truth.
Wringing her hands in wemens pitteous wise,
Tho can she weepe, to stirre up gentle ruth,
Both for her noble bloud, and for her tender youth.

And said, "Ah Sir, my liege Lord and my love,
Shall I accuse the hidden cruell fate,
And mightie causes wrought in heaven above,
Or the blind God, that doth me thus amate,
For hoped love to winne me certaine hate?
Yet thus perforce he bids me do, or die.
Die is my dew: yet rew my wretched state
You, whom my hard avenging destinie
Hath made judge of my life or death indifferently.

"Your owne deare sake forst me at first to leave
My Fathers kingdom," There she stopt with teares;
Her swollen hart her speach seemd to bereave,
And then againe begun, "My weaker yeares
Captiv'd to fortune and frayle worldly feares,
Fly to your faith for succour and sure ayde:
Let me not dye in languor and long teares."
"Why Dame" (quoth he) "what hath ye thus dismayd?
What frayes ye, that were wont to comfort me affrayd?"

"Love of your selfe," she saide, "and deare constraint
Lets me not sleepe, but wast the wearie night
In secret anguish and unpittied plaint,
Whiles you in carelesse sleepe are drowned quight."
Her doubtfull words made that redoubted knight
Suspect her truth: yet since no'untruth he knew,
Her fawning love with foule disdainefull spight
He would not shend, but said, "Dear dame I rew,
That for my sake unknowne such griefe unto you grew.

"Assure your selfe, it fell not all to ground;
For all so deare as life is to my hart,
I deeme your love, and hold me to you bound;
Ne let vaine feares procure your needlesse smart,

Where cause is none, but to your rest depart."
  Not all content, yet seemd she to appease
  Her mournefull plaintes, beguiled of her art,
  And fed with words, that could not chuse but please,
So slyding softly forth, she turnd as to her ease.

Long after lay he musing at her mood,
  Much griev'd to think that gentle Dame so light,
  For whose defence he was to shed his blood.
  At last dull wearinesse of former fight
  Having yrockt a sleepe his irkesome spright,
  That troublous dreame gan freshly tosse his braine,
  With bowres, and beds, and Ladies deare delight:
  But when he saw his labour all was vaine,
With that misformed spright he backe returnd againe.

Walter Raleigh

A FAREWELL TO FALSE LOVE

FAREWELL, false love, the oracle of lies,
A mortal foe and enemy to rest,
An envious boy, from whom all cares arise,
A bastard vile, a beast with rage possessed,
A way of error, a temple full of treason,
In all effects contrary unto reason.

A poisoned serpent covered all with flowers,
Mother of sighs, and murderer of repose,
A sea of sorrows whence are drawn such showers
As moisture lend to every grief that grows;
A school of guile, a net of deep deceit,
A gilded hook that holds a poisoned bait.

A fortress foiled, which reason did defend,
A siren song, a fever of the mind,
A maze wherein affection finds no end,

A raging cloud that runs before the wind,
A substance like the shadow of the sun,
A goal of grief for which the wisest run.

A quenchless fire, a nurse of trembling fear,
A path that leads to peril and mishap,
A true retreat of sorrow and despair,
An idle boy that sleeps in pleasure's lap,
A deep mistrust of that which certain seems,
A hope of that which reason doubtful deems.

Sith then thy trains my younger years betrayed,
And for my faith ingratitude I find;
And sith repentance hath my wrongs bewrayed,
Whose course was ever contrary to kind:
False love, desire, and beauty frail, adieu!
Dead is the root whence all these fancies grew.

A FAREWELL TO THE VANITIES OF THE WORLD

FAREWELL, ye gilded follies, pleasing troubles!
Farewell, ye honoured rags, ye glorious bubbles!
Fame's but a hollow echo; gold, pure clay;
Honour, the darling but of one short day,
Beauty—th' eye's idol—but a damasked skin;
State, but a golden prison to live in
And torture free-born minds; embroidered trains,
But pageants for proud swelling veins;
And blood allied to greatness, is alone
Inherited, not purchased, nor our own:
Fame, honour, beauty, state, train, blood, and birth
Are but the fading blossoms of the earth.

I would be great, but that the sun doth still
Level his rays against the rising hill;
I would be high, but see the proudest oak

Most subject to the rending thunder-stroke
I would be rich, but see men, too unkind,
Dig in the bowels of the richest mind;
I would be wise, but that I often see
The fox suspected whilst the ass goes free;
I would be fair, but see the fair and proud,
Like the bright sun, oft setting in a cloud;
I would be poor, but know the humble grass
Still trampled on by each unworthy ass:
Rich, hated; wise, suspected; scorned, if poor,
Great, feared; fair, tempted; high, still envied more;
I have wished all, but now I wish for neither;
Great, high, rich, wise, nor fair, poor I'll be rather.
Would the World now adopt me for her heir,
Would beauty's queen entitle me the fair,
Fame speak me Fortune's minion, could I vie
Angels with India, with a speaking eye
Command bare heads, bowed knees, strike Justice dumb
As well as blind and lame, or give a tongue
To stones by epitaphs, be called great master
In the loose rimes of every poetaster;
Could I be more than any man that lives,
Great, fair, rich, wise, all in superlatives;
Yet I more freely would these gifts resign,
Than ever Fortune would have made them mine;
And hold one minute of this holy leisure
Beyond the riches of this empty pleasure.

Welcome, pure thoughts! welcome, ye silent groves!
These guests, these courts, my soul most dearly loves.
Now the winged people of the sky shall sing
My cheerful anthems to the gladsome spring;
A prayer-book now shall be my looking-glass,
In which I will adore sweet Virtue's face.
Here dwell no hateful looks, no palace cares,
No broken vows dwell here, nor pale-faced fears,
Then here I'll sit and sigh my hot love's folly,

And learn to affect an holy melancholy;
And if contentment be a stranger then
I'll ne'er look for it, but in heaven, again.

A VISION UPON THE FAIRY QUEEN

METHOUGHT I saw the grave where Laura lay,
Within that temple where the vestal flame
Was wont to burn; and, passing by that way,
To see that buried dust of living fame,
Whose tomb fair Love, and fairer Virtue kept:
All suddenly I saw the Fairy Queen;
At whose approach the soul of Petrarch wept,
And, from thenceforth, those Graces were not seen:
For they this queen attended; in whose stead
Oblivion laid him down on Laura's hearse:
Hereat the hardest stones were seen to bleed,
And groans of buried ghosts the heavens did pierce:
Where Homer's spright did tremble all for grief,
And cursed the access of that celestial thief!

Philip Sidney

ASTROPHIL AND STELLA

I

LOVING IN truth, and fain in verse my love to show,
That she, dear she, might take some pleasure of my pain,—
Pleasure might cause her read, reading might make her know,
Knowledge might pity win, and pity grace obtain,—
I sought fit words to paint the blackest face of woe;
Studying inventions fine her wits to entertain,
Oft turning others' leaves, to see if thence would flow

Some fresh and fruitful showers upon my sunburn'd brain.
But words came halting forth, wanting invention's stay;
Invention, Nature's child, fled step-dame Study's blows;
And others' feet still seem'd but strangers in my way.
Thus great with child to speak and helpless in my throes,
   Biting my truant pen, beating myself for spite,
    "Fool," said my Muse to me, "look in thy heart, and write."

XXXI

With how sad steps, O Moon, thou climb'st the skies!
How silently, and with how wan a face!
What, may it be that even in heav'nly place
That busy archer his sharp arrows tries!
Sure, if that long-with love-acquainted eyes
Can judge of love, thou feel'st a lover's case,
I read it in thy looks; thy languish'd grace
To me, that feel the like, thy state descries.
Then, ev'n of fellowship, O Moon, tell me,
Is constant love deem'd there but want of wit?
Are beauties there as proud as here they be?
Do they above love to be lov'd, and yet
   Those lovers scorn whom that love doth possess?
   Do they call virtue there ungratefulness?

XXXIX

Come Sleep; O Sleep! the certain knot of peace,
The baiting-place of wit, the balm of woe,
The poor man's wealth, the prisoner's release,
Th' indifferent judge between the high and low;
With shield of proof shield me from out the prease
Of those fierce darts Despair at me doth throw:
O make in me those civil wars to cease;
I will good tribute pay, if thou do so.
Take thou of me smooth pillows, sweetest bed,
A chamber deaf to noise and blind of light,
A rosy garland and a weary head;

And if these things, as being thine by right,
    Move not thy heavy grace, thou shalt in me,
    Livelier than elsewhere, Stella's image see.

YE GOATHERD GODS

Strephon:

> YE GOATHERD gods, that love the grassy mountains,
> Ye nymphs which haunt the springs in pleasant valleys,
> Ye satyrs joyed with free and quiet forests,
> Vouchsafe your silent ears to plaining music,
> Which to my woes gives still an early morning,
> And draws the dolor on till weary evening.

Klaius:

> O Mercury, forgoer to the evening,
> O heavenly huntress of the savage mountains,
> O lovely star, entitled of the morning,
> While that my voice doth fill these woeful valleys,
> Vouchsafe you silent ears to plaining music,
> Which oft hath Echo tired in secret forests.

Strephon:

> I, that was once free burgess of the forests,
> Where shade from sun and sport I sought in evening,
> I that was once esteemed for pleasant music,
> Am banished now among the monstrous mountains
> Of huge despair, and foul affliction's valleys,
> Am grown a screech owl to myself each morning.

Klaius:

> I, that was once delighted every morning,
> Hunting the wild inhabiters of forests,
> I, that was once the music of these valleys,
> So darkened am that all my day is evening,
> Heartbroken so that molehills seem high mountains,

And fill the vales with cries instead of music.

Strephon:

> Long since, alas, my deadly swannish music
> Hath made itself a crier of the morning,
> And hath with wailing strength climbed highest mountains;
> Long since my thoughts more desert be than forests,
> Long since I see my joys come to their evening,
> And state thrown down to overtrodden valleys.

Klaius:

> Long since the happy dwellers of these valleys,
> Have prayed me leave my strange exclaiming music
> Which troubles their day's work and joys of evening;
> Long since I hate the night, more hate the morning;
> Long since my thoughts chase me like beasts in forests
> And make me wish myself laid under mountains.

Strephon:

> Meseems I see the high and stately mountains,
> Transform themselves to low dejected valleys;
> Meseems I hear in these ill-changed forests
> The nightingales do learn of owls their music;
> Meseems I feel the comfort of the morning
> Turned to the mortal serene of an evening.

Klaius:

> Meseems I see a filthy cloudy evening
> As soon as sun begins to climb the mountains;
> Meseems I feel a noisome scent, the morning
> When I do smell the flowers of these valleys;
> Meseems I hear, when I do hear sweet music,
> The dreadful cries of murdered men in forests.

Strephon:

> I wish to fire the trees of all these forests;
> I give the sun a last farewell each evening;

I curse the fiddling finders-out of music;
With envy I do hate the lofty mountains,
And with despite despise the humble valleys;
I do detest night, evening, day, and morning.

Klaius:

Curse to myself my prayer is, the morning;
My fire is more than can be made with forests,
My state more base than are the basest valleys.
I wish no evenings more to see, each evening;
Shamed, I hate myself in sight of mountains,
And stop mine ears, lest I grow mad with music.

Strephon:

For she whose parts maintained a perfect music,
Whose beauties shined more than the blushing morning,
Who much did pass in state the stately mountains,
In straightness past the cedars of the forests,
Hath cast me, wretch, into eternal evening
By taking her two suns from these dark valleys.

Klaius:

For she, with whom compared, the Alps are valleys,
She, whose least word brings from the spheres their music,
At whose approach the sun rose in the evening,
Who where she went bore in her forehead morning,
Is gone, is gone, from these our spoiled forests,
Turning to deserts our best pastured mountains.

Strephon:

These mountains witness shall, so shall these valleys,

Klaius:

These forests eke, made wretched by our music,

[Both:]

Our morning hymn this is, and song at evening.

William Shakespeare

SONNETS

XII

WHEN I do count the clock that tells the time,
And see the brave day sunk in hideous night;
When I behold the violet past prime,
And sable curls all silver'd o'er with white;
When lofty trees I see barren of leaves
Which erst from heat did canopy the herd,
And summer's green all girded up in sheaves
Borne on the bier with white and bristly beard,
Then of thy beauty do I question make,
That thou among the wastes of time must go,
Since sweets and beauties do themselves forsake
And die as fast as they see others grow;
    And nothing 'gainst Time's scythe can make defence
    Save breed, to brave him when he takes thee hence.

LXXIII

THAT TIME of year thou mayst in me behold
When yellow leaves, or none, or few, do hang
Upon those boughs which shake against the cold,
Bare ruin'd choirs, where late the sweet birds sang.
In me thou see'st the twilight of such day
As after sunset fadeth in the west,
Which by and by black night doth take away,
Death's second self, that seals up all in rest.
In me thou see'st the glowing of such fire
That on the ashes of his youth doth lie,
As the death-bed whereon it must expire,
Consum'd with that which it was nourish'd by.
    This thou perceiv'st, which makes thy love more strong,
    To love that well which thou must leave ere long.

CXXIX

Th' expense of spirit in a waste of shame
Is lust in action; and till action, lust
Is perjured, murd'rous, bloody, full of blame,
Savage, extreme, rude, cruel, not to trust,
Enjoyed no sooner but despisèd straight,
Past reason hunted; and, no sooner had
Past reason hated as a swallowed bait
On purpose laid to make the taker mad;
Mad in pursuit and in possession so,
Had, having, and in quest to have, extreme;
A bliss in proof and proved, a very woe;
Before, a joy proposed; behind, a dream.
    All this the world well knows; yet none knows well
    To shun the heaven that leads men to this hell.

CXLVI

Poor soul, the centre of my sinful earth,
. . . these rebel powers that thee array,
Why dost thou pine within and suffer dearth,
Painting thy outward walls so costly gay?
Why so large cost, having so short a lease,
Dost thou upon thy fading mansion spend?
Shall worms, inheritors of this excess,
Eat up thy charge? Is this thy body's end?
Then soul, live thou upon thy servant's loss
And let that pine to aggravate thy store;
Buy terms divine in selling hours of dross;
Within be fed, without be rich no more.
    So shalt thou feed on Death, that feeds on men,
    And, Death once dead, there's no more dying then.

John Donne

DEATH, BE NOT PROUD

DEATH, be not proud, though some have called thee
Mighty and dreadful, for thou art not so;
For those whom thou think'st thou dost overthrow
Die not, poor Death, nor yet canst thou kill me.
From rest and sleep, which but thy pictures be,
Much pleasure; then from thee much more must flow,
And soonest our best men with thee do go,
Rest of their bones, and soul's delivery.
Thou art slave to fate, chance, kings, and desperate men,
And dost with poison, war, and sickness dwell,
And poppy or charms can make us sleep as well
And better than thy stroke; why swell'st thou then?
    One short sleep past, we wake eternally
    And death shall be no more; Death, thou shalt die.

NO MAN IS AN ISLAND

No MAN is an island,
Entire of itself;
Every man is a piece of the continent,
A part of the main.

If a clod be washed away by the sea,
Europe is the less,
As well as if a promontory were:
As well as if a manor of thy friend's
Or of thine own were.

Any man's death diminishes me,
Because I am involved in mankind.
And therefore never send to know for whom the bell tolls;
It tolls for thee.

Ben Jonson

A FIT OF RHYME
AGAINST RHYME

RHYME, the rack of finest wits,
That expresseth but by fits
True conceit,
Spoiling senses of their treasure,
Cozening judgment with a measure,
But false weight;
Wresting words from their true calling,
Propping verse for fear of falling
To the ground;
Jointing syllabes, drowning letters,
Fast'ning vowels as with fetters
They were bound!
Soon as lazy thou wert known,
All good poetry hence was flown,
And art banish'd.
For a thousand years together
All Parnassus' green did wither,
And wit vanish'd.
Pegasus did fly away,
At the wells no Muse did stay,
But bewail'd
So to see the fountain dry,
And Apollo's music die,
All light failed!
Starveling rhymes did fill the stage;
Not a poet in an age
Worth crowning;
Not a work deserving bays,
Not a line deserving praise,
Pallas frowning;
Greek was free from rhyme's infection,

Happy Greek by this protection
Was not spoiled.
Whilst the Latin, queen of tongues,
Is not yet free from rhyme's wrongs,
But rests foiled.
Scarce the hill again doth flourish,
Scarce the world a wit doth nourish
To restore
Phoebus to his crown again,
And the Muses to their brain,
As before.
Vulgar languages that want
Words and sweetness, and be scant
Of true measure,
Tyrant rhyme hath so abused,
That they long since have refused
Other cæsure.
He that first invented thee,
May his joints tormented be,
Cramp'd forever.
Still may syllabes jar with time,
Still may reason war with rhyme,
Resting never.
May his sense when it would meet
The cold tumor in his feet,
Grow unsounder;
And his title be long fool,
That in rearing such a school
Was the founder.

AN ODE TO HIMSELF

Where dost thou careless lie,
Buried in ease and sloth?
Knowledge that sleeps doth die;
And this security,

It is the common moth
That eats on wits and arts, and oft destroys them both.

Are all th' Aonian springs
Dried up? lies Thespia waste?
Doth Clarius' harp want strings,
That not a nymph now sings?
Or droop they as disgrac'd,
To see their seats and bowers by chatt'ring pies defac'd?

If hence thy silence be,
As 'tis too just a cause,
Let this thought quicken thee:
Minds that are great and free
Should not on fortune pause;
'Tis crown enough to virtue still, her own applause.

What though the greedy fry
Be taken with false baites
Of worded balladry,
And think it poesy?
They die with their conceits,
And only piteous scorn upon their folly waits.

Then take in hand thy lyre,
Strike in thy proper strain,
With Japhet's line aspire
Sol's chariot for new fire,
To give the world again;
Who aided him will thee, the issue of Jove's brain.

And since our dainty age
Cannot endure reproof,
Make not thyself a page
To that strumpet, the stage,
But sing high and aloof,
Safe from the wolf's black jaw and the dull ass's hoof.

ON GUT

Gut eats all day and lechers all the night;
So all his meat he tasteth over twice;
And, striving so to double his delight,
He makes himself a thoroughfare of vice.
Thus in his belly can he change a sin:
Lust it comes out, that gluttony went in.

ON MY FIRST SON

Farewell, thou child of my right hand, and joy;
My sin was too much hope of thee, lov'd boy.
Seven years tho' wert lent to me, and I thee pay,
Exacted by thy fate, on the just day.
O, could I lose all father now! For why
Will man lament the state he should envy?
To have so soon 'scap'd world's and flesh's rage,
And if no other misery, yet age?
Rest in soft peace, and, ask'd, say, "Here doth lie
Ben Jonson his best piece of poetry."
For whose sake henceforth all his vows be such,
As what he loves may never like too much.

THE SUN RISING

    Busy old fool, unruly sun,
        Why dost thou thus,
Through windows, and through curtains call on us?
Must to thy motions lovers' seasons run?
        Saucy pedantic wretch, go chide
        Late school boys and sour prentices,
    Go tell court huntsmen that the king will ride,
    Call country ants to harvest offices,
Love, all alike, no season knows nor clime,

Nor hours, days, months, which are the rags of time.

> Thy beams, so reverend and strong
> Why shouldst thou think?
I could eclipse and cloud them with a wink,
But that I would not lose her sight so long;
> If her eyes have not blinded thine,
> Look, and tomorrow late, tell me,
> Whether both th' Indias of spice and mine
> Be where thou leftst them, or lie here with me.
Ask for those kings whom thou saw'st yesterday,
And thou shalt hear, All here in one bed lay.

> She's all states, and all princes, I,
> Nothing else is.
Princes do but play us; compared to this,
All honor's mimic, all wealth alchemy.
> Thou, sun, art half as happy as we,
> In that the world's contracted thus.
> Thine age asks ease, and since thy duties be
> To warm the world, that's done in warming us.
Shine here to us, and thou art everywhere;
This bed thy center is, these walls, thy sphere.

Robert Herrick

TO THE VIRGINS, TO MAKE MUCH OF TIME

GATHER YE rose-buds while ye may,
Old Time is still a-flying;
And this same flower that smiles today
Tomorrow will be dying.

The glorious lamp of heaven, the sun,
The higher he's a-getting,
The sooner will his race be run,

And nearer he's to setting.

That age is best which is the first,
When youth and blood are warmer;
But being spent, the worse, and worst
Times still succeed the former.

Then be not coy, but use your time,
And while ye may, go marry;
For having lost but once your prime,
You may forever tarry.

George Herbert

LOVE (III)

LOVE BADE me welcome. Yet my soul drew back
  Guilty of dust and sin.
But quick-eyed Love, observing me grow slack
  From my first entrance in,
Drew nearer to me, sweetly questioning,
  If I lacked any thing.

A guest, I answered, worthy to be here:
  Love said, You shall be he.
I the unkind, ungrateful? Ah my dear,
  I cannot look on thee.
Love took my hand, and smiling did reply,
  Who made the eyes but I?

Truth Lord, but I have marred them: let my shame
  Go where it doth deserve.
And know you not, says Love, who bare the blame?
  My dear, then I will serve.
You must sit down, says Love, and taste my meat:
  So I did sit and eat.

VIRTUE

Sweet day, so cool, so calm, so bright,
The bridal of the earth and sky;
The dew shall weep thy fall to-night,
    For thou must die.

Sweet rose, whose hue angry and brave
Bids the rash gazer wipe his eye;
Thy root is ever in its grave,
    And thou must die.

Sweet spring, full of sweet days and roses,
A box where sweets compacted lie;
My music shows ye have your closes,
    And all must die.

Only a sweet and virtuous soul,
Like season'd timber, never gives;
But though the whole world turn to coal,
    Then chiefly lives.

John Milton

LYCIDAS

Yet once more, O ye laurels, and once more
Ye myrtles brown, with ivy never sere,
I come to pluck your berries harsh and crude,
And with forc'd fingers rude
Shatter your leaves before the mellowing year.
Bitter constraint and sad occasion dear
Compels me to disturb your season due;
For Lycidas is dead, dead ere his prime,
Young Lycidas, and hath not left his peer.
Who would not sing for Lycidas? he knew
Himself to sing, and build the lofty rhyme.

He must not float upon his wat'ry bier
Unwept, and welter to the parching wind,
Without the meed of some melodious tear.

    Begin then, Sisters of the sacred well
That from beneath the seat of Jove doth spring;
Begin, and somewhat loudly sweep the string.
Hence with denial vain and coy excuse!
So may some gentle muse
With lucky words favour my destin'd urn,
And as he passes turn
And bid fair peace be to my sable shroud!

    For we were nurs'd upon the self-same hill,
Fed the same flock, by fountain, shade, and rill;
Together both, ere the high lawns appear'd
Under the opening eyelids of the morn,
We drove afield, and both together heard
What time the gray-fly winds her sultry horn,
Batt'ning our flocks with the fresh dews of night,
Oft till the star that rose at ev'ning bright
Toward heav'n's descent had slop'd his westering wheel.
Meanwhile the rural ditties were not mute,
Temper'd to th'oaten flute;
Rough Satyrs danc'd, and Fauns with clov'n heel,
From the glad sound would not be absent long;
And old Damætas lov'd to hear our song.

    But O the heavy change now thou art gone,
Now thou art gone, and never must return!
Thee, Shepherd, thee the woods and desert caves,
With wild thyme and the gadding vine o'ergrown,
And all their echoes mourn.
The willows and the hazel copses green
Shall now no more be seen
Fanning their joyous leaves to thy soft lays.
As killing as the canker to the rose,
Or taint-worm to the weanling herds that graze,

Or frost to flowers that their gay wardrobe wear
When first the white thorn blows:
Such, Lycidas, thy loss to shepherd's ear.

    Where were ye, Nymphs, when the remorseless deep
Clos'd o'er the head of your lov'd Lycidas?
For neither were ye playing on the steep
Where your old bards, the famous Druids, lie,
Nor on the shaggy top of Mona high,
Nor yet where Deva spreads her wizard stream.
Ay me! I fondly dream
Had ye bin there'—for what could that have done?
What could the Muse herself that Orpheus bore,
The Muse herself, for her enchanting son,
Whom universal nature did lament,
When by the rout that made the hideous roar
His gory visage down the stream was sent,
Down the swift Hebrus to the Lesbian shore?

    Alas! what boots it with incessant care
To tend the homely, slighted shepherd's trade,
And strictly meditate the thankless Muse?
Were it not better done, as others use,
To sport with Amaryllis in the shade,
Or with the tangles of Neæra's hair?
Fame is the spur that the clear spirit doth raise
(That last infirmity of noble mind)
To scorn delights and live laborious days;
But the fair guerdon when we hope to find,
And think to burst out into sudden blaze,
Comes the blind Fury with th'abhorred shears,
And slits the thin-spun life. "But not the praise,"
Phoebus replied, and touch'd my trembling ears;
"Fame is no plant that grows on mortal soil,
Nor in the glistering foil
Set off to th'world, nor in broad rumour lies,
But lives and spreads aloft by those pure eyes
And perfect witness of all-judging Jove;

As he pronounces lastly on each deed,
Of so much fame in Heav'n expect thy meed."

   O fountain Arethuse, and thou honour'd flood,
Smooth-sliding Mincius, crown'd with vocal reeds,
That strain I heard was of a higher mood.
But now my oat proceeds,
And listens to the Herald of the Sea,
That came in Neptune's plea.
He ask'd the waves, and ask'd the felon winds,
"What hard mishap hath doom'd this gentle swain?"
And question'd every gust of rugged wings
That blows from off each beaked promontory.
They knew not of his story;
And sage Hippotades their answer brings,
That not a blast was from his dungeon stray'd;
The air was calm, and on the level brine
Sleek Panope with all her sisters play'd.
It was that fatal and perfidious bark,
Built in th'eclipse, and rigg'd with curses dark,
That sunk so low that sacred head of thine.

   Next Camus, reverend sire, went footing slow,
His mantle hairy, and his bonnet sedge,
Inwrought with figures dim, and on the edge
Like to that sanguine flower inscrib'd with woe.
"Ah! who hath reft," quoth he, "my dearest pledge?"
Last came, and last did go,
The Pilot of the Galilean lake;
Two massy keys he bore of metals twain
(The golden opes, the iron shuts amain).
He shook his mitred locks, and stern bespake:
"How well could I have spar'd for thee, young swain,
Enow of such as for their bellies' sake
Creep and intrude, and climb into the fold?
Of other care they little reck'ning make
Than how to scramble at the shearers' feast
And shove away the worthy bidden guest.

Blind mouths! that scarce themselves know how to hold
A sheep-hook, or have learn'd aught else the least
That to the faithful herdman's art belongs!
What recks it them? What need they? They are sped;
And when they list their lean and flashy songs
Grate on their scrannel pipes of wretched straw,
The hungry sheep look up, and are not fed,
But, swoll'n with wind and the rank mist they draw,
Rot inwardly, and foul contagion spread;
Besides what the grim wolf with privy paw
Daily devours apace, and nothing said,
But that two-handed engine at the door
Stands ready to smite once, and smite no more".

   Return, Alpheus: the dread voice is past
That shrunk thy streams; return, Sicilian Muse,
And call the vales and bid them hither cast
Their bells and flow'rets of a thousand hues.
Ye valleys low, where the mild whispers use
Of shades and wanton winds, and gushing brooks,
On whose fresh lap the swart star sparely looks,
Throw hither all your quaint enamel'd eyes,
That on the green turf suck the honied showers
And purple all the ground with vernal flowers.
Bring the rathe primrose that forsaken dies,
The tufted crow-toe, and pale jessamine,
The white pink, and the pansy freak'd with jet,
The glowing violet,
The musk-rose, and the well attir'd woodbine,
With cowslips wan that hang the pensive head,
And every flower that sad embroidery wears;
Bid amaranthus all his beauty shed,
And daffadillies fill their cups with tears,
To strew the laureate hearse where Lycid lies.
For so to interpose a little ease,
Let our frail thoughts dally with false surmise.
Ay me! Whilst thee the shores and sounding seas

Wash far away, where'er thy bones are hurl'd;
Whether beyond the stormy Hebrides,
Where thou perhaps under the whelming tide
Visit'st the bottom of the monstrous world,
Or whether thou, to our moist vows denied,
Sleep'st by the fable of Bellerus old,
Where the great vision of the guarded mount
Looks toward Namancos and Bayona's hold:
Look homeward Angel now, and melt with ruth;
And, O ye dolphins, waft the hapless youth.

    Weep no more, woeful shepherds, weep no more,
For Lycidas, your sorrow, is not dead,
Sunk though he be beneath the wat'ry floor;
So sinks the day-star in the ocean bed,
And yet anon repairs his drooping head,
And tricks his beams, and with new spangled ore
Flames in the forehead of the morning sky:
So Lycidas sunk low, but mounted high
Through the dear might of him that walk'd the waves;
Where, other groves and other streams along,
With nectar pure his oozy locks he laves,
And hears the unexpressive nuptial song,
In the blest kingdoms meek of joy and love.
There entertain him all the Saints above,
In solemn troops, and sweet societies,
That sing, and singing in their glory move,
And wipe the tears for ever from his eyes.
Now, Lycidas, the shepherds weep no more:
Henceforth thou art the Genius of the shore,
In thy large recompense, and shalt be good
To all that wander in that perilous flood.

    Thus sang the uncouth swain to th'oaks and rills,
While the still morn went out with sandals gray;
He touch'd the tender stops of various quills,
With eager thought warbling his Doric lay;
And now the sun had stretch'd out all the hills,

And now was dropp'd into the western bay;
At last he rose, and twitch'd his mantle blue:
To-morrow to fresh woods, and pastures new.

ON HIS BLINDNESS

When I consider how my light is spent
Ere half my days in this dark world and wide,
And that one talent which is death to hide
Lodg'd with me useless, though my soul more bent
To serve therewith my Maker, and present
My true account, lest he returning chide,
"Doth God exact day-labour, light denied?"
I fondly ask. But Patience, to prevent
That murmur, soon replies: "God doth not need
Either man's work or his own gifts: who best
Bear his mild yoke, they serve him best. His state
Is kingly; thousands at his bidding speed
And post o'er land and ocean without rest:
They also serve who only stand and wait."

ON THE LATE MASSACRE IN PIEDMONT

Avenge, O Lord, thy slaughter'd saints, whose bones
    Lie scatter'd on the Alpine mountains cold,
    Ev'n them who kept thy truth so pure of old,
    When all our fathers worshipp'd stocks and stones;
Forget not: in thy book record their groans
    Who were thy sheep and in their ancient fold
    Slain by the bloody Piemontese that roll'd
    Mother with infant down the rocks. Their moans
The vales redoubl'd to the hills, and they
    To Heav'n. Their martyr'd blood and ashes sow
    O'er all th' Italian fields where still doth sway

The triple tyrant; that from these may grow
  A hundred-fold, who having learnt thy way
Early may fly the Babylonian woe.

From PARADISE LOST

Book 1

Of Man's First Disobedience, and the Fruit
Of that Forbidden Tree, whose mortal tast
Brought Death into the World, and all our woe,
With loss of *Eden*, till one greater Man
Restore us, and regain the blissful Seat,
Sing Heav'nly Muse, that on the secret top
Of *Oreb*, or of *Sinai*, didst inspire
That Shepherd, who first taught the chosen Seed,
In the Beginning how the Heav'ns and Earth
Rose out of *Chaos*: or if *Sion* Hill
Delight thee more, and *Siloa's* brook that flow'd
Fast by the Oracle of God; I thence
Invoke thy aid to my adventrous Song,
That with no middle flight intends to soar
Above th' *Aonian* Mount, while it pursues
Things unattempted yet in Prose or Rhime.
And chiefly Thou, O Spirit, that dost prefer
Before all Temples th' upright heart and pure,
Instruct me, for Thou know'st; Thou from the first
Wast present, and with mighty wings outspread
Dove-like satst brooding on the vast Abyss
And mad'st it pregnant: What in me is dark
Illumin, what is low raise and support;
That to the highth of this great Argument
I may assert Eternal Providence,
And justifie the wayes of God to men.

Say first, for Heav'n hides nothing from thy view
Nor the deep Tract of Hell, say first what cause

Mov'd our Grand Parents in that happy State,
Favour'd of Heav'n so highly, to fall off
From thir Creator, and transgress his Will
For one restraint, Lords of the World besides?
Who first seduc'd them to that foul revolt?
Th' infernal Serpent; he it was, whose guile
Stird up with Envy and Revenge, deceiv'd
The Mother of Mankind, what time his Pride
Had cast him out from Heav'n, with all his Host
Of Rebel Angels, by whose aid aspiring
To set himself in Glory above his Peers,
He trusted to have equal'd the most High,
If he oppos'd; and with ambitious aim
Against the Throne and Monarchy of God
Rais'd impious War in Heav'n and Battel proud
With vain attempt. Him the Almighty Power
Hurld headlong flaming from th' Ethereal Skie
With hideous ruine and combustion down
To bottomless perdition, there to dwell
In Adamantine Chains and penal Fire,
Who durst defie th' Omnipotent to Arms.
Nine times the Space that measures Day and Night
To mortal men, he with his horrid crew
Lay vanquisht, rowling in the fiery Gulfe
Confounded though immortal: But his doom
Reserv'd him to more wrath; for now the thought
Both of lost happiness and lasting pain
Torments him; round he throws his baleful eyes
That witness'd huge affliction and dismay
Mixt with obdurate pride and stedfast hate:
At once as far as Angels kenn he views
The dismal Situation waste and wilde,
A Dungeon horrible, on all sides round
As one great Furnace flam'd, yet from those flames
No light, but rather darkness visible
Serv'd onely to discover sights of woe,
Regions of sorrow, doleful shades, where peace

And rest can never dwell, hope never comes
That comes to all; but torture without end
Still urges, and a fiery Deluge, fed
With ever-burning Sulphur unconsum'd:
Such place Eternal Justice had prepar'd
For those rebellious, here thir prison ordained
In utter darkness, and thir portion set
As far remov'd from God and light of Heav'n
As from the Center thrice to th' utmost Pole.
O how unlike the place from whence they fell!
There the companions of his fall, o'rewhelm'd
With Floods and Whirlwinds of tempestuous fire,
He soon discerns, and weltring by his side
One next himself in power, and next in crime,
Long after known in *Palestine*, and nam'd
Beelzebub. To whom th' Arch-Enemy,
And thence in Heav'n call'd Satan, with bold words
Breaking the horrid silence thus began.

If thou beest he; But O how fall'n! how chang'd
From him, who in the happy Realms of Light
Cloth'd with transcendent brightness didst out-shine
Myriads though bright: If he whom mutual league,
United thoughts and counsels, equal hope
And hazard in the Glorious Enterprize,
Joynd with me once, now misery hath joynd
In equal ruin: into what Pit thou seest
From what highth fall'n, so much the stronger prov'd
He with his Thunder: and till then who knew
The force of those dire Arms?   yet not for those,
Nor what the Potent Victor in his rage
Can else inflict, do I repent or change,
Though chang'd in outward lustre; that fixt mind
And high disdain, from sence of injur'd merit,
That with the mightiest rais'd me to contend,
And to the fierce contention brought along
Innumerable force of Spirits arm'd

That durst dislike his reign, and me preferring,
His utmost power with adverse power oppos'd
In dubious Battel on the Plains of Heav'n,
And shook his throne. What though the field be lost?
All is not lost; the unconquerable Will,
And study of revenge, immortal hate,
And courage never to submit or yield:
And what is else not to be overcome?
That Glory never shall his wrath or might
Extort from me. To bow and sue for grace
With suppliant knee, and deifie his power,
Who from the terrour of this Arm so late
Doubted his Empire, that were low indeed,
That were an ignominy and shame beneath
This downfall; since by Fate the strength of Gods
And this Empyreal substance cannot fail,
Since through experience of this great event
In Arms not worse, in foresight much advanc't,
We may with more successful hope resolve
To wage by force or guile eternal Warr
Irreconcileable, to our grand Foe,
Who now triumphs, and in th' excess of joy
Sole reigning holds the Tyranny of Heav'n.

So spake th' Apostate Angel, though in pain,
Vaunting aloud, but rackt with deep despare:
And him thus answer'd soon his bold Compeer.

O Prince, O Chief of many Throned Powers,
That led th' imbattelld Seraphim to Warr
Under thy conduct, and in dreadful deeds
Fearless, endanger'd Heav'ns perpetual King;
And put to proof his high Supremacy,
Whether upheld by strength, or Chance, or Fate,
Too well I see and rue the dire event,
That with sad overthrow and foul defeat
Hath lost us Heav'n, and all this mighty Host
In horrible destruction laid thus low,

As far as Gods and Heav'nly Essences
Can perish: for the mind and spirit remains
Invincible, and vigour soon returns,
Though all our Glory extinct and happy state
Here swallow'd up in endless misery.
But what if he our Conquerour, (whom I now
Of force believe Almighty, since no less
Then such could hav orepow'rd such force as ours)
Have left us this our spirit and strength intire
Strongly to suffer and support our pains,
That we may so suffice his vengeful ire,
Or do him mightier service as his thralls
By right of Warr, what e're his business be
Here in the heart of Hell to work in Fire,
Or do his Errands in the gloomy Deep;
What can it then avail though yet we feel
Strength undiminisht, or eternal being
To undergo eternal punishment?
Whereto with speedy words th' Arch-fiend reply'd.

Fall'n Cherube, to be weak is miserable
Doing or Suffering: but of this be sure,
To do ought good never will be our task,
But ever to do ill our sole delight,
As being the contrary to his high will
Whom we resist. If then his Providence
Out of our evil seek to bring forth good,
Our labour must be to pervert that end,
And out of good still to find means of evil;
Which oft times may succeed, so as perhaps
Shall grieve him, if I fail not, and disturb
His inmost counsels from thir destind aim.
But see the angry Victor hath recall'd
His Ministers of vengeance and pursuit
Back to the Gates of Heav'n: the Sulphurous Hail
Shot after us in storm, oreblown hath laid
The fiery Surge, that from the Precipice

Of Heav'n receiv'd us falling, and the Thunder,
Wing'd with red Lightning and impetuous rage,
Perhaps hath spent his shafts, and ceases now
To bellow through the vast and boundless Deep.
Let us not slip th' occasion, whether scorn,
Or satiate fury yield it from our Foe.
Seest thou yon dreary Plain, forlorn and wilde,
The seat of desolation, voyd of light,
Save what the glimmering of these livid flames
Casts pale and dreadful?   Thither let us tend
From off the tossing of these fiery waves,
There rest, if any rest can harbour there,
And reassembling our afflicted Powers,
Consult how we may henceforth most offend
Our Enemy, our own loss how repair,
How overcome this dire Calamity,
What reinforcement we may gain from Hope,
If not what resolution from despare.

Thus Satan to his neerest Mate
With Head up-lift above the wave, and Eyes
That sparkling blaz'd, his other Parts besides
Prone on the Flood, extended long and large
Lay floating many a rood, in bulk as huge
As whom the Fables name of monstrous size,
Titanian, or *Earth-born*, that warr'd on *Jove*,
Briareos or *Typhon*, whom the Den
By ancient *Tarsus* held, or that Sea-beast
Leviathan, which God of all his works
Created hugest that swim th' Ocean stream:
Him haply slumbring on the *Norway* foam
The Pilot of some small night-founder'd Skiff,
Deeming some Island, oft, as Sea-men tell,
With fixed Anchor in his skaly rind
Moors by his side under the Lee, while Night
Invests the Sea, and wished Morn delayes:
So stretcht out huge in length the Arch-fiend lay

Chain'd on the burning Lake, nor ever thence
Had ris'n or heav'd his head, but that the will
And high permission of all-ruling Heaven
Left him at large to his own dark designs,
That with reiterated crimes he might
Heap on himself damnation, while he sought
Evil to others, and enrag'd might see
How all his malice serv'd but to bring forth
Infinite goodness, grace and mercy shewn
On Man by him seduc't, but on himself
Treble confusion, wrath and vengeance pour'd.
Forthwith upright he rears from off the Pool
His mighty Stature; on each hand the flames
Drivn backward slope thir pointing spires, and rowld
In billows, leave i'th'midst a horrid Vale.
Then with expanded wings he stears his flight
Aloft, incumbent on the dusky Air
That felt unusual weight, till on dry Land
He lights, as if it were Land that ever burn'd
With solid, as the Lake with liquid fire;
And such appear'd in hue, as when the force
Of subterranean wind transports a Hill
Torn from *Pelorus*, or the shatter'd side
Of thundring *Aetna*, whose combustible
And fewel'd entrals thence conceiving Fire,
Sublim'd with Mineral fury, aid the Winds,
And leave a singed bottom all involv'd
With stench and smoak: Such resting found the sole
Of unblest feet. Him followed his next Mate,
Both glorying to have scap't the *Stygian* flood
As Gods, and by thir own recover'd strength,
Not by the sufferance of supernal Power.

Is this the Region, this the Soil, the Clime,
Said then the lost Arch-Angel, this the seat
That we must change for Heav'n, this mournful gloom
For that celestial light?   Be it so, since he

Who now is Sovran can dispose and bid
What shall be right: fardest from him his best
Whom reason hath equald, force hath made supream
Above his equals. Farewel happy Fields
Where Joy for ever dwells: Hail horrours, hail
Infernal world, and thou profoundest Hell
Receive thy new Possessor: One who brings
A mind not to be chang'd by Place or Time.
The mind is its own place, and in it self
Can make a Heav'n of Hell, a Hell of Heav'n.
What matter where, if I be still the same,
And what I should be, all but less then he
Whom Thunder hath made greater? Here at least
We shall be free; th' Almighty hath not built
Here for his envy, will not drive us hence:
Here we may reign secure, and in my choyce
To reign is worth ambition though in Hell:
Better to reign in Hell, then serve in Heav'n.
But wherefore let we then our faithful friends,
Th' associates and copartners of our loss
Lye thus astonisht on th' oblivious Pool,
And call them not to share with us their part
In this unhappy Mansion, or once more
With rallied Arms to try what may be yet
Regaind in Heav'n, or what more lost in Hell?

So *Satan* spake, and him *Beelzebub*
Thus answer'd. Leader of those Armies bright,
Which but th' Omnipotent none could have foyld,
If once they hear that voyce, thir liveliest pledge
Of hope in fears and dangers, heard so oft
In worst extreams, and on the perilous edge
Of battel when it rag'd, in all assaults
Thir surest signal, they will soon resume
New courage and revive, though now they lye
Groveling and prostrate on yon Lake of Fire,
As we erewhile, astounded and amaz'd,

No wonder, fall'n such a pernicious highth.

He scarce had ceas't when the superiour Fiend
Was moving toward the shoar; his ponderous shield
Ethereal temper, massy, large and round,
Behind him cast; the broad circumference
Hung on his shoulders like the Moon, whose Orb
Through Optic Glass the *Tuscan* Artist views
At Ev'ning from the top of *Fesole*,
Or in *Valdarno*, to descry new Lands,
Rivers or Mountains in her spotty Globe.
His Spear, to equal which the tallest Pine
Hewn on *Norwegian* hills, to be the Mast
Of some great Ammiral, were but a wand,
He walkt with to support uneasie steps
Over the burning Marle, not like those steps
On Heavens Azure, and the torrid Clime
Smote on him sore besides, vaulted with Fire;
Nathless he so endur'd, till on the Beach
Of that inflamed Sea, he stood and call'd
His Legions, Angel Forms, who lay intrans't
Thick as Autumnal Leaves that strow the Brooks
In *Vallombrosa*, where th' *Etrurian* shades
High overarch't imbowr; or scatterd sedge
Afloat, when with fierce Winds *Orion* arm'd
Hath vext the Red-Sea Coast, whose waves orethrew
Busiris and his *Memphian* Chivalry,
While with perfidious hatred they pursu'd
The Sojourners of *Goshen*, who beheld
From the safe shore thir floating Carkases
And broken Chariot Wheels, so thick bestrown
Abject and lost lay these, covering the Flood,
Under amazement of thir hideous change.
He call'd so loud, that all the hollow Deep
Of Hell resounded. Princes, Potentates
Warriers, the Flowr of Heav'n, once yours, now lost,
If such astonishment as this can sieze

Eternal spirits; or have ye chos'n this place
After the toyl of Battel to repose
Your wearied vertue, for the ease you find
To slumber here, as in the Vales of Heav'n?
Or in this abject posture have ye sworn
To adore the Conquerour? who now beholds
Cherube and Seraph rowling in the Flood
With scatter'd Arms and Ensigns, till anon
His swift pursuers from Heav'n Gates discern
Th' advantage, and descending tread us down
Thus drooping, or with linked Thunderbolts
Transfix us to the bottom of this Gulfe.
Awake, arise, or be for ever fall'n.

They heard, and were abasht, and up they sprung
Upon the wing, as when men wont to watch
On duty, sleeping found by whom they dread,
Rouse and bestir themselves ere well awake.
Nor did they not perceave the evil plight
In which they were, or the fierce pains not feel;
Yet to thir Generals Voyce they soon obeyd
Innumerable. As when the potent Rod
Of *Amrams* Son in *Egypts* evill day
Wav'd round the Coast, up call'd a pitchy cloud
Of *Locusts*, warping on the Eastern Wind,
That ore the Realm of impious *Pharaoh* hung
Like Night, and darken'd all the Land of *Nile*:
So numberless were those bad Angels seen
Hovering on wing under the Cope of Hell
'Twixt upper, nether, and surrounding Fires;
Till, as a signal giv'n, th' uplifted Spear
Of thir great Sultan waving to direct
Thir course, in even ballance down they light
On the firm brimstone, and fill all the Plain;
A multitude, like which the populous North
Pour'd never from her frozen loyns, to pass
Rhene or the *Danaw*, when her barbarous Sons

Came like a Deluge on the South, and spread
Beneath *Gibralter* to the *Lybian* sands.
Forthwith from every Squadron and each Band
The Heads and Leaders thither hast where stood
Thir great Commander; Godlike shapes and forms
Excelling human, Princely Dignities,
And Powers that earst in Heaven sat on Thrones;
Though of thir Names in heav'nly Records now
Be no memorial blotted out and ras'd
By thir Rebellion, from the Books of Life.
Nor had they yet among the Sons of *Eve*
Got them new Names, till wandring ore the Earth,
Through Gods high sufferance for the tryal of man,
By falsities and lyes the greatest part
Of Mankind they corrupted to forsake
God thir Creator, and th' invisible
Glory of him that made them, to transform
Oft to the Image of a Brute, adorn'd
With gay Religions full of Pomp and Gold,
And Devils to adore for Deities:
Then were they known to men by various Names,
And various Idols through the Heathen World.
Say, Muse, the Names then known, who first, who last,
Rous'd from the slumber, on that fiery Couch,
At thir great Emperors call, as next in worth
Came singly where he stood on the bare strand,
While the promiscuous croud stood yet aloof?
The chief were those who from the Pit of Hell
Roaming to seek thir prey on earth, durst fix
Thir Seats long after next the Seat of God,
Thir Altars by his Altar, Gods ador'd
Among the Nations round, and durst abide
Jehovah thundring out of *Sion*, thron'd
Between the Cherubim; yea, often plac'd
Within his Sanctuary it self thir Shrines,
Abominations; and with cursed things
His holy Rites, and solemn Feasts profan'd,

And with thir darkness durst affront his light.
First *Moloch*, horrid King besmear'd with blood
Of human sacrifice, and parents tears,
Though for the noyse of Drums and Timbrels loud
Thir childrens cries unheard, that past through fire
To his grim Idol. Him the *Ammonite*
Worshipt in *Rabba* and her watry Plain,
In *Argob* and in *Basan*, to the stream
Of utmost *Arnon*. Not content with such
Audacious neighbourhood, the wisest heart
Of *Solomon* he led by fraud to build
His Temple right against the Temple of God
On that opprobrious Hill, and made his Grove
The pleasant Vally of *Hinnom*, *Tophet* thence
And black *Gehenna* call'd, the Type of Hell.
Next *Chemos*, th' obscene dread of *Moabs* Sons,
From *Aroar* to *Nebo*, and the wild
Of Southmost *Abarim*; in *Hesebon*
And *Heronaim*, *Seons* Realm, beyond
The flowry Dale of *Sibma* clad with Vines,
And *Eleale* to th' *Asphaltick* Pool.
Peor his other Name, when he entic'd
Israel in *Sittim* on thir march from *Nile*
To do him wanton rites, which cost them woe.
Yet thence his lustful Orgies he enlarg'd
Even to that Hill of scandal, but the Grove
Of *Moloch* homicide, lust hard by hate;
Till good *Josiah* drove them hence to Hell.
With these cam they, who from the bordring flood
Of old *Euphrates* to the Brook that parts
Egypt from *Syrian* ground, had general names
Of *Baalim* and *Ashtaroth*, those male,
These Feminine. For Spirits when they please
Can either Sex assume, or both; so soft
And uncompounded is thir Essence pure,
Nor ti'd or manacl'd with joynt or limb,
Nor founded on the brittle strength of bones,

Like cumbrous flesh; but in what shape they choose
Dilated or condens't, bright or obscure,
Can execute thir aerie purposes,
And works of love or enmity fulfill.
For those the Race of *Israel* oft forsook
Thir living strength, and unfrequented left
His righteous Altar, bowing lowly down
To bestial Gods; for which thir heads as low
Bow'd down in Battel, sunk before the Spear
Of despicable foes. With these in troop
Came *Astoreth*, whom the *Phoenicians* call'd
Astarte, Queen of Heav'n, with crescent Horns;
To whose bright Image nightly by the Moon
Sidonian Virgins paid thir Vows and Songs,
In *Sion* also not unsung, where stood
Her Temple on th' offensive Mountain, built
By that uxorious King, whose heart though large,
Beguil'd by fair Idolatresses, fell
To idols foul. *Thammuz* came next behind,
Whose annual wound in *Lebanon* allur'd
The *Syrian* Damsels to lament his fate
In amorous dittyes all a Summers day,
While smooth *Adonis* from his native Rock
Ran purple to the Sea, suppos'd with blood
Of *Thammuz* yearly wounded; the Love-tale
Infected *Sions* daughters with like heat,
Whose wanton passions in the sacred Porch
Ezekial saw, when by the Vision led
His eye survay'd the dark Idolatries
Of alienated *Judah*. Next came one
Who mourn'd in earnest, when the Captive Ark
Maim'd his brute Image, head and hands lopt off
In his own Temple, on the grunsel edge,
Where he fell flat, and sham'd his Worshipers:
Dagon his Name, Sea Monster, upward Man
And downward Fish: yet had his Temple high
Rear'd in *Azotus*, dreaded through the Coast

Of *Palestine*, in *Gath* and *Ascalon*
And *Accaron* and *Gaza's* frontier bounds.
Him follow'd *Rimmon*, whose delightful Seat
Was fair *Damascus*, on the fertil Banks
Of *Abbana* and *Pharphar*, lucid streams.
He also against the house of God was bold:
A Leper once he lost and gain'd a King,
Ahaz his sottish Conquerour, whom he drew
Gods Altar to disparage and displace
For one of *Syrian* mode, whereon to burn
His odious offrings, and adore the Gods
Whom he had vanquisht. After these appear'd
A crew who under Names of old Renown,
Osiris, *Isis*, *Orus* and thir Train
With monstrous shapes and sorceries abus'd
Fanatic *Egypt* and her Priests, to seek
Thir wandring Gods Disguis'd in brutish forms
Rather then human. Nor did *Israel* scape
Th' infection when thir borrow'd Gold compos'd
The Calf in *Oreb*: and the Rebel King
Doubl'd that sin in *Bethel* and in *Dan*,
Lik'ning his Maker to the Grazed Ox,
Jehovah, who in one Night when he pass'd
From *Egypt* marching, equal'd with one stroke
Both her first born and all her bleating Gods
Belial came last, then whom a Spirit more lewd
Fell not from Heaven, or more gross to love
Vice for it self: To him no Temple stood
Or Altar smoak'd; yet who more oft then hee
In Temples and at Altars, when the Priest
Turns Atheist, as did *Ely's* Sons, who fill'd
With lust and violence the house of God.
In Courts and Palaces he also Reigns
And in luxurious Cities, where the noyse
Of riot ascends above thir loftiest Towrs,
And injury and outrage: And when Night
Darkens the Streets, then wander forth the Sons

Of *Belial*, flown with insolence and wine.
Witness the Streets of *Sodom*, and that night
In *Gibeah*, when the hospitable door
Expos'd a Matron to avoid worse rape.
These were the prime in order and in might;
The rest were long to tell, though far renown'd,
Th' *Ionian* Gods, of *Javans* issue held
Gods, yet confest later then Heav'n and Earth
Thir boasted Parents; *Titan Heav'ns* first born
With his enormous brood, and birthright seis'd
By younger *Saturn*, he from mightier *Jove*
His own and *Rhea's* Son like measure found;
So *Jove* usurping reign'd: these first in *Creet*
And *Ida* known, thence on the Snowy top
Of cold *Olympus* rul'd the middle Air
Thir highest Heav'n; or on the *Delphian* Cliff,
Or in *Dodona*, and through all the bounds
Of *Doric* Land; or who with *Saturn* old
Fled over *Adria* to th' *Hesperian* Fields,
And ore the *Celtic* roam'd the utmost Isles.
All these and more came flocking; but with looks
Down cast and damp, yet such wherein appear'd
Obscure some glimps of joy, to have found thir chief
Not in despair, to have found themselves not lost
In loss itself; which on his count'nance cast
Like doubtful hue: but he his wonted pride
Soon recollecting, with high words, that bore
Semblance of worth, not substance, gently rais'd
Thir fanting courage, and dispel'd thir fears.
Then strait commands that at the warlike sound
Of Trumpets loud and Clarions be upreard
His mighty Standard; that proud honour claim'd
Azazel as his right, a Cherube tall:
Who forthwith from the glittering Staff unfurld
Th' Imperial Ensign, which full high advanc't
Shon like a Meteor streaming to the Wind
With Gemms and Golden lustre rich imblaz'd,

Seraphic arms and Trophies: all the while
Sonorous mettal blowing Martial sounds:
At which the universal Host upsent
A shout that tore Hells Concave, and beyond
Frighted the Reign of *Chaos* and old Night.
All in a moment through the gloom were seen
Ten thousand Banners rise into the Air
With Orient Colours waving: with them rose
A Forrest huge of Spears: and thronging Helms
Appear'd, and serried Shields in thick array
Of depth immeasurable: Anon they move
In perfect *Phalanx* to the *Dorian* mood
Of Flutes and soft Recorders; such as rais'd
To hight of noblest temper Hero's old
Arming to Battel, and in stead of rage
Deliberate valour breath'd, firm and unmov'd
With dread of death to flight or foul retreat,
Nor wanting power to mitigate and swage
With solemn touches, troubl'd thoughts, and chase
Anguish and doubt and fear and sorrow and pain
From mortal or immortal minds. Thus they
Breathing united force with fixed thought
Mov'd on in silence to soft Pipes that charm'd
Thir painful steps o're the burnt soyle; and now
Advanc't in view, they stand, a horrid Front
Of dreadful length and dazling Arms, in guise
Of Warriers old with order'd Spear and Shield,
Awaiting what command thir mighty Chief
Had to impose: He through the armed Files
Darts his experienc't eye, and soon traverse
The whole Battalion views, thir order due,
Thir visages and stature as of Gods,
Thir number last he summs. And now his heart
Distends with pride, and hardning in his strength
Glories: For never since created man,
Met such imbodied force, as nam'd with these
Could merit more then that small infantry

Warr'd on by Cranes: though all the Giant brood
Of *Phlegra* with th' Heroic Race were joyn'd
That fought at *Theb's* and *Ilium*, on each side
Mixt with auxiliar Gods;   and what resounds
In Fable or *Romance* of *Uthers* Sons
Begirt with *British* and *Armoric* Knights;
And all who since Baptiz'd or Infidel
Jousted in *Aspramont* or *Montalban*,
Damasco, or *Marocco*, or *Trebisond*
Or whom *Biserta* sent from *Afric* shore
When *Charlemain* with all his Peerage fell
By *Fontarabbia*. Thus far these beyond
Compare of mortal prowess, yet observ'd
Thir dread commander: he above the rest
In shape and gesture proudly eminent
Stood like a Towr; his form had yet not lost
All her Original brightness, nor appear'd
Less then Arch Angel ruind, and th' excess
Of Glory obscur'd;   As when the Sun new ris'n
Looks through the Horizontal misty Air
Shorn of his Beams, or from behind the Moon
In dim Eclips disastrous twilight sheds
On half the Nations, and with fear of change
Perplexes Monarch. Dark'n'd so, yet shon
Above them all th' Arch Angel; but his face
Deep scars of Thunder had intrencht, and care
Sat on his faded cheek, but under Browes
Of dauntless courage, and considerate Pride
Waiting revenge: cruel his eye, but cast
Signs of remorse and passion to behold
The fellows of his crime, the followers rather
(Far other once beheld in bliss) condemn'd
For ever now to have thir lot in pain,
Millions of Spirits for his fault amerc't
Of Heav'n, and from Eternal Splendors flung
For his revolt, yet faithfull how they stood,
Thir Glory witherd. As when Heavens Fire

Hath scath'd the Forrest Oaks, or Mountain Pines,
With singed top thir stately growth though bare
Stands on the blasted Heath. He now prepar'd
To speak; whereat thir doubl'd Ranks they bend
From wing to wing, and half enclose him round
With all his Peers: attention held them mute.
Thrice he assayd, and thrice in spight of scorn,
Tears such as Angels weep, burst forth: at last
Words interwove with sighs found out thir way.

O Myriads of immortal Spirits, O Powers
Matchless, but with th' Almighty, and that strife
Was not inglorious, though th' event was dire,
As this place testifies, and this dire change
Hateful to utter: but what power of mind
Foreseeing or presaging, from the Depth
Of knowledge past or present, could have fear'd,
How such united force of Gods, how such
As stood like these, could ever know repulse?
For who can yet beleeve, though after loss,
That all these puissant Legions, whose exile
Hath emptied Heav'n, shall fail to re-ascend
Self-rais'd, and repossess thir native seat?
For mee be witness all the Host of Heav'n,
If counsels different, or danger shun'd
By mee, have lost our hopes. But he who reigns
Monarch in Heav'n, till then as one secure
Sat on his Throne, upheld by old repute,
Consent or custome, and his Regal State
Put forth at full, but still his strength conceal'd,
Which tempted our attempt, and wrought our fall.
Henceforth his might we know, and know our own
So as not either to provoke, or dread
New warr, provok't; our better part remains
To work in close design, by fraud or guile
What force effected not: that he no less
At length from us may find, who overcomes

By force, hath overcome but half his foe.
Space may produce new Worlds; whereof so rife
There went a fame in Heav'n that he ere long
Intended to create, and therein plant
A generation, whom his choice regard
Should favour equal to the Sons of Heaven:
Thither, if but to pry, shall be perhaps
Our first eruption, thither or elsewhere:
For this Infernal Pit shall never hold
Caelestial Spirits in Bondage, nor th' Abyss
Long under darkness cover. But these thoughts
Full Counsel must mature: Peace is despaird,
For who can think Submission? Warr then, Warr
Open or understood must be resolv'd.

He spake: and to confirm his words, out-flew
Millions of flaming swords, drawn from the thighs
Of mighty Cherubim; the sudden blaze
Far round illumin'd hell: highly they rag'd
Against the Highest, and fierce with grasped Arms
Clash'd on thir sounding Shields the din of war,
Hurling defiance toward the Vault of Heav'n.

There stood a hill not far whose griesly top
Belch'd fire and rowling smoak; the rest entire
Shon with a glossie scurff, undoubted sign
That in his womb was hid metallic Ore,
The work of Sulphur. Thither wing'd with speed
A numerous Brigad hasten'd. As when Bands
Of Pioners with Spade and Pickax arm'd
Forerun the Royal Camp, to trench a Field,
Or cast a Rampart. *Mammon* led them on,
Mammon, the least erected Spirit that fell
From heav'n, for ev'n in heav'n his looks and thoughts
Were always downward bent, admiring more
The riches of Heav'ns pavement, trod'n Gold,
Then aught divine or holy else enjoy'd
In vision beatific: by him first

Men also, and by his suggestion taught
Ransack'd the Center, and with impious hands
Rifl'd the bowels of thir mother Earth
For Treasures better hid. Soon had his crew
Op'nd into the Hill a spacious wound
And dig'd out ribs of Gold. Let none admire
That riches grow in Hell; that soyle may best
Deserve the precious bane. And here let those
Who boast in mortal things, and wond'ring tell
Of *Babel*, and the works of *Memphian* Kings
Learn how thir greatest Monuments of Fame,
And Strength and Art are easily out-done
By Spirits reprobate, and in an hour
What in an age they with incessant toyle
And hands innumerable scarce perform.
Nigh on the Plain in many cells prepar'd
That underneath had veins of liquid fire
Sluc'd from the Lake, a second multitude
With wond'rous Art found out the massie Ore,
Severing each kind, and scum'd the Bullion dross:
A third as soon had form'd within the ground
A various mould, and from the boyling cells
By strange conveyance fill'd each hollow nook,
As in an Organ from one blast of wind
To many a row of Pipes the sound-board breaths.
Anon out of the earth a Fabrick huge
Rose like an Exhalation, with the sound
Of Dulcet Symphonies and voices sweet,
Built like a Temple, where *Pilasters* round
Were set, and Doric pillars overlaid
With Golden Architrave; nor did there want
Cornice or Freeze, with bossy Sculptures grav'n,
The Roof was fretted Gold. Not *Babilon*,
Nor great *Alcairo* such magnificence
Equal'd in all thir glories, to inshrine
Belus or *Serapis* thir Gods, or seat
Thir Kings, when *Aegypt* with *Assyria* strove

In wealth and luxurie. Th' ascending pile
Stood fixt her stately hyghth, and strait the dores
Op'ning thir brazen foulds discover wide
Within, her ample spaces, o're the smooth
And level pavement: from the arched roof
Pendant by suttle Magic many a row
Of Starry Lamps and blazing Cressets fed
With *Naphtha* and *Asphaltus* yeilded light
As from a sky. The hasty multitude
Admiring enter'd, and the work some praise
And some the Architect: his hand was known
In Heav'n by many a Towred structure high,
Where Scepter'd Angels held thir residence,
And sat as Princes, whom the supreme King
Exalted to such power, and gave to rule,
Each in his Hierarchie, the Orders bright.
Nor was his name unheard or unador'd
In ancient Greece; and in *Ausonian* land
Men call'd him *Mulciber*; and how he fell
From Heav'n, they fabl'd, thrown by angry *Jove*
Sheer o're the Chrystal Battlements; from Morn
To Noon he fell, from Noon to dewy Eve,
A Summers day; and with the setting Sun
Dropt from the Zenith like a falling Star,
On *Lemnos* th' *Aegaean* Ile: thus they relate,
Erring; for he with this rebellious rout
Fell long before; nor aught avail'd him now
To have built in Heav'n high Towrs; nor did he scape
By all his Engins, but was headlong sent
With his industrious crew to build in hell.
Mean while the winged Haralds by command
Of Sovran power, with awful Ceremony
And Trumpets sound throughout the Host proclaim
A solemn Councel forthwith to be held
At *Pandaemonium*, the high Capital
Of Satan and his Peers: thir summons call'd
From every Band and squared Regiment

By place or choice the worthiest; they anon
With hunderds and with thousands trooping came
Attended: all access was throng'd, the Gates
And Porches wide, but chief the spacious Hall
(Though like a cover'd field, where Champions bold
Wont ride in arm'd, and at the Soldans chair
Defi'd the best of *Panim* chivalry
To mortal combat or carreer with Lance)
Thick swarm'd, both on the ground and in the air,
Brusht with the hiss of russling wings. As Bees
In spring time, when the Sun with *Taurus* rides,
Pour forth thir populous youth about the Hive
In clusters; they among fresh dews and flowers
Flie to and fro, or on the smoothed Plank,
The suburb of thir Straw-built Cittadel,
New rub'd with Baum, expatiate and confer
Thir State affairs. So thick the aerie crowd
Swarm'd and were straitn'd; till the Signal giv'n
Behold a wonder! they but now who seemd
In bigness to surpass Earths Giant Sons
Now less then smallest Dwarfs, in narrow room
Throng numberless, like that Pigmean Race
Beyond the *Indian* Mount, or Faerie Elves,
Whose midnight Revels, by a Forrest side
Or Fountain some belated Peasant sees,
Or dreams he sees, while over-head the Moon
Sits Arbitress, and neerer to the Earth
Wheels her pale course, they on thir mirth and dance
Intent, with jocond Music charm his ear;
At once with joy and fear his heart rebounds.
Thus incorporeal Spirits to smallest forms
Reduc'd thir shapes immense, and were at large,
Though without number still amidst the Hall
Of that infernal Court. But far within
And in thir own dimensions like themselves
The great Seraphic Lords and Cherubim
In close recess and secret conclave sat

A thousand Demy-Gods on golden seat's,
Frequent and full. After short silence then
And summons read, the great consult began.

Richard Lovelace

LA BELLA BONA ROBA

To My Lady H.

I

Tell me, ye subtill judges in loves treasury,
Inform me, which hath most inricht mine eye,
This diamonds greatnes, or its clarity?

II

Ye cloudy spark lights, whose vast multitude
Of fires are harder to be found then view'd,
Waite on this star in her first magnitude.

III

Calmely or roughly! Ah, she shines too much;
That now I lye (her influence is such),
Chrusht with too strong a hand, or soft a touch.

IV

Lovers, beware! a certaine, double harme
Waits your proud hopes, her looks al-killing charm
Guarded by her as true victorious arme.

V

Thus with her eyes brave Tamyris spake dread,
Which when the kings dull breast not entered,
Finding she could not looke, she strook him dead.

TO ALTHEA, FROM PRISON

When Love with unconfinèd wings
Hovers within my Gates,
And my divine *Althea* brings
To whisper at the Grates;
When I lie tangled in her hair,
And fettered to her eye,
The Gods that wanton in the Air,
Know no such Liberty.

When flowing Cups run swiftly round
With no allaying *Thames*,
Our careless heads with Roses bound,
Our hearts with Loyal Flames;
When thirsty grief in Wine we steep,
When Healths and draughts go free,
Fishes that tipple in the Deep
Know no such Liberty.

When (like committed linnets) I
With shriller throat shall sing
The sweetness, Mercy, Majesty,
And glories of my King;
When I shall voice aloud how good
He is, how Great should be,
Enlargèd Winds, that curl the Flood,
Know no such Liberty.

Stone Walls do not a Prison make,
Nor Iron bars a Cage;
Minds innocent and quiet take
That for an Hermitage.
If I have freedom in my Love,
And in my soul am free,
Angels alone that soar above,
Enjoy such Liberty.

TO LUCASTA,
GOING TO THE WARS

Tell me not (Sweet) I am unkind,
    That from the nunnery
Of thy chaste breast and quiet mind
    To war and arms I fly.
True, a new mistress now I chase,
    The first foe in the field;
And with a stronger faith embrace
    A sword, a horse, a shield.
Yet this inconstancy is such
    As you too shall adore;
I could not love thee (Dear) so much,
    Lov'd I not Honour more.

Andrew Marvell

THE GARDEN

How vainly men themselves amaze
To win the palm, the oak, or bays,
And their uncessant labours see
Crown'd from some single herb or tree,
Whose short and narrow verged shade
Does prudently their toils upbraid;
While all flow'rs and all trees do close
To weave the garlands of repose.

Fair Quiet, have I found thee here,
And Innocence, thy sister dear!
Mistaken long, I sought you then
In busy companies of men;
Your sacred plants, if here below,
Only among the plants will grow.
Society is all but rude,

To this delicious solitude.

No white nor red was ever seen
So am'rous as this lovely green.
Fond lovers, cruel as their flame,
Cut in these trees their mistress' name;
Little, alas, they know or heed
How far these beauties hers exceed!
Fair trees! wheres'e'er your barks I wound,
No name shall but your own be found.

When we have run our passion's heat,
Love hither makes his best retreat.
The gods, that mortal beauty chase,
Still in a tree did end their race:
Apollo hunted Daphne so,
Only that she might laurel grow;
And Pan did after Syrinx speed,
Not as a nymph, but for a reed.

What wond'rous life in this I lead!
Ripe apples drop about my head;
The luscious clusters of the vine
Upon my mouth do crush their wine;
The nectarine and curious peach
Into my hands themselves do reach;
Stumbling on melons as I pass,
Ensnar'd with flow'rs, I fall on grass.

Meanwhile the mind, from pleasure less,
Withdraws into its happiness;
The mind, that ocean where each kind
Does straight its own resemblance find,
Yet it creates, transcending these,
Far other worlds, and other seas;
Annihilating all that's made
To a green thought in a green shade.

Here at the fountain's sliding foot,

Or at some fruit tree's mossy root,
Casting the body's vest aside,
My soul into the boughs does glide;
There like a bird it sits and sings,
Then whets, and combs its silver wings;
And, till prepar'd for longer flight,
Waves in its plumes the various light.

Such was that happy garden-state,
While man there walk'd without a mate;
After a place so pure and sweet,
What other help could yet be meet!
But 'twas beyond a mortal's share
To wander solitary there:
Two paradises 'twere in one
To live in paradise alone.

How well the skillful gard'ner drew
Of flow'rs and herbs this dial new,
Where from above the milder sun
Does through a fragrant zodiac run;
And as it works, th' industrious bee
Computes its time as well as we.
How could such sweet and wholesome hours
Be reckon'd but with herbs and flow'rs!

TO HIS COY MISTRESS

HAD WE but world enough and time,
This coyness, lady, were no crime.
We would sit down, and think which way
To walk, and pass our long love's day.
Thou by the Indian Ganges' side
Shouldst rubies find; I by the tide
Of Humber would complain. I would
Love you ten years before the flood,
And you should, if you please, refuse

Till the conversion of the Jews.
My vegetable love should grow
Vaster than empires and more slow;
An hundred years should go to praise
Thine eyes, and on thy forehead gaze;
Two hundred to adore each breast,
But thirty thousand to the rest;
An age at least to every part,
And the last age should show your heart.
For, lady, you deserve this state,
Nor would I love at lower rate.

   But at my back I always hear
Time's wingèd chariot hurrying near;
And yonder all before us lie
Deserts of vast eternity.
Thy beauty shall no more be found;
Nor, in thy marble vault, shall sound
My echoing song; then worms shall try
That long-preserved virginity,
And your quaint honour turn to dust,
And into ashes all my lust;
The grave's a fine and private place,
But none, I think, do there embrace.

   Now therefore, while the youthful hue
Sits on thy skin like morning dew,
And while thy willing soul transpires
At every pore with instant fires,
Now let us sport us while we may,
And now, like amorous birds of prey,
Rather at once our time devour
Than languish in his slow-chapped power.
Let us roll all our strength and all
Our sweetness up into one ball,
And tear our pleasures with rough strife
Through the iron gates of life:
Thus, though we cannot make our sun

Stand still, yet we will make him run.

Alexander Pope

From THE RAPE OF THE LOCK

Canto I

Nolueram, Belinda, tuos violare capillos;
Sedjuvat, hoc precibus me tribuisse tuis.
(Martial, Epigrams 12.84)

WHAT DIRE offence from am'rous causes springs,
What mighty contests rise from trivial things,
I sing—This verse to Caryl, Muse! is due:
This, ev'n Belinda may vouchsafe to view:
Slight is the subject, but not so the praise,
If she inspire, and he approve my lays.

    Say what strange motive, Goddess! could compel
A well-bred lord t' assault a gentle belle?
O say what stranger cause, yet unexplor'd,
Could make a gentle belle reject a lord?
In tasks so bold, can little men engage,
And in soft bosoms dwells such mighty rage?

    Sol thro' white curtains shot a tim'rous ray,
And op'd those eyes that must eclipse the day;
Now lap-dogs give themselves the rousing shake,
And sleepless lovers, just at twelve, awake:
Thrice rung the bell, the slipper knock'd the ground,
And the press'd watch return'd a silver sound.
Belinda still her downy pillow press'd,
Her guardian sylph prolong'd the balmy rest:
'Twas he had summon'd to her silent bed
The morning dream that hover'd o'er her head;
A youth more glitt'ring than a birthnight beau,

(That ev'n in slumber caus'd her cheek to glow)
Seem'd to her ear his winning lips to lay,
And thus in whispers said, or seem'd to say.

    "Fairest of mortals, thou distinguish'd care
Of thousand bright inhabitants of air!
If e'er one vision touch'd thy infant thought,
Of all the nurse and all the priest have taught,
Of airy elves by moonlight shadows seen,
The silver token, and the circled green,
Or virgins visited by angel pow'rs,
With golden crowns and wreaths of heav'nly flow'rs,
Hear and believe! thy own importance know,
Nor bound thy narrow views to things below.
Some secret truths from learned pride conceal'd,
To maids alone and children are reveal'd:
What tho' no credit doubting wits may give?
The fair and innocent shall still believe.
Know then, unnumber'd spirits round thee fly,
The light militia of the lower sky;
These, though unseen, are ever on the wing,
Hang o'er the box, and hover round the Ring.
Think what an equipage thou hast in air,
And view with scorn two pages and a chair.
As now your own, our beings were of old,
And once inclos'd in woman's beauteous mould;
Thence, by a soft transition, we repair
From earthly vehicles to these of air.
Think not, when woman's transient breath is fled,
That all her vanities at once are dead;
Succeeding vanities she still regards,
And tho' she plays no more, o'erlooks the cards.
Her joy in gilded chariots, when alive,
And love of ombre, after death survive.
For when the fair in all their pride expire,
To their first elements their souls retire:
The sprites of fiery termagants in flame

Mount up, and take a Salamander's name.
Soft yielding minds to water glide away,
And sip with Nymphs, their elemental tea.
The graver prude sinks downward to a Gnome,
In search of mischief still on earth to roam.
The light coquettes in Sylphs aloft repair,
And sport and flutter in the fields of air.

   Know further yet; whoever fair and chaste
Rejects mankind, is by some sylph embrac'd:
For spirits, freed from mortal laws, with ease
Assume what sexes and what shapes they please.
What guards the purity of melting maids,
In courtly balls, and midnight masquerades,
Safe from the treach'rous friend, the daring spark,
The glance by day, the whisper in the dark,
When kind occasion prompts their warm desires,
When music softens, and when dancing fires?
'Tis but their sylph, the wise celestials know,
Though honour is the word with men below.

   Some nymphs there are, too conscious of their face,
For life predestin'd to the gnomes' embrace.
These swell their prospects and exalt their pride,
When offers are disdain'd, and love denied:
Then gay ideas crowd the vacant brain,
While peers, and dukes, and all their sweeping train,
And garters, stars, and coronets appear,
And in soft sounds 'Your Grace' salutes their ear.
'Tis these that early taint the female soul,
Instruct the eyes of young coquettes to roll,
Teach infant cheeks a bidden blush to know,
And little hearts to flutter at a beau.

   Oft, when the world imagine women stray,
The Sylphs through mystic mazes guide their way,
Thro' all the giddy circle they pursue,
And old impertinence expel by new.

What tender maid but must a victim fall
To one man's treat, but for another's ball?
When Florio speaks, what virgin could withstand,
If gentle Damon did not squeeze her hand?
With varying vanities, from ev'ry part,
They shift the moving toyshop of their heart;
Where wigs with wigs, with sword-knots sword-knots strive,
Beaux banish beaux, and coaches coaches drive.
This erring mortals levity may call,
Oh blind to truth! the Sylphs contrive it all.

   Of these am I, who thy protection claim,
A watchful sprite, and Ariel is my name.
Late, as I rang'd the crystal wilds of air,
In the clear mirror of thy ruling star
I saw, alas! some dread event impend,
Ere to the main this morning sun descend,
But Heav'n reveals not what, or how, or where:
Warn'd by the Sylph, oh pious maid, beware!
This to disclose is all thy guardian can.
Beware of all, but most beware of man!"

   He said; when Shock, who thought she slept too long,
Leap'd up, and wak'd his mistress with his tongue.
'Twas then, Belinda, if report say true,
Thy eyes first open'd on a billet-doux;
Wounds, charms, and ardors were no sooner read,
But all the vision vanish'd from thy head.

   And now, unveil'd, the toilet stands display'd,
Each silver vase in mystic order laid.
First, rob'd in white, the nymph intent adores
With head uncover'd, the cosmetic pow'rs.
A heav'nly image in the glass appears,
To that she bends, to that her eyes she rears;
Th' inferior priestess, at her altar's side,
Trembling, begins the sacred rites of pride.
Unnumber'd treasures ope at once, and here

The various off'rings of the world appear;
From each she nicely culls with curious toil,
And decks the goddess with the glitt'ring spoil.
This casket India's glowing gems unlocks,
And all Arabia breathes from yonder box.
The tortoise here and elephant unite,
Transform'd to combs, the speckled and the white.
Here files of pins extend their shining rows,
Puffs, powders, patches, bibles, billet-doux.
Now awful beauty puts on all its arms;
The fair each moment rises in her charms,
Repairs her smiles, awakens ev'ry grace,
And calls forth all the wonders of her face;
Sees by degrees a purer blush arise,
And keener lightnings quicken in her eyes.
The busy Sylphs surround their darling care;
These set the head, and those divide the hair,
Some fold the sleeve, whilst others plait the gown;
And Betty's prais'd for labours not her own.

Canto II

Not with more glories, in th' etherial plain,
The sun first rises o'er the purpled main,
Than, issuing forth, the rival of his beams
Launch'd on the bosom of the silver Thames.
Fair nymphs, and well-dress'd youths around her shone,
But ev'ry eye was fix'd on her alone.
On her white breast a sparkling cross she wore,
Which Jews might kiss, and infidels adore.
Her lively looks a sprightly mind disclose,
Quick as her eyes, and as unfix'd as those:
Favours to none, to all she smiles extends;
Oft she rejects, but never once offends.
Bright as the sun, her eyes the gazers strike,
And, like the sun, they shine on all alike.
Yet graceful ease, and sweetness void of pride,

Might hide her faults, if belles had faults to hide:
If to her share some female errors fall,
Look on her face, and you'll forget 'em all.

   This nymph, to the destruction of mankind,
Nourish'd two locks, which graceful hung behind
In equal curls, and well conspir'd to deck
With shining ringlets the smooth iv'ry neck.
Love in these labyrinths his slaves detains,
And mighty hearts are held in slender chains.
With hairy springes we the birds betray,
Slight lines of hair surprise the finney prey,
Fair tresses man's imperial race ensnare,
And beauty draws us with a single hair.

   Th' advent'rous baron the bright locks admir'd;
He saw, he wish'd, and to the prize aspir'd.
Resolv'd to win, he meditates the way,
By force to ravish, or by fraud betray;
For when success a lover's toil attends,
Few ask, if fraud or force attain'd his ends.

   For this, ere Phoebus rose, he had implor'd
Propitious Heav'n, and ev'ry pow'r ador'd,
But chiefly love—to love an altar built,
Of twelve vast French romances, neatly gilt.
There lay three garters, half a pair of gloves;
And all the trophies of his former loves;
With tender billet-doux he lights the pyre,
And breathes three am'rous sighs to raise the fire.
Then prostrate falls, and begs with ardent eyes
Soon to obtain, and long possess the prize:
The pow'rs gave ear, and granted half his pray'r,
The rest, the winds dispers'd in empty air.

   But now secure the painted vessel glides,
The sun-beams trembling on the floating tides,
While melting music steals upon the sky,
And soften'd sounds along the waters die.

Smooth flow the waves, the zephyrs gently play,
Belinda smil'd, and all the world was gay.
All but the Sylph—with careful thoughts opprest,
Th' impending woe sat heavy on his breast.
He summons strait his denizens of air;
The lucid squadrons round the sails repair:
Soft o'er the shrouds aerial whispers breathe,
That seem'd but zephyrs to the train beneath.
Some to the sun their insect-wings unfold,
Waft on the breeze, or sink in clouds of gold.
Transparent forms, too fine for mortal sight,
Their fluid bodies half dissolv'd in light,
Loose to the wind their airy garments flew,
Thin glitt'ring textures of the filmy dew;
Dipp'd in the richest tincture of the skies,
Where light disports in ever-mingling dyes,
While ev'ry beam new transient colours flings,
Colours that change whene'er they wave their wings.
Amid the circle, on the gilded mast,
Superior by the head, was Ariel plac'd;
His purple pinions op'ning to the sun,
He rais'd his azure wand, and thus begun.

"Ye Sylphs and Sylphids, to your chief give ear!
Fays, Fairies, Genii, Elves, and Dæmons, hear!
Ye know the spheres and various tasks assign'd
By laws eternal to th' aerial kind.
Some in the fields of purest æther play,
And bask and whiten in the blaze of day.
Some guide the course of wand'ring orbs on high,
Or roll the planets through the boundless sky.
Some less refin'd, beneath the moon's pale light
Pursue the stars that shoot athwart the night,
Or suck the mists in grosser air below,
Or dip their pinions in the painted bow,
Or brew fierce tempests on the wintry main,
Or o'er the glebe distil the kindly rain.

Others on earth o'er human race preside,
Watch all their ways, and all their actions guide:
Of these the chief the care of nations own,
And guard with arms divine the British throne.

    "Our humbler province is to tend the fair,
Not a less pleasing, though less glorious care.
To save the powder from too rude a gale,
Nor let th' imprison'd essences exhale,
To draw fresh colours from the vernal flow'rs,
To steal from rainbows e'er they drop in show'rs
A brighter wash; to curl their waving hairs,
Assist their blushes, and inspire their airs;
Nay oft, in dreams, invention we bestow,
To change a flounce, or add a furbelow.

    "This day, black omens threat the brightest fair
That e'er deserv'd a watchful spirit's care;
Some dire disaster, or by force, or slight,
But what, or where, the fates have wrapt in night.
Whether the nymph shall break Diana's law,
Or some frail china jar receive a flaw;
Or stain her honour, or her new brocade,
Forget her pray'rs, or miss a masquerade;
Or lose her heart, or necklace, at a ball;
Or whether Heav'n has doom'd that Shock must fall.
Haste, then, ye spirits! to your charge repair:
The flutt'ring fan be Zephyretta's care;
The drops to thee, Brillante, we consign;
And, Momentilla, let the watch be thine;
Do thou, Crispissa, tend her fav'rite lock;
Ariel himself shall be the guard of Shock.

    "To fifty chosen Sylphs, of special note,
We trust th' important charge, the petticoat:
Oft have we known that sev'n-fold fence to fail,
Though stiff with hoops, and arm'd with ribs of whale.
Form a strong line about the silver bound,

And guard the wide circumference around.

"Whatever spirit, careless of his charge,
His post neglects, or leaves the fair at large,
Shall feel sharp vengeance soon o'ertake his sins,
Be stopp'd in vials, or transfix'd with pins;
Or plung'd in lakes of bitter washes lie,
Or wedg'd whole ages in a bodkin's eye:
Gums and pomatums shall his flight restrain,
While clogg'd he beats his silken wings in vain;
Or alum styptics with contracting pow'r
Shrink his thin essence like a rivell'd flow'r.
Or, as Ixion fix'd, the wretch shall feel
The giddy motion of the whirling mill,
In fumes of burning chocolate shall glow,
And tremble at the sea that froths below!"

He spoke; the spirits from the sails descend;
Some, orb in orb, around the nymph extend,
Some thrid the mazy ringlets of her hair,
Some hang upon the pendants of her ear;
With beating hearts the dire event they wait,
Anxious, and trembling for the birth of fate.

Samuel Johnson

LONDON: A POEM

In Imitation of the Third Satire of Juvenal

> *Quis ineptæ
> Tam patiens urbis, tam ferreus ut teneat se?*
> (Juvenal)

THO' GRIEF and fondness in my breast rebel,
When injur'd Thales bids the town farewell,
Yet still my calmer thoughts his choice commend,
I praise the hermit, but regret the friend,

Who now resolves, from vice and London far,
To breathe in distant fields a purer air,
And, fix'd on Cambria's solitary shore,
Give to St. David one *true Briton* more.

For who would leave, unbrib'd, *Hibernia's* land,
Or change the rocks of *Scotland* for the *Strand*?
There none are swept by sudden fate away,
But all whom hunger spares, with age decay:
Here malice, rapine, accident, conspire,
And now a rabble rages, now a fire;
Their ambush here relentless ruffians lay,
And here the fell attorney prowls for prey;
Here falling houses thunder on your head,
And here a female atheist talks you dead.

While Thales waits the wherry that contains
Of dissipated wealth the small remains,
On *Thames's* banks, in silent thought we stood,
Where Greenwich smiles upon the silver flood:
Struck with the seat that gave Eliza birth,
We kneel, and kiss the consecrated earth;
In pleasing dreams the blissful age renew,
And call Britannia's glories back to view;
Behold her cross triumphant on the main,
The guard of commerce, and the dread of Spain,
Ere masquerades debauch'd, excise oppress'd,
Or *English* honour grew a standing jest.

A transient calm the happy scenes bestow,
And for a moment lull the sense of woe.
At length awaking, with contemptuous frown,
Indignant Thales eyes the neighb'ring town.

Since worth, he cries, in these degen'rate days,
Wants ev'n the cheap reward of empty praise;
In those curs'd walls, devote to vice and gain,
Since unrewarded science toils in vain;
Since hope but sooths to double my distress,

And ev'ry moment leaves my little less;
While yet my steddy steps no staff sustains,
And life still vig'rous revels in my veins;
Grant me, kind heaven, to find some happier place,
Where honesty and sense are no disgrace;
Some pleasing bank where verdant osiers play,
Some peaceful vale with mature's paintings gay;
Where once the harass'd Briton found repose,
And safe in poverty defy'd his foes;
Some secret cell, ye pow'rs, indulgent give.
Let —— live here, for —— has learn'd to live.
Here let those reign, whom pensions can incite
To vote a patriot black, a courtier white;
Explain their country's dear-bought rights away,
And plead for pirates in the face of day;
With slavish tenets taint our poison'd youth,
And lend a lye the confidence of truth.

Let such raise palaces, and manors buy,
Collect a tax, or farm a lottery,
With warbling eunuchs fill a licens'd stage,
And lull to servitude a thoughtless age.

Heroes, proceed! what bounds your pride shall hold?
What check restrain your thirst of pow'r and gold?
Behold rebellious virtue quite o'erthrown,
Behold our fame, our wealth, our lives your own.

To such, a groaning nation's spoils are giv'n,
When publick crimes inflame the wrath of heav'n:
But what, my friend, what hope remains for me,
Who start at theft, and blush at perjury?
Who scarce forbear, tho' Britain's Court he sing,
To pluck a titled poet's borrow'd wing;
A statesman's logick unconvinc'd can hear,
And dare to slumber o'er the *Gazetteer*;
Despise a fool in half his pension dress'd,
And strive in vain to laugh at H—*y's* jest.

Others with softer smiles, and subtler art,
Can sap the principles, or taint the heart;
With more address a lover's note convey,
Or bribe a virgin's innocence away.
Well may they rise, while I, whose rustick tongue
Ne'er knew to puzzle right, or varnish wrong,
Spurn'd as a begger, dreaded as a spy,
Live unregarded, unlamented die.

For what but social guilt the friend endears?
Who shares Orgilio's crimes, his fortune shares.
But thou, should tempting villainy present
All *Marlb'rough* hoarded, or all *Villiers* spent;
Turn from the glitt'ring bribe thy scornful eye,
Nor sell for gold, what gold could never buy,
The peaceful slumber, self-approving day,
Unsullied fame, and conscience ever gay.

The cheated nation's happy fav'rites, see!
Mark whom the great caress, who frown on me!
London! the needy villain's gen'ral home,
The common shore of Paris and of Rome;
With eager thirst, by folly or by fate,
Sucks in the dregs of each corrupted state.
Forgive my transports on a theme like this,
I cannot bear a *French* metropolis.

Illustrious Edward! from the realms of day,
The land of heroes and of saints survey;
Nor hope the *British* lineaments to trace,
The rustick grandeur, or the surly grace;
But lost in thoughtless ease, and empty show,
Behold the warriour dwindled to a beau;
Sense, freedom, piety, refin'd away,
Of France the mimick, and of Spain the prey.

All that at home no more can beg or steal,
Or like a gibbet better than a wheel;
Hiss'd from the stage, or hooted from the court,

Their air, their dress, their politicks import;
Obsequious, artful, voluble and gay,
On Britain's fond credulity they prey.
No gainful trade their industry can 'scape,
They sing, they dance, clean shoes, or cure a clap;
All sciences a fasting Monsieur knows,
And bid him go to hell, to hell he goes.

Ah! what avails it, that, from slav'ry far,
I drew the breath of life in *English* air;
Was early taught a *Briton's* right to prize,
And lisp the tale of Henry's victories;
If the gull'd conqueror receives the chain,
And flattery subdues when arms are vain?

Studious to please, and ready to submit,
The supple *Gaul* was born a parasite:
Still to his int'rest true, where'er he goes,
Wit, brav'ry, worth, his lavish tongue bestows;
In ev'ry face a thousand graces shine,
From ev'ry tongue flows harmony divine.
These arts in vain our rugged natives try,
Strain out with fault'ring diffidence a lye,
And gain a kick for aukward flattery.

Besides, with justice, this discerning age
Admires their wond'rous talents for the stage:
Well may they venture on the mimick's art,
Who play from morn to night a borrow'd part;
Practis'd their master's notions to embrace,
Repeat his maxims, and reflect his face;
With ev'ry wild absurdity comply,
And view each object with another's eye;
To shake with laughter ere the jest they hear,
To pour at will the counterfeited tear;
And as their patron hints the cold or heat,
To shake in dog-days, in *December* sweat.

How, when competitors like these contend,

Can surly virtue hope to fix a friend?
Slaves that with serious impudence beguile,
And lye without a blush, without a smile;
Exalt each trifle, ev'ry vice adore,
Your taste in snuff, your judgment in a whore;
Can *Balbo's* eloquence applaud, and swear
He gropes his breeches with a monarch's air.

For arts like these preferr'd, admir'd, caress'd,
They first invade your table, then your breast;
Explore your secrets with insidious art,
Watch the weak hour, and ransack all the heart;
Then soon your ill-plac'd confidence repay,
Commence your lords, and govern or betray.

By numbers here from shame or censure free,
All crimes are safe, but hated poverty.
This, only this, the rigid law pursues,
This, only this, provokes the snarling muse;
The sober trader at a tatter'd cloak,
Wakes from his dream, and labours for a joke;
With brisker air the silken courtiers gaze,
And turn the varied taunt a thousand ways.
Of all the griefs that harrass the distress'd,
Sure the most bitter is a scornful jest;
Fate never wounds more deep the gen'rous heart,
Than when a blockhead's insult points the dart.

Has heaven reserv'd, in pity to the poor,
No pathless waste, or undiscover'd shore;
No secret island in the boundless main?
No peaceful desart yet unclaim'd by Spain?
Quick let us rise, the happy seats explore,
And bear oppression's insolence no more.
This mournful truth is ev'ry where confess'd,
SLOW RISES WORTH, BY POVERTY DEPRESS'D:
But here more slow, where all are slaves to gold,
Where looks are merchandise, and smiles are sold,

Where won by bribes, by flatteries implor'd,
The groom retails the favours of his lord.

But hark! th' affrighted crowd's tumultuous cries
Roll thro' the streets, and thunder to the skies;
Rais'd from some pleasing dream of wealth and pow'r,
Some pompous palace, or some blissful bow'r,
Aghast you start, and scarce with aking sight,
Sustain th' approaching fire's tremendous light;
Swift from pursuing horrors take your way,
And leave your little ALL to flames a prey;
Then thro' the world a wretched vagrant roam,
For where can starving merit find a home?
In vain your mournful narrative disclose,
While all neglect, and most insult your woes.

Should heaven's just bolts *Orgilio's* wealth confound,
And spread his flaming palace on the ground,
Swift o'er the land the dismal rumour flies,
And publick mournings pacify the skies;
The laureat tribe in servile verse relate,
How virtue wars with persecuting fate;
With well-feign'd gratitude the pension'd band
Refund the plunder of the begger'd land.
See! while he builds, the gaudy vassals come,
And crowd with sudden wealth the rising dome;
The price of boroughs and of souls restore,
And raise his treasures higher than before.
Now bless'd with all the baubles of the great,
The polish'd marble, and the shining plate,
Orgilio sees the golden pile aspire,
And hopes from angry heav'n another fire.

Could'st thou resign the park and play content,
For the fair banks of *Severn* or of *Trent*;
There might'st thou find some elegant retreat,
Some hireling senator's deserted seat;
And stretch thy prospects o'er the smiling land,

For less than rent the dungeons of the *Strand*;
There prune thy walks, support thy drooping flow'rs,
Direct thy rivulets, and twine thy bow'rs;
And, while thy beds a cheap repast afford,
Despise the dainties of a venal lord:
There ev'ry bush with nature's musick rings,
There ev'ry breeze bears health upon its wings;
On all thy hours security shall smile,
And bless thine evening walk and morning toil.

Prepare for death, if here at night you roam,
And sign your will before you sup from home.
Some fiery fop, with new commission vain,
Who sleeps on brambles till he kills his man;
Some frolick drunkard, reeling from a feast,
Provokes a broil, and stabs you for a jest.
Yet ev'n these heroes, mischievously gay,
Lords of the street, and terrors of the way;
Flush'd as they are with folly, youth and wine,
Their prudent insults to the poor confine;
Afar they mark the flambeau's bright approach,
And shun the shining train, and golden coach.

In vain, these dangers past, your doors you close,
And hope the balmy blessings of repose:
Cruel with guilt, and daring with despair,
The midnight murd'rer bursts the faithless bar;
Invades the sacred hour of silent rest,
And plants, unseen, a dagger in your breast.

Scarce can our fields, such crowds at Tyburn die,
With hemp the gallows and the fleet supply.
Propose your schemes, ye Senatorian band,
Whose *Ways and Means* support the sinking land;
Lest ropes be wanting in the tempting spring,
To rig another convoy for the k—g.

A single jail, in Alfred's golden reign,
Could half the nation's criminals contain;

Fair justice then, without constraint ador'd,
Held high the steady scale, but drop'd the sword;
No spies were paid, no *special juries* known,
Blest age! but ah! how diff'rent from our own!

Much could I add,—but see the boat at hand,
The tide retiring, calls me from the land:
Farewel!—When youth, and health, and fortune spent,
Thou fly'st for refuge to the wilds of *Kent*;
And tir'd like me with follies and with crimes,
In angry numbers warn'st succeeding times;
Then shall thy friend, nor thou refuse his aid,
Still foe to vice forsake his *Cambrian* shade;
In virtue's cause once more exert his rage,
Thy satire point, and animate thy page.

THE VANITY
OF HUMAN WISHES

The tenth satire of Juvenal imitated.

LET OBSERVATION with extensive view,
Survey mankind, from China to Peru;
Remark each anxious toil, each eager strife,
And watch the busy scenes of crowded life;
Then say how hope and fear, desire and hate,
O'erspread with snares the clouded maze of fate,
Where wav'ring man, betray'd by vent'rous pride,
To tread the dreary paths without a guide,
As treach'rous phantoms in the mist delude,
Shuns fancied ills, or chases airy good.
How rarely reason guides the stubborn choice,
Rules the bold hand, or prompts the suppliant voice,
How nations sink, by darling schemes oppress'd,
When vengeance listens to the fool's request.
Fate wings with ev'ry wish th' afflictive dart,

Each gift of nature, and each grace of art,
With fatal heat impetuous courage glows,
With fatal sweetness elocution flows,
Impeachment stops the speaker's pow'rful breath,
And restless fire precipitates on death.

But scarce observ'd, the knowing and the bold,
Fall in the gen'ral massacre of gold;
Wide-wasting pest! that rages unconfin'd,
And crowds with crimes the records of mankind;
For gold his sword the hireling ruffian draws,
For gold the hireling judge distorts the laws;
Wealth heap'd on wealth, nor truth nor safety buys,
The dangers gather as the treasures rise.

Let hist'ry tell where rival kings command,
And dubious title shakes the madded land,
When statutes glean the refuse of the sword,
How much more safe the vassal than the lord:
Low sculks the hind beneath the rage of pow'r,
And leaves the wealthy traitor in the Tow'r,
Untouch'd his cottage, and his slumbers sound,
Tho' confiscation's vultures hover round.

The needy traveller, serene and gay,
Walks the wild heath, and sings his toil away.
Does envy seize thee? crush th' upbraiding joy,
Increase his riches and his peace destroy,
New fears in dire vicissitude invade,
The rustling brake alarms, and quiv'ring shade,
Nor light nor darkness bring his pain relief.
One shews the plunder, and one hides the thief.

Yet still one gen'ral cry the skies assails,
And gain and grandeur load the tainted gales,
Few know the toiling statesman's fear or care,
Th' insidious rival and the gaping heir.

Once more, Democritus, arise on earth,

With cheerful wisdom and instructive mirth,
See motley life in modern trappings dress'd,
And feed with varied fools th' eternal jest:
Thou who couldst laugh where want enchain'd caprice,
Toil crush'd conceit, and man was of a piece;
Where wealth unlov'd without a mourner died;
And scarce a sycophant was fed by pride;
Where ne'er was known the form of mock debate,
Or seen a new-made mayor's unwieldy state;
Where change of fav'rites made no change of laws,
And senates heard before they judg'd a cause;
How wouldst thou shake at Britain's modish tribe,
Dart the quick taunt, and edge the piercing gibe?
Attentive truth and nature to descry,
And pierce each scene with philosophic eye.
To thee were solemn toys or empty show,
The robes of pleasure and the veils of woe:
All aid the farce, and all thy mirth maintain,
Whose joys are causeless, or whose griefs are vain.

Such was the scorn that fill'd the sage's mind,
Renew'd at ev'ry glance on humankind;
How just that scorn ere yet thy voice declare,
Search every state, and canvas ev'ry pray'r.

Unnumber'd suppliants crowd Preferment's gate,
Athirst for wealth, and burning to be great;
Delusive Fortune hears the incessant call,
They mount, they shine, evaporate, and fall.
On ev'ry stage the foes of peace attend,
Hate dogs their flight, and insult mocks their end.
Love ends with hope, the sinking statesman's door
Pours in the morning worshiper no more;
For growing names the weekly scribbler lies,
To growing wealth the dedicator flies,
From every room descends the painted face,
That hung the bright palladium of the place,
And smok'd in kitchens or in auctions sold,

To better features yields the frame of gold;
For now no more we trace in ev'ry line,
Heroic worth, benevolence divine:
The form distorted justifies the fall,
And detestation rids th' indignant wall.

But will not Britain hear the last appeal,
Sign her foes doom, or guard her fav'rites' zeal?
Through freedom's sons no more remonstrance rings,
Degrading nobles, and controlling kings;
Our supple tribes repress their patriot throats,
And ask no question but the price of votes;
With weekly libels and septennial ale,
Their wish is full to riot and to rail.

In full-blown dignity see Wolsey stand,
Law in his voice, and fortune in his hand;
To him the church, the realm, their powers consign,
Through him the rays of regal bounty shine;
Turn'd by his nod the stream of honour flows,
His smile alone security bestows:
Still to new heights his restless wishes tour;
Claim leads to claim, and pow'r advances pow'r;
Till conquest unresisted ceas'd to please,
And rights submitted, left him none to seize.
At length his sov'reign frowns—the train of state
Mark the keen glance, and watch the sign to hate;
Where'er he turns he meets a stranger's eye,
His suppliants scorn him, and his followers fly;
Now drops at once the pride of awful state,
The golden canopy, the glitt'ring plate,
The regal palace, the luxurious board,
The liv'ried army, and the menial lord.
With age, with cares, with maladies oppress'd,
He seeks the refuge of monastic rest.
Grief aids disease, remember'd folly stings,
And his last sighs reproach the faith of kings.

Speak thou, whose thoughts at humble peace repine,
Shall Wolsey's wealth, with Wolsey's end, be thine?
Or liv'st thou now, with safer pride content,
The wisest justice on the banks of Trent?
For why did Wolsey, near the steeps of fate,
On weak foundations raise th' enormous weight?
Why but to sink beneath misfortune's blow
With louder ruin to the gulphs below?

What gave great Villiers to the assassin's knife,
And fix'd disease on Harley's closing life?
What murder'd Wentworth, and what exil'd Hyde,
By kings protected, and to kings ally'd?
What but their wish indulg'd, in courts to shine,
And pow'r too great to keep or to resign?

When first the college rolls receive his name,
The young enthusiast quits his ease for fame;
Resistless burns the fever of renown,
Caught from the strong contagion of the gown:
O'er Bodley's dome his future labours spread,
And Bacon's mansion trembles o'er his head.
Are these thy views? proceed, illustrious youth,
And virtue guard thee to the throne of Truth!
Yet should thy soul indulge the gen'rous heat,
Till captive Science yields her last retreat;
Should Reason guide thee with her brightest ray,
And pour on misty doubt resistless day;
Should no false kindness lure to loose delight,
Nor praise relax, nor difficulty fright;
Should tempting novelty thy cell refrain,
And sloth effuse her opiate fumes in vain;
Should beauty blunt on fops her fatal dart,
Nor claim the triumph of a letter'd heart;
Should no disease thy torpid veins invade,
Nor melancholy's phantoms haunt thy shade;
Yet hope not life from grief or danger free,
Nor think the doom of man revers'd for thee:

Deign on the passing world to turn thine eyes,
And pause awhile from learning, to be wise;
There mark what ills the scholar's life assail,
Toil, envy, want, the patron, and the jail.
See nations slowly wise, and meanly just,
To buried merit raise the tardy bust.
If dreams yet flatter, once again attend,
Hear Lydiat's life, and Galileo's end.

Nor deem, when learning her last prize bestows
The glitt'ring eminence exempt from foes;
See when the vulgar 'scapes despis'd or aw'd,
Rebellion's vengeful talons seize on Laud.
From meaner minds, though smaller fines content,
The plunder'd palace, or sequester'd rent;
Mark'd out by dangerous parts he meets the shock,
And fatal learning leads him to the block:
Around his tomb let art and genius weep,
But hear his death, ye blockheads, hear and sleep.

The festal blazes, the triumphal show,
The ravish'd standard, and the captive foe,
The senate's thanks, the Gazette's pompous tale,
With force resistless o'er the brave prevail.
Such bribes the rapid Greek o'er Asia whirl'd,
For such the steady Romans shook the world;
For such in distant lands the Britons shine,
And stain with blood the Danube or the Rhine;
This power has praise, that virtue scarce can warm,
Till fame supplies the universal charm.
Yet reason frowns on war's unequal game,
Where wasted nation's raise a single name,
And mortgag'd states their grandsire's wreaths regret,
From age to age in everlasting debt;
Wreaths which at last the dear-bought right convey,
To rust on medals, or on stones decay.

On what foundation stands the warrior's pride,

How just his hopes, let Swedish Charles decide;
A frame of adamant, a soul of fire,
No dangers fright him, and no labours tire;
O'er love, o'er fear, extends his wide domain,
Unconquer'd lord of pleasure and of pain;
No joys to him pacific scepters yield,
War sounds the trump, he rushes to the field;
Behold surrounding kings their power combine,
And one capitulate, and one resign;
Peace courts his hand, but spreads her charms in vain;
"Think nothing gain'd," he cries, "till nought remain,
"On Muscow's walls till Gothic standards fly,
"And all be mine beneath the polar sky."
The march begins in military state,
And nations on his eye suspended wait;
Stern famine guards the solitary coast,
And winter barricades the realms of frost;
He comes, nor want nor cold his course delay;
Hide, blushing glory, hide Pultowa's day:
The vanquish'd hero leaves his broken bands,
And shews his miseries in distant lands;
Condemn'd a needy supplicant to wait,
While ladies interpose, and slaves debate.
But did not chance at length her error mend?
Did no subverted empire mark his end?
Did rival monarchs give the fatal wound?
Or hostile millions press him to the ground?
His fall was destin'd to a barren strand,
A petty fortress, and a dubious hand;
He left the name at which the world grew pale,
To point a moral, or adorn a tale.

All times their scenes of pompous woes afford,
From Persia's tyrant to Bavaria's lord,
In gay hostility, and barb'rous pride,
With half mankind embattled at his side,
Great Xerxes comes to seize the certain prey,

And starves exhausted regions in his way;
Attendant flattery counts his myriads o'er,
Till counted myriads sooth his pride no more;
Fresh praise is try'd, till madness fires his mind,
The waves he lashes, and enchains the wind;

New pow'rs are claim'd, new pow'rs are still bestow'd,
Till rude resistance lops the spreading god;
The daring Greeks deride the marital show,
And heap their valleys with the gaudy foe;
Th' insulted sea with humbler thoughts he gains,
A single skiff to speed his flight remains:
Th' encumber'd oar scarce leaves the dreaded coast
Through purple billows and a floating host.

The bold Bavarian, in a luckless hour,
Tries the dread summits of Caesarean power,
With unexpected legions bursts away,
And sees defenceless realms receive his sway;
Short sway! fair Austria spreads her mournful charms,
The queen, the beauty, sets the world in arms;
From hill to hill the beacon's rousing blaze
Spreads wide the hope of plunder and of praise.
The fierce Croatian, and the wild Hussar,
With all the sons of ravage crowd the war;
The baffled prince in honour's flattering bloom
Of hasty greatness finds the fatal doom;
His foes' derision, and his subjects' blame,
And steals to death from anguish and from shame.

Enlarge my life with multitude of days,
In health, in sickness, thus the suppliant prays;
Hides from himself his state, and shuns to know
That life protracted is protracted woe.
Time hovers o'er, impatient to destroy,
And shuts up all the passages of joy:
In vain their gifts the bounteous seasons pour,
The fruit autumnal, and the vernal flower,

With listless eyes the dotard views the store,
He views, and wonders that they please no more;
Now pall the tasteless meats, and joyless wines,
And luxury with sighs her slave resigns.
Approach, ye minstrels, try the soothing strain,
And yield the tuneful lenitives of pain:
No sounds, alas! would touch th' impervious ear,
Though dancing mountains witness'd Orpheus near;
Nor lute nor lyre his feeble pow'rs attend,
Nor sweeter music of a virtuous friend,
But everlasting dictates crowd his tongue,
Perversely grave, or positively wrong.
The still returning tale, and ling'ring jest,
Perplex the fawning niece and pamper'd guest;
While growing hopes scarce awe the gathering sneer,
And scarce a legacy can bribe to hear;
The watchful guests still hint the last offence,
The daughter's petulance, the son's expence,
Improve his heady rage with treach'rous skill,
And mould his passions till they make his will.

Unnumber'd maladies his joints invade,
Lay siege to life and press the dire blockade;
But unextinguish'd Av'rice still remains,
And dreaded losses aggravate his pains;
He turns, with anxious heart and crippled hands,
His bonds of debt, and mortgages of lands;
Or views his coffers with suspicious eyes,
Unlocks his gold, and counts it till he dies.

But grant, the virtues of a temp'rate prime
Bless with an age exempt from scorn or crime;
An age that melts with unperceiv'd decay,
And glides in modest innocence away;
Whose peaceful day benevolence endears,
Whose night congratulating conscience cheers;
The gen'ral fav'rite as the gen'ral friend:

Such age there is, and who could wish its end?

Yet ev'n on this her load misfortune flings,
To press the weary minutes' flagging wings:
New sorrow rises as the day returns,
A sister sickens, or a daughter mourns.
Now kindred merit fills the sable bier,
Now lacerated friendship claims a tear.
Year chases year, decay pursues decay,
Still drops some joy from with'ring life away;
New forms arise, and diff'rent views engage,
Superfluous lags the vet'ran on the stage,
Till pitying nature signs the last release,
And bids afflicted worth retire to peace.

But few there are whom hours like these await,
Who set unclouded in the gulfs of fate.
From Lydia's monarch should the search descend,
By Solon caution'd to regard his end,
In life's last scene what prodigies surprise,
Fears of the brave, and follies of the wise?
From Marlb'rough's eyes the streams of dotage flow,
And Swift expires a driv'ler and a show.

The teeming mother, anxious for her race,
Begs for each birth the fortune of a face:
Yet Vane could tell what ills from beauty spring;
And Sedley curs'd the form that pleas'd a king.
Ye nymphs of rosy lips and radiant eyes,
Whom Pleasure keeps too busy to be wise,
Whom Joys with soft varieties invite,
By day the frolic, and the dance by night,
Who frown with vanity, who smile with art,
And ask the latest fashion of the heart,
What care, what rules your heedless charms shall save,
Each nymph your rival, and each youth your slave?
Against your fame with fondness hate combines,
The rival batters, and the lover mines.

With distant voice neglected virtue calls,
Less heard and less, the faint remonstrance falls;
Tir'd with contempt, she quits the slipp'ry reign,
And pride and prudence take her seat in vain.
In crowd at once, where none the pass defend,
The harmless freedom, and the private friend.
The guardians yield, by force superior plied;
To int'rest, prudence; and by flatt'ry, pride.
Here beauty falls betray'd, despis'd, distress'd,
And hissing infamy proclaims the rest.

Where then shall hope and fear their objects find?
Must dull suspense corrupt the stagnant mind?
Must helpless man, in ignorance sedate,
Roll darkling down the torrent of his fate?
Must no dislike alarm, no wishes rise,
No cries attempt the mercies of the skies?
Inquirer, cease, petitions yet remain,
Which heaven may hear, nor deem religion vain.
Still raise for good the supplicating voice,
But leave to heaven the measure and the choice.
Safe in his pow'r, whose eyes discern afar
The secret ambush of a specious pray'r.
Implore his aid, in his decisions rest,
Secure whate'er he gives, he gives the best.
Yet when the sense of sacred presence fires,
And strong devotion to the skies aspires,
Pour forth thy fervors for a healthful mind,
Obedient passions, and a will resign'd;
For love, which scarce collective man can fill;
For patience, sov'reign o'er transmuted ill;
For faith, that panting for a happier seat,
Counts death kind nature's signal of retreat:
These goods for man the laws of heaven ordain,
These goods he grants, who grants the pow'r to gain;
With these celestial wisdom calms the mind,
And makes the happiness she does not find.

Thomas Gray

ELEGY WRITTEN
IN A COUNTRY CHURCHYARD

The curfew tolls the knell of parting day,
    The lowing herd wind slowly o'er the lea,
The plowman homeward plods his weary way,
    And leaves the world to darkness and to me.

Now fades the glimm'ring landscape on the sight,
    And all the air a solemn stillness holds,
Save where the beetle wheels his droning flight,
    And drowsy tinklings lull the distant folds;

Save that from yonder ivy-mantled tow'r
    The moping owl does to the moon complain
Of such, as wand'ring near her secret bow'r,
    Molest her ancient solitary reign.

Beneath those rugged elms, that yew-tree's shade,
    Where heaves the turf in many a mould'ring heap,
Each in his narrow cell for ever laid,
    The rude forefathers of the hamlet sleep.

The breezy call of incense-breathing Morn,
    The swallow twitt'ring from the straw-built shed,
The cock's shrill clarion, or the echoing horn,
    No more shall rouse them from their lowly bed.

For them no more the blazing hearth shall burn,
    Or busy housewife ply her evening care:
No children run to lisp their sire's return,
    Or climb his knees the envied kiss to share.

Oft did the harvest to their sickle yield,
    Their furrow oft the stubborn glebe has broke;
How jocund did they drive their team afield!
    How bow'd the woods beneath their sturdy stroke!

Let not Ambition mock their useful toil,
   Their homely joys, and destiny obscure;
Nor Grandeur hear with a disdainful smile
   The short and simple annals of the poor.

The boast of heraldry, the pomp of pow'r,
   And all that beauty, all that wealth e'er gave,
Awaits alike th' inevitable hour.
   The paths of glory lead but to the grave.

Nor you, ye proud, impute to these the fault,
   If Mem'ry o'er their tomb no trophies raise,
Where thro' the long-drawn aisle and fretted vault
   The pealing anthem swells the note of praise.

Can storied urn or animated bust
   Back to its mansion call the fleeting breath?
Can Honour's voice provoke the silent dust,
   Or Flatt'ry soothe the dull cold ear of Death?

Perhaps in this neglected spot is laid
   Some heart once pregnant with celestial fire;
Hands, that the rod of empire might have sway'd,
   Or wak'd to ecstasy the living lyre.

But Knowledge to their eyes her ample page
   Rich with the spoils of time did ne'er unroll;
Chill Penury repress'd their noble rage,
   And froze the genial current of the soul.

Full many a gem of purest ray serene,
   The dark unfathom'd caves of ocean bear:
Full many a flow'r is born to blush unseen,
   And waste its sweetness on the desert air.

Some village-Hampden, that with dauntless breast
   The little tyrant of his fields withstood;
Some mute inglorious Milton here may rest,
   Some Cromwell guiltless of his country's blood.

Th' applause of list'ning senates to command,

> The threats of pain and ruin to despise,
> To scatter plenty o'er a smiling land,
> And read their hist'ry in a nation's eyes,
>
> Their lot forbade: nor circumscrib'd alone
> Their growing virtues, but their crimes confin'd;
> Forbade to wade through slaughter to a throne,
> And shut the gates of mercy on mankind,
>
> The struggling pangs of conscious truth to hide,
> To quench the blushes of ingenuous shame,
> Or heap the shrine of Luxury and Pride
> With incense kindled at the Muse's flame.
>
> Far from the madding crowd's ignoble strife,
> Their sober wishes never learn'd to stray;
> Along the cool sequester'd vale of life
> They kept the noiseless tenor of their way.
>
> Yet ev'n these bones from insult to protect,
> Some frail memorial still erected nigh,
> With uncouth rhymes and shapeless sculpture deck'd,
> Implores the passing tribute of a sigh.
>
> Their name, their years, spelt by th' unletter'd muse,
> The place of fame and elegy supply:
> And many a holy text around she strews,
> That teach the rustic moralist to die.
>
> For who to dumb Forgetfulness a prey,
> This pleasing anxious being e'er resign'd,
> Left the warm precincts of the cheerful day,
> Nor cast one longing, ling'ring look behind?
>
> On some fond breast the parting soul relies,
> Some pious drops the closing eye requires;
> Ev'n from the tomb the voice of Nature cries,
> Ev'n in our ashes live their wonted fires.
>
> For thee, who mindful of th' unhonour'd Dead
> Dost in these lines their artless tale relate;

If chance, by lonely contemplation led,
   Some kindred spirit shall inquire thy fate,

Haply some hoary-headed swain may say,
   "Oft have we seen him at the peep of dawn
Brushing with hasty steps the dews away
   To meet the sun upon the upland lawn.

"There at the foot of yonder nodding beech
   That wreathes its old fantastic roots so high,
His listless length at noontide would he stretch,
   And pore upon the brook that babbles by.

"Hard by yon wood, now smiling as in scorn,
   Mutt'ring his wayward fancies he would rove,
Now drooping, woeful wan, like one forlorn,
   Or craz'd with care, or cross'd in hopeless love.

"One morn I miss'd him on the custom'd hill,
   Along the heath and near his fav'rite tree;
Another came; nor yet beside the rill,
   Nor up the lawn, nor at the wood was he;

"The next with dirges due in sad array
   Slow thro' the church-way path we saw him borne.
Approach and read (for thou canst read) the lay,
   Grav'd on the stone beneath yon aged thorn."

The Epitaph

Here rests his head upon the lap of Earth
   A youth to Fortune and to Fame unknown.
Fair Science frown'd not on his humble birth,
   And Melancholy mark'd him for her own.

Large was his bounty, and his soul sincere,
   Heav'n did a recompense as largely send:
He gave to Mis'ry all he had, a tear,
   He gain'd from Heav'n ('twas all he wish'd) a friend.

No farther seek his merits to disclose,

Or draw his frailties from their dread abode,
(There they alike in trembling hope repose)
The bosom of his Father and his God.

THE BARD:
A PINDARIC ODE

I.1

"Ruin seize thee, ruthless King!
Confusion on thy banners wait,
Tho' fann'd by Conquest's crimson wing
They mock the air with idle state.
Helm, nor hauberk's twisted mail,
Nor even thy virtues, tyrant, shall avail
To save thy secret soul from nightly fears,
From Cambria's curse, from Cambria's tears!"
Such were the sounds, that o'er the crested pride
Of the first Edward scatter'd wild dismay,
As down the steep of Snowdon's shaggy side
He wound with toilsome march his long array.
Stout Glo'ster stood aghast in speechless trance;
To arms! cried Mortimer, and couch'd his quiv'ring lance.

I.2

On a rock, whose haughty brow
Frowns o'er old Conway's foaming flood,
Rob'd in the sable garb of woe,
With haggard eyes the poet stood;
(Loose his beard, and hoary hair
Stream'd, like a meteor, to the troubled air)
And with a master's hand, and prophet's fire,
Struck the deep sorrows of his lyre;
"Hark, how each giant-oak, and desert cave,
Sighs to the torrent's awful voice beneath!
O'er thee, O King! their hundred arms they wave,

Revenge on thee in hoarser murmurs breathe;
Vocal no more, since Cambria's fatal day,
To high-born Hoel's harp, or soft Llewellyn's lay.

I.3

"Cold is Cadwallo's tongue,
That hush'd the stormy main;
Brave Urien sleeps upon his craggy bed:
Mountains, ye mourn in vain
Modred, whose magic song
Made huge Plinlimmon bow his cloud-topp'd head.
On dreary Arvon's shore they lie,
Smear'd with gore, and ghastly pale:
Far, far aloof th' affrighted ravens sail;
The famish'd eagle screams, and passes by.
Dear lost companions of my tuneful art,
Dear, as the light that visits these sad eyes,
Dear, as the ruddy drops that warm my heart,
Ye died amidst your dying country's cries—
No more I weep. They do not sleep.
On yonder cliffs, a griesly band,
I see them sit, they linger yet,
Avengers of their native land:
With me in dreadful harmony they join,
And weave with bloody hands the tissue of thy line:—

II.1

"'Weave the warp, and weave the woof,
The winding sheet of Edward's race.
Give ample room, and verge enough
The characters of hell to trace.
Mark the year, and mark the night,
When Severn shall re-echo with affright
The shrieks of death, thro' Berkley's roofs that ring,
Shrieks of an agonising King!
She-Wolf of France, with unrelenting fangs,

That tear'st the bowels of thy mangled mate,
From thee be born, who o'er thy country hangs
The scourge of Heav'n. What terrors round him wait!
Amazement in his van, with Flight combin'd,
And Sorrow's faded form, and Solitude behind.

II.2

"'Mighty victor, mighty lord,
Low on his funeral couch he lies!
No pitying heart, no eye, afford
A tear to grace his obsequies.
Is the Sable Warrior fled?
Thy son is gone. He rests among the dead.
The swarm, that in thy noon-tide beam were born?
Gone to salute the rising Morn.
Fair laughs the Morn, and soft the Zephyr blows,
While proudly riding o'er the azure realm
In gallant trim the gilded vessel goes;
Youth on the prow, and Pleasure at the helm;
Regardless of the sweeping Whirlwind's sway,
That, hush'd in grim repose, expects his evening prey.

II.3

"'Fill high the sparkling bowl,
The rich repast prepare;
Reft of a crown, he yet may share the feast.
Close by the regal chair
Fell Thirst and Famine scowl
A baleful smile upon their baffled guest.
Heard ye the din of battle bray,
Lance to lance, and horse to horse?
Long years of havoc urge their destin'd course
And thro' the kindred squadrons mow their way.
Ye towers of Julius, London's lasting shame,
With many a foul and midnight murther fed,
Revere his consort's faith, his father's fame,

And spare the meek usurper's holy head.
Above, below, the rose of snow,
Twined with her blushing foe, we spread:
The bristled Boar in infant-gore
Wallows beneath the thorny shade.
Now, brothers, bending o'er th' accursed loom
Stamp we our vengeance deep, and ratify his doom.

III.1

"'Edward, lo! to sudden fate
(Weave we the woof. The thread is spun)
Half of thy heart we consecrate.
(The web is wove. The work is done.)'
Stay, oh stay! nor thus forlorn
Leave me unbless'd, unpitied, here to mourn!
In yon bright track, that fires the western skies!
They melt, they vanish from my eyes.
But oh! what solemn scenes on Snowdon's height
Descending slow their glitt'ring skirts unroll?
Visions of glory, spare my aching sight,
Ye unborn Ages, crowd not on my soul!
No more our long-lost Arthur we bewail.
All-hail, ye genuine kings, Britannia's issue, hail!

III.2

"Girt with many a baron bold
Sublime their starry fronts they rear;
And gorgeous dames, and statesmen old
In bearded majesty appear.
In the midst a form divine!
Her eye proclaims her of the Briton-line;
Her lion-port, her awe-commanding face,
Attemper'd sweet to virgin-grace.
What strings symphonious tremble in the air,
What strings of vocal transport round her play!
Hear from the grave, great Taliessin, hear;

They breathe a soul to animate thy clay.
Bright Rapture calls, and soaring, as she sings,
Waves in the eye of Heav'n her many-colour'd wings.

III.3

"The verse adorn again
Fierce War, and faithful Love,
And Truth severe, by fairy Fiction drest.
In buskin'd measures move
Pale Grief, and pleasing Pain,
With Horror, tyrant of the throbbing breast.
A voice, as of the cherub-choir,
Gales from blooming Eden bear;
And distant warblings lessen on my ear,
That lost in long futurity expire.
Fond impious man, think'st thou, yon sanguine cloud,
Rais'd by thy breath, has quench'd the orb of day?
To-morrow he repairs the golden flood,
And warms the nations with redoubled ray.
Enough for me: with joy I see
The different doom our Fates assign.
Be thine Despair, and scept'red Care,
To triumph, and to die, are mine."
He spoke, and headlong from the mountain's height
Deep in the roaring tide he plung'd to endless night.

William Blake

AUGURIES OF INNOCENCE

To SEE a World in a Grain of Sand
And a Heaven in a Wild Flower
Hold Infinity in the palm of your hand
And Eternity in an hour
A Robin Red breast in a Cage

Puts all Heaven in a Rage
A Dove house filld with Doves & Pigeons
Shudders Hell thr' all its regions
A dog starvd at his Masters Gate
Predicts the ruin of the State
A Horse misusd upon the Road
Calls to Heaven for Human blood
Each outcry of the hunted Hare
A fibre from the Brain does tear
A Skylark wounded in the wing
A Cherubim does cease to sing
The Game Cock clipd & armd for fight
Does the Rising Sun affright
Every Wolfs & Lions howl
Raises from Hell a Human Soul
The wild deer, wandring here & there
Keeps the Human Soul from Care
The Lamb misusd breeds Public Strife
And yet forgives the Butchers knife
The Bat that flits at close of Eve
Has left the Brain that wont Believe
The Owl that calls upon the Night
Speaks the Unbelievers fright
He who shall hurt the little Wren
Shall never be belovd by Men
He who the Ox to wrath has movd
Shall never be by Woman lovd
The wanton Boy that kills the Fly
Shall feel the Spiders enmity
He who torments the Chafers Sprite
Weaves a Bower in endless Night
The Catterpiller on the Leaf
Repeats to thee thy Mothers grief
Kill not the Moth nor Butterfly
For the Last Judgment draweth nigh
He who shall train the Horse to War
Shall never pass the Polar Bar

The Beggars Dog & Widows Cat
Feed them & thou wilt grow fat
The Gnat that sings his Summers Song
Poison gets from Slanders tongue
The poison of the Snake & Newt
Is the sweat of Envys Foot
The poison of the Honey Bee
Is the Artists Jealousy
The Princes Robes & Beggars Rags
Are Toadstools on the Misers Bags
A Truth thats told with bad intent
Beats all the Lies you can invent
It is right it should be so
Man was made for Joy & Woe
And when this we rightly know
Thro the World we safely go
Joy & Woe are woven fine
A Clothing for the soul divine
Under every grief & pine
Runs a joy with silken twine
The Babe is more than swadling Bands
Throughout all these Human Lands
Tools were made & Born were hands
Every Farmer Understands
Every Tear from Every Eye
Becomes a Babe in Eternity
This is caught by Females bright
And returnd to its own delight
The Bleat the Bark Bellow & Roar
Are Waves that Beat on Heavens Shore
The Babe that weeps the Rod beneath
Writes Revenge in realms of Death
The Beggars Rags fluttering in Air
Does to Rags the Heavens tear
The Soldier armd with Sword & Gun
Palsied strikes the Summers Sun
The poor Mans Farthing is worth more

Than all the Gold on Africs Shore
One Mite wrung from the Labrers hands
Shall buy & sell the Misers Lands
Or if protected from on high
Does that whole Nation sell & buy
He who mocks the Infants Faith
Shall be mockd in Age & Death
He who shall teach the Child to Doubt
The rotting Grave shall neer get out
He who respects the Infants faith
Triumphs over Hell & Death
The Childs Toys & the Old Mans Reasons
Are the Fruits of the Two seasons
The Questioner who sits so sly
Shall never know how to Reply
He who replies to words of Doubt
Doth put the Light of Knowledge out
The Strongest Poison ever known
Came from Caesars Laurel Crown
Nought can Deform the Human Race
Like to the Armours iron brace
When Gold & Gems adorn the Plow
To peaceful Arts shall Envy Bow
A Riddle or the Crickets Cry
Is to Doubt a fit Reply
The Emmets Inch & Eagles Mile
Make Lame Philosophy to smile
He who Doubts from what he sees
Will neer Believe do what you Please
If the Sun & Moon should Doubt
Theyd immediately Go out
To be in a Passion you Good may Do
But no Good if a Passion is in you
The Whore & Gambler by the State
Licencd build that Nations Fate
The Harlots cry from Street to Street
Shall weave Old Englands winding Sheet

The Winners Shout the Losers Curse
Dance before dead Englands Hearse
Every Night & every Morn
Some to Misery are Born
Every Morn and every Night
Some are Born to sweet delight
Some are Born to sweet delight
Some are Born to Endless Night
We are led to Believe a Lie
When we see not Thro the Eye
Which was Born in a Night to perish in a Night
When the Soul Slept in Beams of Light
God Appears & God is Light
To those poor Souls who dwell in Night
But does a Human Form Display
To those who Dwell in Realms of day

JERUSALEM

AND DID those feet in ancient time
Walk upon England's mountains green?
And was the holy Lamb of God
On England's pleasant pastures seen?

And did the Countenance Divine
Shine forth upon our clouded hills?
And was Jerusalem builded here
Among these dark Satanic mills?

Bring me my bow of burning gold:
Bring me my arrows of desire:
Bring me my spear: O clouds unfold!
Bring me my chariot of fire.

I will not cease from mental fight,
Nor shall my sword sleep in my hand
Till we have built Jerusalem

In England's green and pleasant land.

MOCK ON, MOCK ON, VOLTAIRE, ROUSSEAU

Mock on, Mock on, Voltaire, Rousseau;
Mock on, Mock on, 'tis all in vain.
You throw the sand against the wind,
And the wind blows it back again.

And every sand becomes a Gem
Reflected in the beams divine;
Blown back, they blind the mocking Eye,
But still in Israel's paths they shine.

The Atoms of Democritus
And Newton's Particles of light
Are sands upon the Red sea shore
Where Israel's tents do shine so bright.

THE CLOD AND THE PEBBLE

"Love seeketh not itself to please,
Nor for itself hath any care,
But for another gives its ease,
And builds a Heaven in Hell's despair."

So sung a little Clod of Clay
Trodden with the cattle's feet,
But a Pebble of the brook
Warbled out these metres meet:

"Love seeketh only self to please,
To bind another to its delight,
Joys in another's loss of ease,
And builds a Hell in Heaven's despite."

THE TYGER

Tyger Tyger, burning bright,
In the forests of the night;
What immortal hand or eye,
Could frame thy fearful symmetry?

In what distant deeps or skies.
Burnt the fire of thine eyes?
On what wings dare he aspire?
What the hand, dare seize the fire?

And what shoulder, & what art,
Could twist the sinews of thy heart?
And when thy heart began to beat.
What dread hand? & what dread feet?

What the hammer? what the chain,
In what furnace was thy brain?
What the anvil? what dread grasp.
Dare its deadly terrors clasp?

When the stars threw down their spears
And water'd heaven with their tears:
Did he smile his work to see?
Did he who made the Lamb make thee?

Tyger Tyger burning bright,
In the forests of the night:
What immortal hand or eye,
Dare frame thy fearful symmetry?

Robert Burns

COMIN THRO' THE RYE

First Setting

Comin thro' the rye, poor body,
    Comin thro' the rye,
She draigl't a' her petticoatie   *draggled*
    Comin thro' the rye.

Chorus

    Oh Jenny's a' weet poor body   *all wet*
        Jenny's seldom dry,
    She draigl't a' her petticoatie
        Comin thro' the rye.

Gin a body meet a body   *Should*
    Comin thro' the rye,
Gin a body kiss a body —
    Need a body cry.
        Oh Jenny's a' weet, &c.

Gin a body meet a body
    Comin thro' the glen;
Gin a body kiss a body —
    Need the warld ken!   *world know*
        Oh Jenny's a' weet, &c.

Second Setting

Gin a body meet a body, comin thro' the rye,
Gin a body kiss a body, need a body cry;
Ilka body has a body, ne'er a ane hae I;   *Every : one*
But a' the lads they loe me, and what the waur   *love : worse off*
  am I.

Gin a body meet a body, comin frae the well,   *from*
Gin a body kiss a body, need a body tell;

Ilka body has a body, ne'er a ane hae I,
But a the lads they loe me, and what the waur
   am I.

Gin a body meet a body, comin frae the town,
Gin a body kiss a body, need a body gloom;   *be sullen*
Ilka Jenny has her Jockey, ne'er a ane hae I,
But a' the lads they loe me, and what the waur
   am I.

TAM O' SHANTER

WHEN CHAPMAN billies leave the street,	*fellows*
And drouthy neebors neebors meet,	*thirsty*
As market-days are wearing late,	
And folk begin to tak the gate;	*road*
While we sit bousin, at the nappy,	*boozing : ale*
And gettin fou and unco happy,	*full : uncommon*
We think na on the lang Scots miles,	
The mosses, waters, slaps, and stiles,	*hedgerows*
That lie between us and our hame,	
Whare sits our sulky, sullen dame,	
Gathering her brows like gathering storm,	
Nursing her wrath to keep it warm.	
This truth fand honest Tam o' Shanter,	*tested*
As he frae Ayr ae night did canter:	*from*
(Auld Ayr, wham ne'er a town surpasses,	
For honest men and bonie lasses.)	
O Tam! had'st thou but been sae wise	
As taen thy ain wife Kate's advice!	*taken : own*
She tauld thee weel thou was a skellum,	*ne'er-do-well*
A bletherin, blusterin, drunken blellum;	*babbler*
That frae November till October,	
Ae market-day thou was na sober;	
That ilka melder wi' the miller,	*every wheat load*
Thou sat as lang as thou had siller;	*silver*

That ev'ry naig was ca'd a shoe on,   *horse : driven*
The smith and thee gat roarin fou on;   *full*
That at the Lord's house, ev'n on Sunday,
Thou drank wi' Kirkton Jean till Monday.
She prophesied, that, late or soon,
Thou would be found deep drown'd in Doon;
Ot catch'd wi' warlocks in the mirk,   *dark*
By Alloway's auld haunted kirk.   *church*

  Ah, gentle dames! it gars me greet,   *makes me weep*
To think how mony counsels sweet,
How mony lengthen'd sage advices,
The husband frae the wife despises!

  But to our tale:—Ae market night,   *One*
Tam had got planted unco right,   *uncommonly*
Fast by an ingle, bleezing finely,   *hearth : blazing*
Wi' reaming swats that drank divinely;   *foaming ale*
And at his elbow, Souter Johnie,   *Cobbler*
His ancient, trusty, drouthy crony: *thirsty*
Tam lo'ed him like a vera brither;   *very*
They had been fou for weeks thegither.   *full : together*
The night drave on wi' sangs and clatter;
And ay the ale was growing better:
The landlady and Tam grew gracious
Wi' secret favours, sweet, and precious:
The souter tauld his queerest stories;   *cobbler*
The landlord's laugh was ready chorus:
The storm without might rair and rustle,   *roar*
Tam did na mind the storm a whistle.

  Care, mad to see a man sae happy,
E'en drown'd himsel amang the nappy: *ale*
As bees flee hame wi' lades o' treasure,
The minutes wing'd their way wi' pleasure;
Kings may be blest, but Tam was glorious,
O'er a' the ills o' life victorious!

  But pleasures are like poppies spread,

You seize the flow'r, its bloom is shed;
Or like the snow falls in the river,
A moment white—then melts forever;
Or like the borealis race,
That flit ere you can point their place;
Or like the rainbow's lovely form
Evanishing amid the storm.
Nae man can tether time or tide:
The hour approaches Tam maun ride,— *must*
That hour, o' night's black arch the key-stane
That dreary hour he mounts his beast in;
And sic a night he taks the road in,
As ne'er poor sinner was abroad in.

The wind blew as 'twad blawn its last; *it would*
The rattling show'rs rose on the blast;
The speedy gleams the darkness swallow'd;
Loud, deep, and lang the thunder bellow'd:
That night, a child might understand,
The Deil had business on his hand.

Weel mounted on his grey mare, Meg,—
A better never lifted leg,—
Tam skelpit on thro' dub and mire, *darted : puddle*
Despising wind and rain and fire;
Whiles holding fast his guid blue bonnet,
Whiles crooning o'er some auld Scots sonnet,
Whiles glowrin round wi' prudent cares, *staring*
Lest bogles catch him unawares. *spirits*
Kirk-Alloway was drawing nigh,
Whare ghaists and houlets nightly cry. *owls*

By this time he was cross the ford,
Whare in the snaw the chapman smoor'd; *smothered*
And past the birks and meikle stane, *birches : big*
Whare drucken Charlie brak's neckbane: *drunken*
And thro' the whins, and by the cairn, *furze*
Whare hunters fand the murder'd bairn; *child*

And near the thorn, aboon the well,   *above*
Whare Mungo's mither hang'd hersel.
Before him Doon pours all his floods;
The doubling storm roars thro' the woods;
The lightnings flash from pole to pole,
Near and more near the thunders roll;
When, glimmering thro' the groaning trees,
Kirk-Alloway seem'd in a bleeze: *blaze*
Thro' ilka bore the beams were glancing,   *every hole*
And loud resounded mirth and dancing.

   Inspiring bold John Barleycorn!
What dangers thou can'st make us scorn!
Wi' tippenny we fear nae evil;   *weak ale*
Wi' usquebae we'll face the devil!   *whiskey*
The swats sae ream'd in Tammie's noddle,   *weak beer : head*
Fair play, he car'd na deils a boddle.   *farthing*
But Maggie stood right sair astonish'd,   *sore*
Till, by the heel and hand admonish'd,
She ventur'd forward on the light;
And, wow! Tam saw an unco sight!   *uncommon*

   Warlocks and witches in a dance;
Nae cotillion brent-new frae France,   *brand-new*
But hornpipes, jigs, strathspeys, and reels
Put life and mettle in their heels.
A winnock bunker in the east,   *window-seat*
There sat Auld Nick in shape o' beast:
A towzie tyke, black, grim, and large,   *shaggy dog*
To gie them music was his charge;
He screw'd the pipes and gart them skirl,   *made the scream*
Till roof and rafters a' did dirl.—   *resound*
Coffins stood round like open presses,
That shaw'd the dead in their last dresses;
And by some devilish cantraip sleight   *magic*
Each in its cauld hand held a light,
By which heroic Tam was able
To note upon the haly table

A murderer's banes in gibbet airns; *irons*
Twa span-lang, wee, unchristen'd bairns; *children*
A thief, new-cutted frae the rape— *from*
Wi' his last gasp his gab did gape; *mouth*
Five tomahawks, wi' blude red-rusted;
Five scimitars, wi' murder crusted;
A garter, which a babe had strangled;
A knife, a father's throat had mangled,
Whom his ain son o' life bereft—
The grey hairs yet stack to the heft;
Wi' mair o' horrible and awfu',
Which ev'n to name wad be unlawfu'.

As Tammie glowr'd, amaz'd and curious,
The mirth and fun grew fast and furious:
The piper loud and louder blew,
The dancers quick and quicker flew;
They reel'd, they set, they cross'd, they cleekit *joined arms*
Till ilka carlin swat and reekit *every woman*
And coost her duddies to the wark *clothes*
And linket at it in her sark! *tripped : shirt*

Now Tam, O Tam! had thae been queans, *wenches*
A' plump and strapping in their teens!
Their sarks, instead o' creeshie flannen, *greasy*
Been snaw-white seventeen hunder linen!— *fine linen*
Thir breeks o' mine, my only pair, *breeches*
That ance were plush, o' gude blue hair,
I wad hae gien them aff y hurdies, *half my buttocks*
For ae blink o' the bonie burdies! *one : girls*

But wither'd beldams, auld and droll,
Rigwoodie hags wad spean a foal, *wean*
Lowping and flinging on a crummock. *leaping : staff*
I wonder didna turn thy stomach.

But Tam ken'd what was what fu' brawlie; *knew : enough*
There was ae winsom wench and walie, *choice*
That night enlisted in the core

(Lang after ken'd on Carrick shore.
For mony a beast to dead she shot,
And perish'd mony a bonie boat,
And shook baith meikle corn and bear,   *much : barley*
And kept the country-side in fear);
Her cutty sark o' Paisley harn,   *short skirt : cloth*
That while a lassie she had worn,
In longitude tho' sorely scanty,
It was her best, and she was vauntie.   *proud*
Ah! little ken'd thy reverend grannie,
That sark she coft for her wee Nannie,   *bought*
Wi' twa pund Scots ('twas a' her riches),
Wad ever grac'd a dance of witches!

  But here my Muse her wing maun cow'r,   *must*
Sic flights are far beyond her pow'r;
To sing how Nannie lap and flang,   *leapt and flung*
(A souple jad she was and strang),   *supple youth*
And how Tam stood like ane bewitch'd,   *one*
And thought his very een enrich'd;
Even Satan glowr'd and fidg'd fu' fain,   *fidgeted eagerly*
And hotch'd and blew wi' might and main: *jerked*
Till first ae caper, syne anither,   *then*
Tam tint his reason a' thegither,   *lost : altogether*
And roars out, "Weel done, Cutty-sark!"   *short skirt*
And in an instant all was dark:
And scarcely had he Maggie rallied,
When out the hellish legion sallied.

  As bees bizz out wi' angry fyke,   *wrath*
When plundering herds assail their byke;   *hive*
As open pussie's mortal foes,   *wild hare's*
When, pop! she starts before their nose;
As eager runs the market-crowd,
When "Catch the thief!" resounds aloud;
So Maggie runs, the witches follow,
Wi' mony an eldritch skriech and hollo.   *unearthly*

Ah, Tam! ah, Tam! thou'll get thy fairin!	*get what's coming*
In hell they'll roast thee like a herrin!	
In vain thy Kate awaits thy comin!	
Kate soon will be a woefu' woman!	
Now, do thy speedy utmost, Meg,	
And win the key-stane of the brig:	*bridge*
There at them thou thy tail may toss,	
A running stream they dare na cross.	
But ere the key-stane she could make,	
The fient a tail she had to shake!	
For Nannie far before the rest,	
Hard upon noble Maggie prest,	
And flew at Tam wi' furious ettle;	*aim*
But little wist she Maggie's mettle—	
Ae spring brought aff her master hale	*One*
But left behind her ain grey tail:	*own*
The carlin claught her by the rump,	*witch*
And left poor Maggie scarce a stump.	
Now, wha this tale o' truth shall read,	
Ilk man and mother's son, take heed,	*Each*
Whene'er to drink you are inclin'd,	
Or cutty-sarks run in your mind,	
Think, ye may buy the joys o'er dear,	
Remember Tam o' Shanter's mear.	*mare*

TO A MOUSE

On Turning her up in her Nest, with the Plough, November 1785.

Wee, sleekit, cowran, tim'rous beastie,	*sleek*
O, what a panic's in thy breastie!	
Thou need na start awa sae hasty,	
Wi' bickerin brattle!	*scamper*
I wad be laith to rin an' chase thee	*loath*
Wi' murd'ring pattle!	*spade*

I'm truly sorry Man's dominion
Has broken Nature's social union,
An' justifies that ill opinion,
   Which makes thee startle,
At me, thy poor, earth-born companion,
   An' fellow-mortal!

I doubt na, whyles, but thou may thieve;   *sometimes*
What then? poor beastie, thou maun live!   *must*
A daimen-icker in a thrave   *odd ear of corn*
   'S a sma' request:
I'll get a blessin wi' the lave,   *the rest*
   An' never miss 't!

Thy wee-bit housie, too, in ruin!
It's silly wa's the win's are strewin!   *feeble walls*
An' naething, now, to big a new ane,   *one*
   O' foggage green!   *coarse grass*
An' bleak December's winds ensuin,
   Baith snell an' keen!   *Both bitter*

Thou saw the fields laid bare an' waste,
An' weary Winter comin fast,
An' cozie here, beneath the blast,
   Thou thought to dwell,
Till crash! the cruel coulter past   *plow*
   Out thro' thy cell.

That wee-bit heap o' leaves an' stibble
Has cost thee monie a weary nibble!
Now thou's turn'd out, for a' thy trouble,
   But house or hald,   *holding*
To thole the Winter's sleety dribble,   *endure*
   An' cranreuch cauld!   *hoar-frost*

But Mousie, thou art no thy-lane,   *not alone*
In proving foresight may be vain:
The best laid schemes o' Mice an' Men
   Gang aft agley,   *often awry*

An' lea'e us nought but grief an' pain,
    For promis'd joy!

Still, thou art blest, compar'd wi' me!
The present only toucheth thee:
But Och! I backward cast my e'e,   *eye*
    On prospects drear!
An' forward tho' I canna see,
    I guess an' fear!

William Wordsworth

SHE WAS A PHANTOM OF DELIGHT

SHE WAS a Phantom of delight
When first she gleamed upon my sight;
A lovely Apparition, sent
To be a moment's ornament;
Her eyes as stars of Twilight fair;
Like Twilight's, too, her dusky hair;
But all things else about her drawn
From May-time and the cheerful Dawn;
A dancing Shape, an Image gay,
To haunt, to startle, and way-lay.
I saw her upon nearer view,
A Spirit, yet a Woman too!
Her household motions light and free,
And steps of virgin-liberty;
A countenance in which did meet
Sweet records, promises as sweet;
A Creature not too bright or good
For human nature's daily food;
For transient sorrows, simple wiles,
Praise, blame, love, kisses, tears, and smiles.
And now I see with eye serene

The very pulse of the machine;
A Being breathing thoughtful breath,
A Traveller between life and death;
The reason firm, the temperate will,
Endurance, foresight, strength, and skill;
A perfect Woman, nobly planned,
To warn, to comfort, and command;
And yet a Spirit still, and bright
With something of angelic light.

THE SOLITARY REAPER

BEHOLD HER, single in the field,
Yon solitary Highland Lass!
Reaping and singing by herself;
Stop here, or gently pass!
Alone she cuts and binds the grain,
And sings a melancholy strain;
O listen! for the Vale profound
Is overflowing with the sound.

No Nightingale did ever chaunt
More welcome notes to weary bands
Of travellers in some shady haunt,
Among Arabian sands:
A voice so thrilling ne'er was heard
In spring-time from the Cuckoo-bird,
Breaking the silence of the seas
Among the farthest Hebrides.

Will no one tell me what she sings?—
Perhaps the plaintive numbers flow
For old, unhappy, far-off things,
And battles long ago:
Or is it some more humble lay,
Familiar matter of to-day?
Some natural sorrow, loss, or pain,

That has been, and may be again?

Whate'er the theme, the Maiden sang
As if her song could have no ending;
I saw her singing at her work,
And o'er the sickle bending;—
I listened, motionless and still;
And, as I mounted up the hill,
The music in my heart I bore,
Long after it was heard no more.

THE WORLD IS TOO MUCH WITH US

THE WORLD is too much with us; late and soon,
Getting and spending, we lay waste our powers;—
Little we see in Nature that is ours;
We have given our hearts away, a sordid boon!
This Sea that bares her bosom to the moon;
The winds that will be howling at all hours,
And are up-gathered now like sleeping flowers;
For this, for everything, we are out of tune;
It moves us not. Great God! I'd rather be
A Pagan suckled in a creed outworn;
So might I, standing on this pleasant lea,
Have glimpses that would make me less forlorn;
Have sight of Proteus rising from the sea;
Or hear old Triton blow his wreathèd horn.

LINES COMPOSED
A FEW MILES ABOVE
TINTERN ABBEY

On Revisiting the Banks of the Wye during a Tour, July 13, 1798.

FIVE YEARS have past; five summers, with the length
Of five long winters! and again I hear
These waters, rolling from their mountain-springs
With a soft inland murmur. —Once again
Do I behold these steep and lofty cliffs,
That on a wild secluded scene impress
Thoughts of more deep seclusion; and connect
The landscape with the quiet of the sky.
The day is come when I again repose
Here, under this dark sycamore, and view
These plots of cottage-ground, these orchard-tufts,
Which at this season, with their unripe fruits,
Are clad in one green hue, and lose themselves
'Mid groves and copses. Once again I see
These hedge-rows, hardly hedge-rows, little lines
Of sportive wood run wild: these pastoral farms,
Green to the very door; and wreaths of smoke
Sent up, in silence, from among the trees!
With some uncertain notice, as might seem
Of vagrant dwellers in the houseless woods,
Or of some Hermit's cave, where by his fire
The Hermit sits alone.

   These beauteous forms,
Through a long absence, have not been to me
As is a landscape to a blind man's eye:
But oft, in lonely rooms, and 'mid the din
Of towns and cities, I have owed to them,
In hours of weariness, sensations sweet,
Felt in the blood, and felt along the heart;
And passing even into my purer mind

With tranquil restoration:—feelings too
Of unremembered pleasure: such, perhaps,
As have no slight or trivial influence
On that best portion of a good man's life,
His little, nameless, unremembered, acts
Of kindness and of love. Nor less, I trust,
To them I may have owed another gift,
Of aspect more sublime; that blessed mood,
In which the burthen of the mystery,
In which the heavy and the weary weight
Of all this unintelligible world,
Is lightened:—that serene and blessed mood,
In which the affections gently lead us on,—
Until, the breath of this corporeal frame
And even the motion of our human blood
Almost suspended, we are laid asleep
In body, and become a living soul:
While with an eye made quiet by the power
Of harmony, and the deep power of joy,
We see into the life of things.

              If this
Be but a vain belief, yet, oh! how oft—
In darkness and amid the many shapes
Of joyless daylight; when the fretful stir
Unprofitable, and the fever of the world,
Have hung upon the beatings of my heart—
How oft, in spirit, have I turned to thee,
O sylvan Wye! thou wanderer thro' the woods,
   How often has my spirit turned to thee!

   And now, with gleams of half-extinguished thought,
With many recognitions dim and faint,
And somewhat of a sad perplexity,
The picture of the mind revives again:
While here I stand, not only with the sense
Of present pleasure, but with pleasing thoughts
That in this moment there is life and food

For future years. And so I dare to hope,
Though changed, no doubt, from what I was when first
I came among these hills; when like a roe
I bounded o'er the mountains, by the sides
Of the deep rivers, and the lonely streams,
Wherever nature led: more like a man
Flying from something that he dreads, than one
Who sought the thing he loved. For nature then
(The coarser pleasures of my boyish days
And their glad animal movements all gone by)
To me was all in all.—I cannot paint
What then I was. The sounding cataract
Haunted me like a passion: the tall rock,
The mountain, and the deep and gloomy wood,
Their colours and their forms, were then to me
An appetite; a feeling and a love,
That had no need of a remoter charm,
By thought supplied, nor any interest
Unborrowed from the eye.—That time is past,
And all its aching joys are now no more,
And all its dizzy raptures. Not for this
Faint I, nor mourn nor murmur; other gifts
Have followed; for such loss, I would believe,
Abundant recompense. For I have learned
To look on nature, not as in the hour
Of thoughtless youth; but hearing oftentimes
The still sad music of humanity,
Nor harsh nor grating, though of ample power
To chasten and subdue.—And I have felt
A presence that disturbs me with the joy
Of elevated thoughts; a sense sublime
Of something far more deeply interfused,
Whose dwelling is the light of setting suns,
And the round ocean and the living air,
And the blue sky, and in the mind of man:
A motion and a spirit, that impels
All thinking things, all objects of all thought,

And rolls through all things. Therefore am I still
A lover of the meadows and the woods
And mountains; and of all that we behold
From this green earth; of all the mighty world
Of eye, and ear,—both what they half create,
And what perceive; well pleased to recognise
In nature and the language of the sense
The anchor of my purest thoughts, the nurse,
The guide, the guardian of my heart, and soul
Of all my moral being.

              Nor perchance,
If I were not thus taught, should I the more
Suffer my genial spirits to decay:
For thou art with me here upon the banks
Of this fair river; thou my dearest Friend,
My dear, dear Friend; and in thy voice I catch
The language of my former heart, and read
My former pleasures in the shooting lights
Of thy wild eyes. Oh! yet a little while
May I behold in thee what I was once,
My dear, dear Sister! and this prayer I make,
Knowing that Nature never did betray
The heart that loved her; 'tis her privilege,
Through all the years of this our life, to lead
From joy to joy: for she can so inform
The mind that is within us, so impress
With quietness and beauty, and so feed
With lofty thoughts, that neither evil tongues,
Rash judgments, nor the sneers of selfish men,
Nor greetings where no kindness is, nor all
The dreary intercourse of daily life,
Shall e'er prevail against us, or disturb
Our cheerful faith, that all which we behold
Is full of blessings. Therefore let the moon
Shine on thee in thy solitary walk;
And let the misty mountain-winds be free

To blow against thee: and, in after years,
When these wild ecstasies shall be matured
Into a sober pleasure; when thy mind
Shall be a mansion for all lovely forms,
Thy memory be as a dwelling-place
For all sweet sounds and harmonies; oh! then,
If solitude, or fear, or pain, or grief,
Should be thy portion, with what healing thoughts
Of tender joy wilt thou remember me,
And these my exhortations! Nor, perchance—
If I should be where I no more can hear
Thy voice, nor catch from thy wild eyes these gleams
Of past existence—wilt thou then forget
That on the banks of this delightful stream
We stood together; and that I, so long
A worshipper of Nature, hither came
Unwearied in that service: rather say
With warmer love—oh! with far deeper zeal
Of holier love. Nor wilt thou then forget,
That after many wanderings, many years
Of absence, these steep woods and lofty cliffs,
And this green pastoral landscape, were to me
More dear, both for themselves and for thy sake!

Samuel Taylor Coleridge

DEJECTION: AN ODE

Late, late yestreen I saw the new Moon,
With the old Moon in her arms;
And I fear, I fear, my Master dear!
We shall have a deadly storm.
  (Ballad of Sir Patrick Spence)

I

WELL! If the Bard was weather-wise, who made
　The grand old ballad of Sir Patrick Spence,
　This night, so tranquil now, will not go hence
Unroused by winds, that ply a busier trade
Than those which mould yon cloud in lazy flakes,
Or the dull sobbing draft, that moans and rakes
Upon the strings of this Æolian lute,
　　Which better far were mute.
　For lo! the New-moon winter-bright!
　And overspread with phantom light,
　　(With swimming phantom light o'erspread
　But rimmed and circled by a silver thread)
I see the old Moon in her lap, foretelling
　The coming-on of rain and squally blast.
And oh! that even now the gust were swelling,
　And the slant night-shower driving loud and fast!
Those sounds which oft have raised me, whilst they awed,
　　And sent my soul abroad,
Might now perhaps their wonted impulse give,
Might startle this dull pain, and make it move and live!

II

A grief without a pang, void, dark, and drear,
　A stifled, drowsy, unimpassioned grief,
　Which finds no natural outlet, no relief,

        In word, or sigh, or tear—
O Lady! in this wan and heartless mood,
To other thoughts by yonder throstle woo'd,
   All this long eve, so balmy and serene,
Have I been gazing on the western sky,
   And its peculiar tint of yellow green:
And still I gaze—and with how blank an eye!
And those thin clouds above, in flakes and bars,
That give away their motion to the stars;
Those stars, that glide behind them or between,
Now sparkling, now bedimmed, but always seen:
Yon crescent Moon, as fixed as if it grew
In its own cloudless, starless lake of blue;
I see them all so excellently fair,
I see, not feel, how beautiful they are!

III

     My genial spirits fail;
        And what can these avail
To lift the smothering weight from off my breast?
       It were a vain endeavour,
         Though I should gaze for ever
On that green light that lingers in the west:
I may not hope from outward forms to win
The passion and the life, whose fountains are within.

IV

O Lady! we receive but what we give,
And in our life alone does Nature live:
Ours is her wedding garment, ours her shroud!
   And would we aught behold, of higher worth,
Than that inanimate cold world allowed
To the poor loveless ever-anxious crowd,
   Ah! from the soul itself must issue forth
A light, a glory, a fair luminous cloud
        Enveloping the Earth—

And from the soul itself must there be sent
   A sweet and potent voice, of its own birth,
Of all sweet sounds the life and element!

V

O pure of heart! thou need'st not ask of me
What this strong music in the soul may be!
What, and wherein it doth exist,
This light, this glory, this fair luminous mist,
This beautiful and beauty-making power.
   Joy, virtuous Lady! Joy that ne'er was given,
Save to the pure, and in their purest hour,
Life, and Life's effluence, cloud at once and shower,
Joy, Lady! is the spirit and the power,
Which wedding Nature to us gives in dower
   A new Earth and new Heaven,
Undreamt of by the sensual and the proud—
Joy is the sweet voice, Joy the luminous cloud—
     We in ourselves rejoice!
And thence flows all that charms or ear or sight,
   All melodies the echoes of that voice,
All colours a suffusion from that light.

VI

There was a time when, though my path was rough,
   This joy within me dallied with distress,
And all misfortunes were but as the stuff
   Whence Fancy made me dreams of happiness:
For hope grew round me, like the twining vine,
And fruits, and foliage, not my own, seemed mine.
But now afflictions bow me down to earth:
Nor care I that they rob me of my mirth;
     But oh! each visitation
Suspends what nature gave me at my birth,
   My shaping spirit of Imagination.
For not to think of what I needs must feel,

But to be still and patient, all I can;
And haply by abstruse research to steal
    From my own nature all the natural man—
    This was my sole resource, my only plan:
Till that which suits a part infects the whole,
And now is almost grown the habit of my soul.

VII

Hence, viper thoughts, that coil around my mind,
        Reality's dark dream!
I turn from you, and listen to the wind,
    Which long has raved unnoticed. What a scream
Of agony by torture lengthened out
That lute sent forth! Thou Wind, that rav'st without,
    Bare crag, or mountain-tairn, or blasted tree,
Or pine-grove whither woodman never clomb,
Or lonely house, long held the witches' home,
    Methinks were fitter instruments for thee,
Mad Lutanist! who in this month of showers,
Of dark-brown gardens, and of peeping flowers,
Mak'st Devils' yule, with worse than wintry song,
The blossoms, buds, and timorous leaves among.
    Thou Actor, perfect in all tragic sounds!
Thou mighty Poet, e'en to frenzy bold!
        What tell'st thou now about?
        'Tis of the rushing of an host in rout,
    With groans, of trampled men, with smarting wounds—
At once they groan with pain, and shudder with the cold!
But hush! there is a pause of deepest silence!
    And all that noise, as of a rushing crowd,
With groans, and tremulous shudderings—all is over—
    It tells another tale, with sounds less deep and loud!
        A tale of less affright,
        And tempered with delight,
As Otway's self had framed the tender lay,—
        'Tis of a little child

    Upon a lonesome wild,
Nor far from home, but she hath lost her way:
And now moans low in bitter grief and fear,
And now screams loud, and hopes to make her mother hear.

VIII

'Tis midnight, but small thoughts have I of sleep:
Full seldom may my friend such vigils keep!
Visit her, gentle Sleep! with wings of healing,
   And may this storm be but a mountain-birth,
May all the stars hang bright above her dwelling,
   Silent as though they watched the sleeping Earth!
      With light heart may she rise,
      Gay fancy, cheerful eyes,
   Joy lift her spirit, joy attune her voice;
To her may all things live, from pole to pole,
Their life the eddying of her living soul!
   O simple spirit, guided from above,
Dear Lady! friend devoutest of my choice,
Thus mayest thou ever, evermore rejoice.

KUBLA KHAN

Or, a vision in a dream. A Fragment.

In Xanadu did Kubla Khan
A stately pleasure-dome decree:
Where Alph, the sacred river, ran
Through caverns measureless to man
   Down to a sunless sea.
So twice five miles of fertile ground
With walls and towers were girdled round;
And there were gardens bright with sinuous rills,
Where blossomed many an incense-bearing tree;
And here were forests ancient as the hills,

Enfolding sunny spots of greenery.

But oh! that deep romantic chasm which slanted
Down the green hill athwart a cedarn cover!
A savage place! as holy and enchanted
As e'er beneath a waning moon was haunted
By woman wailing for her demon-lover!
And from this chasm, with ceaseless turmoil seething,
As if this earth in fast thick pants were breathing,
A mighty fountain momently was forced:
Amid whose swift half-intermitted burst
Huge fragments vaulted like rebounding hail,
Or chaffy grain beneath the thresher's flail:
And mid these dancing rocks at once and ever
It flung up momently the sacred river.
Five miles meandering with a mazy motion
Through wood and dale the sacred river ran,
Then reached the caverns measureless to man,
And sank in tumult to a lifeless ocean;
And 'mid this tumult Kubla heard from far
Ancestral voices prophesying war!

    The shadow of the dome of pleasure
    Floated midway on the waves;
    Where was heard the mingled measure
    From the fountain and the caves.
It was a miracle of rare device,
A sunny pleasure-dome with caves of ice!

    A damsel with a dulcimer
    In a vision once I saw:
    It was an Abyssinian maid
    And on her dulcimer she played,
    Singing of Mount Abora.
    Could I revive within me
    Her symphony and song,
    To such a deep delight 'twould win me,
That with music loud and long,
I would build that dome in air,

That sunny dome! those caves of ice!
And all who heard should see them there,
And all should cry, Beware! Beware!
His flashing eyes, his floating hair!
Weave a circle round him thrice,
And close your eyes with holy dread
For he on honey-dew hath fed,
And drunk the milk of Paradise.

THE RIME OF
THE ANCIENT MARINER

Argument

How a Ship having passed the Line was driven by storms to the cold Country towards the South Pole; and how from thence she made her course to the tropical Latitude of the Great Pacific Ocean; and of the strange things that befell; and in what manner the Ancyent Marinere came back to his own Country.

I

IT IS an ancient Mariner,
And he stoppeth one of three.
'By thy long grey beard and glittering eye,
Now wherefore stopp'st thou me?

The Bridegroom's doors are opened wide,
And I am next of kin;
The guests are met, the feast is set:
May'st hear the merry din.'

He holds him with his skinny hand,
'There was a ship,' quoth he.
'Hold off! unhand me, grey-beard loon!'
Eftsoons his hand dropt he.

He holds him with his glittering eye—
The Wedding-Guest stood still,

And listens like a three years' child:
The Mariner hath his will.

The Wedding-Guest sat on a stone:
He cannot choose but hear;
And thus spake on that ancient man,
The bright-eyed Mariner.

'The ship was cheered, the harbour cleared,
Merrily did we drop
Below the kirk, below the hill,
Below the lighthouse top.

The Sun came up upon the left,
Out of the sea came he!
And he shone bright, and on the right
Went down into the sea.

Higher and higher every day,
Till over the mast at noon—'
The Wedding-Guest here beat his breast,
For he heard the loud bassoon.

The bride hath paced into the hall,
Red as a rose is she;
Nodding their heads before her goes
The merry minstrelsy.

The Wedding-Guest he beat his breast,
Yet he cannot choose but hear;
And thus spake on that ancient man,
The bright-eyed Mariner.

And now the STORM-BLAST came, and he
Was tyrannous and strong:
He struck with his o'ertaking wings,
And chased us south along.

With sloping masts and dipping prow,
As who pursued with yell and blow
Still treads the shadow of his foe,

And forward bends his head,
The ship drove fast, loud roared the blast,
And southward aye we fled.

And now there came both mist and snow,
And it grew wondrous cold:
And ice, mast-high, came floating by,
As green as emerald.

And through the drifts the snowy clifts
Did send a dismal sheen:
Nor shapes of men nor beasts we ken—
The ice was all between.

The ice was here, the ice was there,
The ice was all around:
It cracked and growled, and roared and howled,
Like noises in a swound!

At length did cross an Albatross,
Thorough the fog it came;
As if it had been a Christian soul,
We hailed it in God's name.

It ate the food it ne'er had eat,
And round and round it flew.
The ice did split with a thunder-fit;
The helmsman steered us through!

And a good south wind sprung up behind;
The Albatross did follow,
And every day, for food or play,
Came to the mariner's hollo!

In mist or cloud, on mast or shroud,
It perched for vespers nine;
Whiles all the night, through fog-smoke white,
Glimmered the white Moon-shine.'

'God save thee, ancient Mariner!
From the fiends, that plague thee thus!—

Why look'st thou so?'—With my cross-bow
I shot the ALBATROSS.

II

The Sun now rose upon the right:
Out of the sea came he,
Still hid in mist, and on the left
Went down into the sea.

And the good south wind still blew behind,
But no sweet bird did follow,
Nor any day for food or play
Came to the mariner's hollo!

And I had done a hellish thing,
And it would work 'em woe:
For all averred, I had killed the bird
That made the breeze to blow.
Ah wretch! said they, the bird to slay,
That made the breeze to blow!

Nor dim nor red, like God's own head,
The glorious Sun uprist:
Then all averred, I had killed the bird
That brought the fog and mist.
'Twas right, said they, such birds to slay,
That bring the fog and mist.

The fair breeze blew, the white foam flew,
The furrow followed free;
We were the first that ever burst
Into that silent sea.

Down dropt the breeze, the sails dropt down,
'Twas sad as sad could be;
And we did speak only to break
The silence of the sea!

All in a hot and copper sky,
The bloody Sun, at noon,

Right up above the mast did stand,
No bigger than the Moon.

Day after day, day after day,
We stuck, nor breath nor motion;
As idle as a painted ship
Upon a painted ocean.

Water, water, every where,
And all the boards did shrink;
Water, water, every where,
Nor any drop to drink.

The very deep did rot: O Christ!
That ever this should be!
Yea, slimy things did crawl with legs
Upon the slimy sea.

About, about, in reel and rout
The death-fires danced at night;
The water, like a witch's oils,
Burnt green, and blue and white.

And some in dreams assurèd were
Of the Spirit that plagued us so;
Nine fathom deep he had followed us
From the land of mist and snow.

And every tongue, through utter drought,
Was withered at the root;
We could not speak, no more than if
We had been choked with soot.

Ah! well a-day! what evil looks
Had I from old and young!
Instead of the cross, the Albatross
About my neck was hung.

III

There passed a weary time. Each throat

Was parched, and glazed each eye.
A weary time! a weary time!
How glazed each weary eye,

When looking westward, I beheld
A something in the sky.

At first it seemed a little speck,
And then it seemed a mist;
It moved and moved, and took at last
A certain shape, I wist.

A speck, a mist, a shape, I wist!
And still it neared and neared:
As if it dodged a water-sprite,
It plunged and tacked and veered.

With throats unslaked, with black lips baked,
We could nor laugh nor wail;
Through utter drought all dumb we stood!
I bit my arm, I sucked the blood,
And cried, A sail! a sail!

With throats unslaked, with black lips baked,
Agape they heard me call:
Gramercy! they for joy did grin,
And all at once their breath drew in.
As they were drinking all.

See! see! (I cried) she tacks no more!
Hither to work us weal;
Without a breeze, without a tide,
She steadies with upright keel!

The western wave was all a-flame.
The day was well nigh done!
Almost upon the western wave
Rested the broad bright Sun;
When that strange shape drove suddenly
Betwixt us and the Sun.

And straight the Sun was flecked with bars,
(Heaven's Mother send us grace!)
As if through a dungeon-grate he peered
With broad and burning face.

Alas! (thought I, and my heart beat loud)
How fast she nears and nears!
Are those her sails that glance in the Sun,
Like restless gossameres?

Are those her ribs through which the Sun
Did peer, as through a grate?
And is that Woman all her crew?
Is that a DEATH? and are there two?
Is DEATH that woman's mate?

Her lips were red, her looks were free,
Her locks were yellow as gold:
Her skin was as white as leprosy,
The Night-mare LIFE-IN-DEATH was she,
Who thicks man's blood with cold.

The naked hulk alongside came,
And the twain were casting dice;
'The game is done! I've won! I've won!'
Quoth she, and whistles thrice.

The Sun's rim dips; the stars rush out;
At one stride comes the dark;
With far-heard whisper, o'er the sea,
Off shot the spectre-bark.

We listened and looked sideways up!
Fear at my heart, as at a cup,
My life-blood seemed to sip!
The stars were dim, and thick the night,
The steersman's face by his lamp gleamed white;
From the sails the dew did drip—
Till clomb above the eastern bar
The hornèd Moon, with one bright star

Within the nether tip.

One after one, by the star-dogged Moon,
Too quick for groan or sigh,
Each turned his face with a ghastly pang,
And cursed me with his eye.

Four times fifty living men,
(And I heard nor sigh nor groan)
With heavy thump, a lifeless lump,
They dropped down one by one.

The souls did from their bodies fly,—
They fled to bliss or woe!
And every soul, it passed me by,
Like the whizz of my cross-bow!

IV

'I fear thee, ancient Mariner!
I fear thy skinny hand!
And thou art long, and lank, and brown,
As is the ribbed sea-sand.

I fear thee and thy glittering eye,
And thy skinny hand, so brown.'—
Fear not, fear not, thou Wedding-Guest!
This body dropt not down.

Alone, alone, all, all alone,
Alone on a wide wide sea!
And never a saint took pity on
My soul in agony.

The many men, so beautiful!
And they all dead did lie:
And a thousand thousand slimy things
Lived on; and so did I.

I looked upon the rotting sea,
And drew my eyes away;

I looked upon the rotting deck,
And there the dead men lay.

I looked to heaven, and tried to pray;
But or ever a prayer had gusht,
A wicked whisper came, and made
My heart as dry as dust.

I closed my lids, and kept them close,
And the balls like pulses beat;
For the sky and the sea, and the sea and the sky
Lay dead like a load on my weary eye,
And the dead were at my feet.

The cold sweat melted from their limbs,
Nor rot nor reek did they:
The look with which they looked on me
Had never passed away.

An orphan's curse would drag to hell
A spirit from on high;
But oh! more horrible than that
Is the curse in a dead man's eye!
Seven days, seven nights, I saw that curse,
And yet I could not die.

The moving Moon went up the sky,
And no where did abide:
Softly she was going up,
And a star or two beside—

Her beams bemocked the sultry main,
Like April hoar-frost spread;
But where the ship's huge shadow lay,
The charmèd water burnt alway
A still and awful red.

Beyond the shadow of the ship,
I watched the water-snakes:
They moved in tracks of shining white,

And when they reared, the elfish light
Fell off in hoary flakes.

Within the shadow of the ship
I watched their rich attire:
Blue, glossy green, and velvet black,
They coiled and swam; and every track
Was a flash of golden fire.

O happy living things! no tongue
Their beauty might declare:
A spring of love gushed from my heart,
And I blessed them unaware:
Sure my kind saint took pity on me,
And I blessed them unaware.

The self-same moment I could pray;
And from my neck so free
The Albatross fell off, and sank
Like lead into the sea.

V

Oh sleep! it is a gentle thing,
Beloved from pole to pole!
To Mary Queen the praise be given!
She sent the gentle sleep from Heaven,
That slid into my soul.

The silly buckets on the deck,
That had so long remained,
I dreamt that they were filled with dew;
And when I awoke, it rained.

My lips were wet, my throat was cold,
My garments all were dank;
Sure I had drunken in my dreams,
And still my body drank.

I moved, and could not feel my limbs:
I was so light—almost

I thought that I had died in sleep,
And was a blessed ghost.

And soon I heard a roaring wind:
It did not come anear;
But with its sound it shook the sails,
That were so thin and sere.

The upper air burst into life!
And a hundred fire-flags sheen,
To and fro they were hurried about!
And to and fro, and in and out,
The wan stars danced between.

And the coming wind did roar more loud,
And the sails did sigh like sedge,
And the rain poured down from one black cloud;
The Moon was at its edge.

The thick black cloud was cleft, and still
The Moon was at its side:
Like waters shot from some high crag,
The lightning fell with never a jag,
A river steep and wide.

The loud wind never reached the ship,
Yet now the ship moved on!
Beneath the lightning and the Moon
The dead men gave a groan.

They groaned, they stirred, they all uprose,
Nor spake, nor moved their eyes;
It had been strange, even in a dream,
To have seen those dead men rise.

The helmsman steered, the ship moved on;
Yet never a breeze up-blew;
The mariners all 'gan work the ropes,
Where they were wont to do;
They raised their limbs like lifeless tools—

We were a ghastly crew.

The body of my brother's son
Stood by me, knee to knee:
The body and I pulled at one rope,
But he said nought to me.

'I fear thee, ancient Mariner!'
Be calm, thou Wedding-Guest!
'Twas not those souls that fled in pain,
Which to their corses came again,
But a troop of spirits blest:

For when it dawned—they dropped their arms,
And clustered round the mast;
Sweet sounds rose slowly through their mouths,
And from their bodies passed.

Around, around, flew each sweet sound,
Then darted to the Sun;
Slowly the sounds came back again,
Now mixed, now one by one.

Sometimes a-dropping from the sky
I heard the sky-lark sing;
Sometimes all little birds that are,
How they seemed to fill the sea and air
With their sweet jargoning!

And now 'twas like all instruments,
Now like a lonely flute;
And now it is an angel's song,
That makes the heavens be mute.

It ceased; yet still the sails made on
A pleasant noise till noon,
A noise like of a hidden brook
In the leafy month of June,
That to the sleeping woods all night
Singeth a quiet tune.

Till noon we quietly sailed on,
Yet never a breeze did breathe:
Slowly and smoothly went the ship,
Moved onward from beneath.

Under the keel nine fathom deep,
From the land of mist and snow,
The spirit slid: and it was he
That made the ship to go.
The sails at noon left off their tune,
And the ship stood still also.

The Sun, right up above the mast,
Had fixed her to the ocean:
But in a minute she 'gan stir,
With a short uneasy motion—
Backwards and forwards half her length
With a short uneasy motion.

Then like a pawing horse let go,
She made a sudden bound:
It flung the blood into my head,
And I fell down in a swound.

How long in that same fit I lay,
I have not to declare;
But ere my living life returned,
I heard and in my soul discerned
Two voices in the air.

'Is it he?' quoth one, 'Is this the man?
By him who died on cross,
With his cruel bow he laid full low
The harmless Albatross.

The spirit who bideth by himself
In the land of mist and snow,
He loved the bird that loved the man
Who shot him with his bow.'

The other was a softer voice,
As soft as honey-dew:
Quoth he, 'The man hath penance done,
And penance more will do.'

VI

First Voice
'But tell me, tell me! speak again,
Thy soft response renewing—
What makes that ship drive on so fast?
What is the ocean doing?'

Second Voice
Still as a slave before his lord,
The ocean hath no blast;
His great bright eye most silently
Up to the Moon is cast—

If he may know which way to go;
For she guides him smooth or grim.
See, brother, see! how graciously
She looketh down on him.'

First Voice
'But why drives on that ship so fast,
Without or wave or wind?'

Second Voice
'The air is cut away before,
And closes from behind.

Fly, brother, fly! more high, more high!
Or we shall be belated:
For slow and slow that ship will go,
When the Mariner's trance is abated.'

I woke, and we were sailing on
As in a gentle weather:
'Twas night, calm night, the moon was high;

The dead men stood together.

All stood together on the deck,
For a charnel-dungeon fitter:
All fixed on me their stony eyes,
That in the Moon did glitter.

The pang, the curse, with which they died,
Had never passed away:
I could not draw my eyes from theirs,
Nor turn them up to pray.

And now this spell was snapt: once more
I viewed the ocean green,
And looked far forth, yet little saw
Of what had else been seen—

Like one, that on a lonesome road
Doth walk in fear and dread,
And having once turned round walks on,
And turns no more his head;
Because he knows, a frightful fiend
Doth close behind him tread.

But soon there breathed a wind on me,
Nor sound nor motion made:
Its path was not upon the sea,
In ripple or in shade.

It raised my hair, it fanned my cheek
Like a meadow-gale of spring—
It mingled strangely with my fears,
Yet it felt like a welcoming.

Swiftly, swiftly flew the ship,
Yet she sailed softly too:
Sweetly, sweetly blew the breeze—
On me alone it blew.

Oh! dream of joy! is this indeed
The light-house top I see?

Is this the hill? is this the kirk?
Is this mine own countree?

We drifted o'er the harbour-bar,
And I with sobs did pray—
O let me be awake, my God!
Or let me sleep alway.

The harbour-bay was clear as glass,
So smoothly it was strewn!
And on the bay the moonlight lay,
And the shadow of the Moon.

The rock shone bright, the kirk no less,
That stands above the rock:
The moonlight steeped in silentness
The steady weathercock.

And the bay was white with silent light,
Till rising from the same,
Full many shapes, that shadows were,
In crimson colours came.

A little distance from the prow
Those crimson shadows were:
I turned my eyes upon the deck—
Oh, Christ! what saw I there!

Each corse lay flat, lifeless and flat,
And, by the holy rood!
A man all light, a seraph-man,
On every corse there stood.

This seraph-band, each waved his hand:
It was a heavenly sight!
They stood as signals to the land,
Each one a lovely light;

This seraph-band, each waved his hand,
No voice did they impart—
No voice; but oh! the silence sank

Like music on my heart.

But soon I heard the dash of oars,
I heard the Pilot's cheer;
My head was turned perforce away
And I saw a boat appear.

The Pilot and the Pilot's boy,
I heard them coming fast:
Dear Lord in Heaven! it was a joy
The dead men could not blast.

I saw a third—I heard his voice:
It is the Hermit good!
He singeth loud his godly hymns
That he makes in the wood.
He'll shrieve my soul, he'll wash away
The Albatross's blood.

VII

This Hermit good lives in that wood
Which slopes down to the sea.
How loudly his sweet voice he rears!
He loves to talk with marineres
That come from a far countree.

He kneels at morn, and noon, and eve—
He hath a cushion plump:
It is the moss that wholly hides
The rotted old oak-stump.

The skiff-boat neared: I heard them talk,
'Why, this is strange, I trow!
Where are those lights so many and fair,
That signal made but now?'

'Strange, by my faith!' the Hermit said—
'And they answered not our cheer!
The planks looked warped! and see those sails,
How thin they are and sere!

I never saw aught like to them,
Unless perchance it were

Brown skeletons of leaves that lag
My forest-brook along;
When the ivy-tod is heavy with snow,
And the owlet whoops to the wolf below,
That eats the she-wolf's young.'

'Dear Lord! it hath a fiendish look—
(The Pilot made reply)
I am a-feared'—'Push on, push on!'
Said the Hermit cheerily.

The boat came closer to the ship,
But I nor spake nor stirred;
The boat came close beneath the ship,
And straight a sound was heard.

Under the water it rumbled on,
Still louder and more dread:
It reached the ship, it split the bay;
The ship went down like lead.

Stunned by that loud and dreadful sound,
Which sky and ocean smote,
Like one that hath been seven days drowned
My body lay afloat;
But swift as dreams, myself I found
Within the Pilot's boat.

Upon the whirl, where sank the ship,
The boat spun round and round;
And all was still, save that the hill
Was telling of the sound.

I moved my lips—the Pilot shrieked
And fell down in a fit;
The holy Hermit raised his eyes,
And prayed where he did sit.

I took the oars: the Pilot's boy,
Who now doth crazy go,
Laughed loud and long, and all the while
His eyes went to and fro.
'Ha! ha!' quoth he, 'full plain I see,
The Devil knows how to row.'

And now, all in my own countree,
I stood on the firm land!
The Hermit stepped forth from the boat,
And scarcely he could stand.

'O shrieve me, shrieve me, holy man!'
The Hermit crossed his brow.
'Say quick,' quoth he, 'I bid thee say—
What manner of man art thou?'

Forthwith this frame of mine was wrenched
With a woful agony,
Which forced me to begin my tale;
And then it left me free.

Since then, at an uncertain hour,
That agony returns:
And till my ghastly tale is told,
This heart within me burns.
I pass, like night, from land to land;
I have strange power of speech;
That moment that his face I see,
I know the man that must hear me:
To him my tale I teach.

What loud uproar bursts from that door!
The wedding-guests are there:
But in the garden-bower the bride
And bride-maids singing are:
And hark the little vesper bell,
Which biddeth me to prayer!

O Wedding-Guest! this soul hath been

Alone on a wide wide sea:
So lonely 'twas, that God himself
Scarce seemèd there to be.

O sweeter than the marriage-feast,
'Tis sweeter far to me,
To walk together to the kirk
With a goodly company!—

To walk together to the kirk,
And all together pray,
While each to his great Father bends,
Old men, and babes, and loving friends
And youths and maidens gay!

Farewell, farewell! but this I tell
To thee, thou Wedding-Guest!
He prayeth well, who loveth well
Both man and bird and beast.

He prayeth best, who loveth best
All things both great and small;
For the dear God who loveth us,
He made and loveth all.

The Mariner, whose eye is bright,
Whose beard with age is hoar,
Is gone: and now the Wedding-Guest
Turned from the bridegroom's door.

He went like one that hath been stunned,
And is of sense forlorn:
A sadder and a wiser man,
He rose the morrow morn.

Lord Byron

DARKNESS

I HAD a dream, which was not all a dream.
The bright sun was extinguish'd, and the stars
Did wander darkling in the eternal space,
Rayless, and pathless, and the icy earth
Swung blind and blackening in the moonless air;
Morn came and went—and came, and brought no day,
And men forgot their passions in the dread
Of this their desolation; and all hearts
Were chill'd into a selfish prayer for light:
And they did live by watchfires—and the thrones,
The palaces of crowned kings—the huts,
The habitations of all things which dwell,
Were burnt for beacons; cities were consum'd,
And men were gather'd round their blazing homes
To look once more into each other's face;
Happy were those who dwelt within the eye
Of the volcanos, and their mountain-torch:
A fearful hope was all the world contain'd;
Forests were set on fire—but hour by hour
They fell and faded—and the crackling trunks
Extinguish'd with a crash—and all was black.
The brows of men by the despairing light
Wore an unearthly aspect, as by fits
The flashes fell upon them; some lay down
And hid their eyes and wept; and some did rest
Their chins upon their clenched hands, and smil'd;
And others hurried to and fro, and fed
Their funeral piles with fuel, and look'd up
With mad disquietude on the dull sky,
The pall of a past world; and then again
With curses cast them down upon the dust,
And gnash'd their teeth and howl'd: the wild birds shriek'd
And, terrified, did flutter on the ground,

And flap their useless wings; the wildest brutes
Came tame and tremulous; and vipers crawl'd
And twin'd themselves among the multitude,
Hissing, but stingless—they were slain for food.
And War, which for a moment was no more,
Did glut himself again: a meal was bought
With blood, and each sate sullenly apart
Gorging himself in gloom: no love was left;
All earth was but one thought—and that was death
Immediate and inglorious; and the pang
Of famine fed upon all entrails—men
Died, and their bones were tombless as their flesh;
The meagre by the meagre were devour'd,
Even dogs assail'd their masters, all save one,
And he was faithful to a corse, and kept
The birds and beasts and famish'd men at bay,
Till hunger clung them, or the dropping dead
Lur'd their lank jaws; himself sought out no food,
But with a piteous and perpetual moan,
And a quick desolate cry, licking the hand
Which answer'd not with a caress—he died.
The crowd was famish'd by degrees; but two
Of an enormous city did survive,
And they were enemies: they met beside
The dying embers of an altar-place
Where had been heap'd a mass of holy things
For an unholy usage; they rak'd up,
And shivering scrap'd with their cold skeleton hands
The feeble ashes, and their feeble breath
Blew for a little life, and made a flame
Which was a mockery; then they lifted up
Their eyes as it grew lighter, and beheld
Each other's aspects—saw, and shriek'd, and died—
Even of their mutual hideousness they died,
Unknowing who he was upon whose brow
Famine had written Fiend. The world was void,
The populous and the powerful was a lump,

Seasonless, herbless, treeless, manless, lifeless—
A lump of death—a chaos of hard clay.
The rivers, lakes and ocean all stood still,
And nothing stirr'd within their silent depths;
Ships sailorless lay rotting on the sea,
And their masts fell down piecemeal: as they dropp'd
They slept on the abyss without a surge—
The waves were dead; the tides were in their grave,
The moon, their mistress, had expir'd before;
The winds were wither'd in the stagnant air,
And the clouds perish'd; Darkness had no need
Of aid from them—She was the Universe.

From DON JUAN

Canto XI

I

When Bishop Berkeley said "there was no matter,"
    And proved it—'twas no matter what he said:
They say his system 'tis in vain to batter,
    Too subtle for the airiest human head;
And yet who can believe it! I would shatter
    Gladly all matters down to stone or lead,
Or adamant, to find the World a spirit,
And wear my head, denying that I wear it.

II

What a sublime discovery 'twas to make the
    Universe universal egotism,
That all's ideal—all ourselves: I'll stake the
    World (be it what you will) that that's no schism.
Oh Doubt!—if thou be'st Doubt, for which some take thee,
    But which I doubt extremely—thou sole prism
Of the Truth's rays, spoil not my draught of spirit!

Heaven's brandy, though our brain can hardly bear it.

III

For ever and anon comes Indigestion
    (Not the most "dainty Ariel") and perplexes
Our soarings with another sort of question:
    And that which after all my spirit vexes,
Is, that I find no spot where Man can rest eye on,
    Without confusion of the sorts and sexes,
Of beings, stars, and this unriddled wonder,
The World, which at the worst's a glorious blunder—

IV

If it be chance—or, if it be according
    To the Old Text, still better: lest it should
Turn out so, we'll say nothing 'gainst the wording,
    As several people think such hazards rude.
They're right; our days are too brief for affording
    Space to dispute what no one ever could
Decide, and everybody one day will
Know very clearly—or at least lie still.

V

And therefore will I leave off metaphysical
    Discussion, which is neither here nor there:
If I agree that what is, is; then this I call
    Being quite perspicuous and extremely fair.
The truth is, I've grown lately rather phthisical:
    I don't know what the reason is—the air
Perhaps; but as I suffer from the shocks
Of illness, I grow much more orthodox.

VI

The first attack at once prov'd the Divinity
    (But that I never doubted, nor the Devil);

The next, the Virgin's mystical virginity;
    The third, the usual Origin of Evil;
The fourth at once establish'd the whole Trinity
    On so uncontrovertible a level,
That I devoutly wish'd the three were four—
On purpose to believe so much the more.

VII

To our theme.—The man who has stood on the Acropolis,
    And look'd down over Attica; or he
Who has sail'd where picturesque Constantinople is,
    Or seen Timbuctoo, or hath taken tea
In small-ey'd China's crockery-ware metropolis,
    Or sat amidst the bricks of Nineveh,
May not think much of London's first appearance—
But ask him what he thinks of it a year hence!

VIII

Don Juan had got out on Shooter's Hill;
    Sunset the time, the place the same declivity
Which looks along that vale of good and ill
    Where London streets ferment in full activity,
While everything around was calm and still,
    Except the creak of wheels, which on their pivot he
Heard, and that bee-like, bubbling, busy hum
Of cities, that boil over with their scum—

IX

I say, Don Juan, wrapp'd in contemplation,
    Walk'd on behind his carriage, o'er the summit,
And lost in wonder of so great a nation,
    Gave way to't, since he could not overcome it.
"And here," he cried, "is Freedom's chosen station;
    Here peals the People's voice nor can entomb it
Racks, prisons, inquisitions; resurrection

Awaits it, each new meeting or election.

X

"Here are chaste wives, pure lives; her people pay
    But what they please; and if that things be dear,
'Tis only that they love to throw away
    Their cash, to show how much they have a-year.
Here laws are all inviolate; none lay
    Traps for the traveller; every highway's clear;
Here"—he was interrupted by a knife,
With—"Damn your eyes! your money or your life!"

XI

These free-born sounds proceeded from four pads
    In ambush laid, who had perceiv'd him loiter
Behind his carriage; and, like handy lads,
    Had seiz'd the lucky hour to reconnoitre,
In which the heedless gentleman who gads
    Upon the road, unless he prove a fighter
May find himself within that isle of riches
Expos'd to lose his life as well as breeches.

XII

Juan, who did not understand a word
    Of English, save their shibboleth, "God damn!"
And even that he had so rarely heard,
    He sometimes thought 'twas only their Salam,"
Or "God be with you!"—and 'tis not absurd
    To think so, for half English as I am
(To my misfortune) never can I say
I heard them wish "God with you," save that way—

XIII

Juan yet quickly understood their gesture,
    And being somewhat choleric and sudden,

Drew forth a pocket pistol from his vesture,
    And fired it into one assailant's pudding,
Who fell, as rolls an ox o'er in his pasture,
    And roar'd out, as he writh'd his native mud in,
Unto his nearest follower or henchman,
"Oh Jack! I'm floor'd by that ere bloody Frenchman!"

XIV

On which Jack and his train set off at speed,
    And Juan's suite, late scatter'd at a distance,
Came up, all marvelling at such a deed,
    And offering, as usual, late assistance.
Juan, who saw the moon's late minion bleed
    As if his veins would pour out his existence,
Stood calling out for bandages and lint,
And wish'd he had been less hasty with his flint.

XV

"Perhaps," thought he, "it is the country's wont
    To welcome foreigners in this way: now
I recollect some innkeepers who don't
    Differ, except in robbing with a bow,
In lieu of a bare blade and brazen front.
    But what is to be done? I can't allow
The fellow to lie groaning on the road:
So take him up, I'll help you with the load."

XVI

But ere they could perform this pious duty,
    The dying man cried, "Hold! I've got my gruel!
Oh! for a glass of max ! We've miss'd our booty—
    Let me die where I am!" And as the fuel
Of life shrunk in his heart, and thick and sooty
    The drops fell from his death-wound, and he drew ill
His breath, he from his swelling throat untied

A kerchief, crying "Give Sal that!"—and died.

XVII

The cravat stain'd with bloody drops fell down
　　Before Don Juan's feet: he could not tell
Exactly why it was before him thrown,
　　Nor what the meaning of the man's farewell.
Poor Tom was once a kiddy upon town,
　　A thorough varmint, and a real swell,
Full flash, all fancy, until fairly diddled,
His pockets first and then his body riddled.

XVIII

Don Juan, having done the best he could
　　In all the circumstances of the case,
As soon as "Crowner's 'quest" allow'd, pursu'd
　　His travels to the capital apace;
Esteeming it a little hard he should
　　In twelve hours' time, and very little space,
Have been oblig'd to slay a free-born native
In self-defence: this made him meditative.

XIX

He from the world had cut off a great man,
　　Who in his time had made heroic bustle.
Who in a row like Tom could lead the van,
　　Booze in the ken, or at the spellken hustle?
Who queer a flat? Who (spite of Bowstreet's ban)
　　On the high toby-spice so flash the muzzle?
Who on a lark, with black-eyed Sal (his blowing),
So prime, so swell, so nutty, and so knowing?

XX

But Tom's no more—and so no more of Tom.
　　Heroes must die; and by God's blessing 'tis

Not long before the most of them go home.
    Hail! Thamis, hail! Upon thy verge it is
That Juan's chariot, rolling like a drum
    In thunder, holds the way it can't well miss,
Through Kennington and all the other "tons,"
Which make us wish ourselves in town at once;

XXI

Through Groves, so called as being void of trees,
    (Like lucus from no light); through prospects nam'd
Mount Pleasant, as containing nought to please,
    Nor much to climb; through little boxes fram'd
Of bricks, to let the dust in at your ease,
    With "To be let," upon their doors proclaim'd;
Through "Rows" most modestly call'd "Paradise,"
Which Eve might quit without much sacrifice;

XXII

Through coaches, drays, chok'd turnpikes, and a whirl
    Of wheels, and roar of voices, and confusion;
Here taverns wooing to a pint of "purl,"
    There mails fast flying off like a delusion;
There barbers' blocks with periwigs in curl
    In windows; here the lamplighter's infusion
Slowly distill'd into the glimmering glass
(For in those days we had not got to gas);

XXIII

Through this, and much, and more, is the approach
    Of travellers to mighty Babylon:
Whether they come by horse, or chaise, or coach,
    With slight exceptions, all the ways seem one.
I could say more, but do not choose to encroach
    Upon the guide-book's privilege. The sun
Had set some time, and night was on the ridge

Of twilight, as the party cross'd the bridge.

XXIV

That's rather fine, the gentle sound of Thamis—
    Who vindicates a moment, too, his stream—
Though hardly heard through multifarious "damme's":
    The lamps of Westminster's more regular gleam,
The breadth of pavement, and yon shrine where Fame is
    A spectral resident—whose pallid beam
In shape of moonshine hovers o'er the pile—
Make this a sacred part of Albion's Isle.

XXV

The Druid's groves are gone—so much the better:
    Stonehenge is not—but what the devil is it?—
But Bedlam still exists with its sage fetter,
    That madmen may not bite you on a visit;
The Bench too seats or suits full many a debtor;
    The Mansion House too (though some people quiz it)
To me appears a stiff yet grand erection;
But then the Abbey's worth the whole collection.

XXVI

The line of lights too, up to Charing Cross,
    Pall Mall, and so forth, have a coruscation
Like gold as in comparison to dross,
    Match'd with the Continent's illumination,
Whose cities Night by no means deigns to gloss.
    The French were not yet a lamp-lighting nation,
And when they grew so—on their new-found lantern,
Instead of wicks, they made a wicked man turn.

XXVII

A row of Gentlemen along the streets
    Suspended may illuminate mankind,

As also bonfires made of country seats;
    But the old way is best for the purblind:
The other looks like phosphorus on sheets,
    A sort of ignis fatuus to the mind,
Which, though 'tis certain to perplex and frighten,
Must burn more mildly ere it can enlighten.

XXVIII

But London's so well lit, that if Diogenes
    Could recommence to hunt his honest man
And found him not amidst the various progenies
    Of this enormous city's spreading spawn,
'Twere not for want of lamps to aid his dodging his
    Yet undiscover'd treasure. What I can,
I've done to find the same throughout life's journey,
But see the World is only one attorney.

XXIX

Over the stones still rattling, up Pall Mall,
    Through crowds and carriages, but waxing thinner
As thunder'd knockers broke the long seal'd spell
    Of doors 'gainst duns, and to an early dinner
Admitted a small party as night fell,
    Don Juan, our young diplomatic sinner,
Pursu'd his path, and drove past some hotels,
St. James's Palace, and St. James's "Hells."

XXX

They reach'd the hotel: forth stream'd from the front door
    A tide of well-clad waiters, and around
The mob stood, and as usual several score
    Of those pedestrian Paphians who abound
In decent London when the daylight's o'er;
    Commodious but immoral, they are found
Useful, like Malthus, in promoting marriage:

But Juan now is stepping from his carriage

XXXI

Into one of the sweetest of hotels,
    Especially for foreigners—and mostly
For those whom favour or whom fortune swells,
    And cannot find a bill's small items costly.
There many an envoy either dwelt or dwells
    (The den of many a diplomatic lost lie),
Until to some conspicuous square they pass,
And blazon o'er the door their names in brass.

XXXII

Juan, whose was a delicate commission,
    Private, though publicly important, bore
No title to point out with due precision
    The exact affair on which he was sent o'er.
'Twas merely known, that on a secret mission
    A foreigner of rank had grac'd our shore,
Young, handsome and accomplish'd, who was said
(In whispers) to have turn'd his Sovereign's head.

XXXIII

Some rumour also of some strange adventures
    Had gone before him, and his wars and loves;
And as romantic heads are pretty painters,
    And, above all, an Englishwoman's roves
Into the excursive, breaking the indentures
    Of sober reason, wheresoe'er it moves,
He found himself extremely in the fashion,
Which serves our thinking people for a passion.

XXXIV

I don't mean that they are passionless, but quite
    The contrary; but then 'tis in the head;

Yet as the consequences are as bright
    As if they acted with the heart instead,
What after all can signify the site
    Of ladies' lucubrations? So they lead
In safety to the place for which you start,
What matters if the road be head or heart?

XXXV

Juan presented in the proper place,
    To proper placement, every Russ credential;
And was receiv'd with all the due grimace
    By those who govern in the mood potential,
Who, seeing a handsome stripling with smooth face,
    Thought (what in state affairs is most essential)
That they as easily might do the youngster,
As hawks may pounce upon a woodland songster.

XXXVI

They err'd, as aged men will do; but by
    And by we'll talk of that; and if we don't,
'T will be because our notion is not high
    Of politicians and their double front,
Who live by lies, yet dare not boldly lie:
    Now, what I love in women is, they won't
Or can't do otherwise than lie, but do it
So well, the very truth seems falsehood to it.

XXXVII

And, after all, what is a lie? 'Tis but
    The truth in masquerade; and I defy
Historians, heroes, lawyers, priests, to put
    A fact without some leaven of a lie.
The very shadow of true Truth would shut
    Up annals, revelations, poesy,
And prophecy—except it should be dated

Some years before the incidents related.

XXXVIII

Prais'd be all liars and all lies! Who now
    Can tax my mild Muse with misanthropy?
She rings the World's "Te Deum," and her brow
    Blushes for those who will not: but to sigh
Is idle; let us like most others bow,
    Kiss hands, feet, any part of Majesty,
After the good example of "Green Erin,"
Whose shamrock now seems rather worse for wearing.

XXXIX

Don Juan was presented, and his dress
    And mien excited general admiration;
I don't know which was more admir'd or less:
    One monstrous diamond drew much observation,
Which Catherine in a moment of "ivresse"
    (In love or brandy's fervent fermentation)
Bestow'd upon him, as the public learn'd;
And, to say truth, it had been fairly earn'd.

XL

Besides the ministers and underlings,
    Who must be courteous to the accredited
Diplomatists of rather wavering kings,
    Until their royal riddle's fully read,
The very clerks—those somewhat dirty springs
    Of Office, or the House of Office, fed
By foul corruption into streams—even they
Were hardly rude enough to earn their pay.

XLI

And insolence no doubt is what they are
    Employ'd for, since it is their daily labour,

In the dear offices of peace or war;
    And should you doubt, pray ask of your next neighbour,
When for a passport, or some other bar
    To freedom, he applied (a grief and a bore),
If he found not this spawn of tax-born riches,
Like lap-dogs, the least civil sons of b——s.

XLII

But Juan was receiv'd with much "empressement" —
    These phrases of refinement I must borrow
From our next neighbours' land, where, like a chessman,
    There is a move set down for joy or sorrow,
Not only in mere talking, but the press. Man
    In islands is, it seems, downright and thorough,
More than on continents—as if the sea
(See Billingsgate) made even the tongue more free.

XLIII

And yet the British "Damme" 's rather Attic,
    Your continental oaths are but incontinent,
And turn on things which no aristocratic
    Spirit would name, and therefore even I won't anent
This subject quote; as it would be schismatic
    In politesse, and have a sound affronting in 't;
But "Damme" 's quite ethereal, though too daring—
Platonic blasphemy, the soul of swearing.

XLIV

For downright rudeness, ye may stay at home;
    For true or false politeness (and scarce that
Now) you may cross the blue deep and white foam:
    The first the emblem (rarely though) of what
You leave behind, the next of much you come
    To meet. However, 'tis no time to chat
On general topics: poems must confine

Themselves to Unity, like this of mine.

XLV

In the great world—which, being interpreted,
    Meaneth the West or worst end of a city,
And about twice two thousand people bred
    By no means to be very wise or witty,
But to sit up while others lie in bed,
    And look down on the Universe with pity—
Juan, as an inveterate patrician,
Was well receiv'd by persons of condition.

XLVI

He was a bachelor, which is a matter
    Of import both to virgin and to bride,
The former's hymeneal hopes to flatter;
    And (should she not hold fast by love or pride)
'Tis also of some momemt to the latter:
    A rib's a thorn in a wed gallant's side,
Requires decorum, and is apt to double
The horrid sin—and what's still worse the trouble.

XLVII

But Juan was a bachelor—of arts,
    And parts, and hearts: he danc'd and sung, and had
An air as sentimental as Mozart's
    Softest of melodies; and could be sad
Or cheerful, without any "flaws or starts,"
    Just at the proper time; and though a lad,
Had seen the world—which is a curious sight,
And very much unlike what people write.

XLVIII

Fair virgins blush'd upon him; wedded dames
    Bloom'd also in less transitory hues;

For both commodities dwell by the Thames
    The painting and the painted; Youth, Ceruse,
Against his heart preferr'd their usual claims,
    Such as no gentleman can quite refuse;
Daughters admir'd his dress, and pious mothers
Inquir'd his income, and if he had brothers.

XLIX

The milliners who furnish "drapery Misses"
    Throughout the season, upon speculation
Of payment ere the Honeymoon's last kisses
    Have wan'd into a crescent's coruscation,
Thought such an opportunity as this is,
    Of a rich foreigner's initiation,
Not to be overlook'd—and gave such credit,
That future bridegrooms swore, and sigh'd, and paid it.

L

The Blues, that tender tribe, who sigh o'er sonnets,
    And with the pages of the last Review
Line the interior of their heads or bonnets,
    Advanc'd in all their azure's highest hue:
They talk'd bad French or Spanish, and upon its
    Late authors ask'd him for a hint or two;
And which was softest, Russian or Castilian?
And whether in his travels he saw Ilion?

LI

Juan, who was a little superficial,
    And not in literature a great Drawcansir,
Examin'd by this learned and especial
    Jury of matrons, scarce knew what to answer:
His duties warlike, loving or official,
    His steady application as a dancer,
Had kept him from the brink of Hippocrene,

Which now he found was blue instead of green.

LII

However, he replied at hazard, with
    A modest confidence and calm assurance,
Which lent his learned lucubrations pith,
    And pass'd for arguments of good endurance.
That prodigy, Miss Araminta Smith
    (Who at sixteen translated "Hercules Furens"
Into as furious English), with her best look,
Set down his sayings in her common-place book.

LIII

Juan knew several languages—as well
    He might—and brought them up with skill, in time
To save his fame with each accomplish'd belle,
    Who still regretted that he did not rhyme.
There wanted but this requisite to swell
    His qualities (with them) into sublime:
Lady Fitz-Frisky, and Miss M{ae}via Mannish,
Both long'd extremely to be sung in Spanish.

LIV

However, he did pretty well, and was
    Admitted as an aspirant to all
The coteries, and, as in Banquo's glass,
    At great assemblies or in parties small,
He saw ten thousand living authors pass,
    That being about their average numeral;
Also the eighty "greatest living poets,"
As every paltry magazine can show it's .

LV

In twice five years the "greatest living poet,"
    Like to the champion in the fisty ring,

Is call'd on to support his claim, or show it,
　　Although 'tis an imaginary thing,
Even I—albeit I'm sure I did not know it,
　　Nor sought of foolscap subjects to be king—
Was reckon'd, a considerable time,
The grand Napoleon of the realms of rhyme.

LVI

But Juan was my Moscow, and Faliero
　　My Leipsic, and my Mont Saint Jean seem Cain:
"La Belle Alliance" of dunces down at zero,
　　Now that the Lion's fall'n, may rise again,
But I will fall at least as fell my hero;
　　Nor reign at all, or as a monarch reign;
Or to some lonely isle of jailors go,
With turncoat Southey for my turnkey Lowe.

LVII

Sir Walter reign'd before me; Moore and Campbell
　　Before and after; but now grown more holy,
The Muses upon Sion's hill must ramble
　　With poets almost clergymen, or wholly;
And Pegasus has a psalmodic amble
　　Beneath the very Reverend Rowley Powley,
Who shoes the glorious animal with stilts,
A modern Ancient Pistol—"by the hilts!"

LVIII

Still he excels that artificial hard
　　Labourer in the same vineyard, though the vine
Yields him but vinegar for his reward—
　　That neutralis'd dull Dorus of the Nine;
That swarthy Sporus, neither man nor bard;
　　That ox of verse, who ploughs for every line:
Cambyses' roaring Romans beat at least

The howling Hebrews of Cybele's priest.

LIX

Then there's my gentle Euphues, who, they say,
    Sets up for being a sort of moral me;
He'll find it rather difficult some day
    To turn out both, or either, it may be.
Some persons think that Coleridge hath the sway;
    And Wordsworth has supporters, two or three;
And that deep-mouth'd Boeotian "Savage Landor"
Has taken for a swan rogue Southey's gander.

LX

John Keats, who was kill'd off by one critique,
    Just as he really promis'd something great,
If not intelligible, without Greek
    Contriv'd to talk about the gods of late,
Much as they might have been suppos'd to speak.
    Poor fellow! His was an untoward fate;
'Tis strange the mind, that very fiery particle,
Should let itself be snuff'd out by an article.

LXI

The list grows long of live and dead pretenders
    To that which none will gain—or none will know
The conqueror at least; who, ere Time renders
    His last award, will have the long grass grow
Above his burnt-out brain, and sapless cinders.
    If I might augur, I should rate but low
Their chances; they're too numerous, like the thirty
Mock tyrants, when Rome's annals wax'd but dirty.

LXII

This is the literary lower empire,
    Where the pr{ae}torian bands take up the matter;

A "dreadful trade," like his who "gathers samphire,"
    The insolent soldiery to soothe and flatter,
With the same feelings as you'd coax a vampire,
    Now, were I once at home, and in good satire,
I'd try conclusions with those Janizaries,
And show them what an intellectual war is.

LXIII

I think I know a trick or two, would turn
    Their flanks; but it is hardly worth my while,
With such small gear to give myself concern:
    Indeed I've not the necessary bile;
My natural temper's really aught but stern,
    And even my Muse's worst reproof's a smile;
And then she drops a brief and modern curtsy,
And glides away, assur'd she never hurts ye.

LXIV

My Juan, whom I left in deadly peril
    Amongst live poets and blue ladies, pass'd
With some small profit through that field so sterile,
    Being tir'd in time, and, neither least nor last,
Left it before he had been treated very ill;
    And henceforth found himself more gaily class'd
Amongst the higher spirits of the day,
The sun's true son, no vapour, but a ray.

LXV

His morns he pass'd in business—which dissected,
    Was, like all business, a laborious nothing
That leads to lassitude, the most infected
    And Centaur-Nessus garb of mortal clothing,
And on our sofas makes us lie dejected,
    And talk in tender horrors of our loathing
All kinds of toil, save for our country's good—

Which grows no better, though 'tis time it should.

LXVI

His afternoons he pass'd in visits, luncheons,
    Lounging and boxing; and the twilight hour
In riding round those vegetable puncheons
    Call'd "Parks," where there is neither fruit nor flower
Enough to gratify a bee's slight munchings;
    But after all it is the only "bower"
(In Moore's phrase) where the fashionable fair
Can form a slight acquaintance with fresh air.

LXVII

Then dress, then dinner, then awakes the world!
    Then glare the lamps, then whirl the wheels, then roar
Through street and square fast flashing chariots hurl'd
    Like harness'd meteors; then along the floor
Chalk mimics painting; then festoons are twirl'd;
    Then roll the brazen thunders of the door,
Which opens to the thousand happy few
An earthly Paradise of "Or Molu."

LXVIII

There stands the noble hostess, nor shall sink
    With the three-thousandth curtsy; there the waltz,
The only dance which teaches girls to think,
    Makes one in love even with its very faults.
Saloon, room, hall, o'erflow beyond their brink,
    And long the latest of arrivals halts,
'Midst royal dukes and dames condemn'd to climb,
And gain an inch of staircase at a time.

LXIX

Thrice happy he who, after a survey
    Of the good company, can win a corner,

A door that's in or boudoir out of the way,
    Where he may fix himself like small "Jack Horner,"
And let the Babel round run as it may,
    And look on as a mourner, or a scorner,
Or an approver, or a mere spectator,
Yawning a little as the night grows later.

LXX

But this won't do, save by and by; and he
    Who, like Don Juan, takes an active share
Must steer with care through all that glittering sea
    Of gems and plumes and pearls and silks, to where
He deems it is his proper place to be;
    Dissolving in the waltz to some soft air,
Or proudlier prancing with mercurial skill,
Where Science marshals forth her own quadrille.

LXXI

Or, if he dance not, but hath higher views
    Upon an heiress or his neighbour's bride,
Let him take care that that which he pursues
    Is not at once too palpably descried.
Full many an eager gentleman oft rues
    His haste; impatience is a blundering guide
Amongst a people famous for reflection,
Who like to play the fool with circumspection.

LXXII

But, if you can contrive, get next at supper;
    Or, if forestalled, get opposite and ogle:
Oh, ye ambrosial moments! always upper
    In mind, a sort of sentimental bogle,
Which sits for ever upon Memory's crupper,
    The ghost of vanish'd pleasures once in vogue! Ill
Can tender souls relate the rise and fall

Of hopes and fears which shake a single ball.

LXXIII

But these precautionary hints can touch
   Only the common run, who must pursue,
And watch and ward; whose plans a word too much
   Or little overturns; and not the few
Or many (for the number's sometimes such)
   Whom a good mien, especially if new,
Or fame, or name, for wit, war, sense or nonsense,
Permits whate'er they please, or did not long since.

LXXIV

Our hero, as a hero young and handsome,
   Noble, rich, celebrated, and a stranger,
Like other slaves of course must pay his ransom
   Before he can escape from so much danger
As will environ a conspicuous man. Some
   Talk about poetry, and "rack and manger,"
And ugliness, disease, as toil and trouble—
I wish they knew the life of a young noble.

LXXV

They are young, but know not youth—it is anticipated;
   Handsome but wasted, rich without a sou;
Their vigour in a thousand arms is dissipated;
   Their cash comes from, their wealth goes to a Jew;
Both senates see their nightly votes participated
   Between the tyrant's and the tribunes' crew;
And having voted, din'd, drunk, gam'd and whor'd,
The family vault receives another lord.

LXXVI

"Where is the World," cries Young, "at eighty? Where
   The World in which a man was born?" Alas!

Where is the world of eight years past? 'Twas there—
    I look for it—'tis gone, a Globe of Glass!
Crack'd, shiver'd, vanish'd, scarcely gaz'd on, ere
    A silent change dissolves the glittering mass.
Statesmen, chiefs, orators, queens, patriots, kings,
And dandies—all are gone on the wind's wings.

LXXVII

Where is Napoleon the Grand? God knows:
    Where little Castlereagh? The devil can tell:
Where Grattan, Curran, Sheridan, all those
    Who bound the Bar or Senate in their spell?
Where is the unhappy Queen, with all her woes?
    And where the Daughter, whom the Isles lov'd well?
Where are those martyr'd saints the Five per Cents?
And where—oh, where the devil are the Rents?

LXXVIII

Where's Brummell? Dish'd. Where's Long Pole Wellesley?
  Diddled.
    Where's Whitbread? Romilly? Where's George the Third?
Where is his will? (That's not so soon unriddled.)
    And where is "Fum" the Fourth, our "royal bird"?
Gone down, it seems, to Scotland to be fiddled
    Unto by Sawney's violin, we have heard:
"Caw me, caw thee"—for six months hath been hatching
This scene of royal itch and loyal scratching.

LXXIX

Where is Lord This? And where my Lady That?
    The Honourable Mistresses and Misses?
Some laid aside like an old Opera hat,
    Married, unmarried, and remarried (this is
An evolution oft perform'd of late).
    Where are the Dublin shouts—and London hisses?
Where are the Grenvilles? Turn'd as usual. Where

My friends the Whigs? Exactly where they were.

LXXX

Where are the Lady Carolines and Franceses?
    Divorc'd or doing thereanent. Ye annals
So brilliant, where the list of routs and dances is,
    Thou Morning Post, sole record of the panels
Broken in carriages, and all the phantasies
    Of fashion, say what streams now fill those channels?
Some die, some fly, some languish on the Continent,
Because the times have hardly left them one tenant.

LXXXI

Some who once set their caps at cautious dukes,
    Have taken up at length with younger brothers:
Some heiresses have bit at sharpers' hooks:
    Some maids have been made wives, some merely mothers:
Others have lost their fresh and fairy looks:
    In short, the list of alterations bothers.
There's little strange in this, but something strange is
The unusual quickness of these common changes.

LXXXII

Talk not of seventy years as age! in seven
    I have seen more changes, down from monarchs to
The humblest individuals under heaven,
    Than might suffice a moderate century through.
I knew that nought was lasting, but now even
    Change grows too changeable, without being new:
Nought's permanent among the human race,
Except the Whigs not getting into place.

LXXXIII

I have seen Napoleon, who seem'd quite a Jupiter,
    Shrink to a Saturn. I have seen a Duke

(No matter which) turn politician stupider,
   If that can well be, than his wooden look.
But it is time that I should hoist my "blue Peter,"
   And sail for a new theme: I have seen—and shook
To see it—the King hiss'd, and then caress'd;
But don't pretend to settle which was best.

LXXXIV

I have seen the Landholders without a rap—
   I have seen Joanna Southcote—I have seen
The House of Commons turn'd to a taxtrap—
   I have seen that sad affair of the late Queen—
I have seen crowns worn instead of a fool's cap—
   I have seen a Congress doing all that's mean—
I have seen some nations, like o'erloaded asses,
Kick off their burthens—meaning the high classes.

LXXXV

I have seen small poets, and great prosers, and
   Interminable—not eternal—speakers—
I have seen the funds at war with house and land—
   I have seen the country gentlemen turn squeakers—
I have seen the people ridden o'er like sand
   By slaves on horseback—I have seen malt liquors
Exchang'd for "thin potations" by John Bull—
I have seen John half detect himself a fool.

LXXXVI

But "carpe diem," Juan, "carpe, carpe!"
   To-morrow sees another race as gay
And transient, and devour'd by the same harpy.
   "Life's a poor player"—then "play out the play,
Ye villains!" and above all keep a sharp eye
   Much less on what you do than what you say:
Be hypocritical, be cautious, be

Not what you seem, but always what you see.

LXXXVII

But how shall I relate in other cantos
    Of what befell our hero in the land,
Which 'tis the common cry and lie to vaunt as
    A moral country? But I hold my hand—
For I disdain to write an Atalantis;
    But 'tis as well at once to understand,
You are not a moral people, and you know it,
Without the aid of too sincere a poet.

LXXXVIII

What Juan saw and underwent shall be
    My topic, with of course the due restriction
Which is requir'd by proper courtesy;
    And recollect the work is only fiction,
And that I sing of neither mine nor me,
    Though every scribe, in some slight turn of diction,
Will hint allusions never meant. Ne'er doubt
This—when I speak, I don't hint, but speak out.

LXXXIX

Whether he married with the third or fourth
    Offspring of some sage husband-hunting countess,
Or whether with some virgin of more worth
    (I mean in Fortune's matrimonial bounties),
He took to regularly peopling Earth,
    Of which your lawful, awful wedlock fount is—
Or whether he was taken in for damages,
For being too excursive in his homages—

XC

Is yet within the unread events of time.
    Thus far, go forth, thou Lay, which I will back

Against the same given quantity of rhyme,
    For being as much the subject of attack
As ever yet was any work sublime,
    By those who love to say that white is black.
So much the better!—I may stand alone,
But would not change my free thoughts for a throne.

SHE WALKS IN BEAUTY

She walks in beauty, like the night
Of cloudless climes and starry skies;
And all that's best of dark and bright
Meet in her aspect and her eyes;
Thus mellowed to that tender light
Which heaven to gaudy day denies.

One shade the more, one ray the less,
Had half impaired the nameless grace
Which waves in every raven tress,
Or softly lightens o'er her face;
Where thoughts serenely sweet express,
How pure, how dear their dwelling-place.

And on that cheek, and o'er that brow,
So soft, so calm, yet eloquent,
The smiles that win, the tints that glow,
But tell of days in goodness spent,
A mind at peace with all below,
A heart whose love is innocent!

Percy Bysshe Shelley

ODE TO THE WEST WIND

I

O WILD West Wind, thou breath of Autumn's being,
Thou, from whose unseen presence the leaves dead
Are driven, like ghosts from an enchanter fleeing,

Yellow, and black, and pale, and hectic red,
Pestilence-stricken multitudes: O thou,
Who chariotest to their dark wintry bed

The winged seeds, where they lie cold and low,
Each like a corpse within its grave, until
Thine azure sister of the Spring shall blow

Her clarion o'er the dreaming earth, and fill
(Driving sweet buds like flocks to feed in air)
With living hues and odours plain and hill:

Wild Spirit, which art moving everywhere;
Destroyer and preserver; hear, oh hear!

II

Thou on whose stream, mid the steep sky's commotion,
Loose clouds like earth's decaying leaves are shed,
Shook from the tangled boughs of Heaven and Ocean,

Angels of rain and lightning: there are spread
On the blue surface of thine aëry surge,
Like the bright hair uplifted from the head

Of some fierce Maenad, even from the dim verge
Of the horizon to the zenith's height,
The locks of the approaching storm. Thou dirge

Of the dying year, to which this closing night
Will be the dome of a vast sepulchre,

Vaulted with all thy congregated might

Of vapours, from whose solid atmosphere
Black rain, and fire, and hail will burst: oh hear!

III

Thou who didst waken from his summer dreams
The blue Mediterranean, where he lay,
Lull'd by the coil of his crystalline streams,

Beside a pumice isle in Baiae's bay,
And saw in sleep old palaces and towers
Quivering within the wave's intenser day,

All overgrown with azure moss and flowers
So sweet, the sense faints picturing them! Thou
For whose path the Atlantic's level powers

Cleave themselves into chasms, while far below
The sea-blooms and the oozy woods which wear
The sapless foliage of the ocean, know

Thy voice, and suddenly grow gray with fear,
And tremble and despoil themselves: oh hear!

IV

If I were a dead leaf thou mightest bear;
If I were a swift cloud to fly with thee;
A wave to pant beneath thy power, and share

The impulse of thy strength, only less free
Than thou, O uncontrollable! If even
I were as in my boyhood, and could be

The comrade of thy wanderings over Heaven,
As then, when to outstrip thy skiey speed
Scarce seem'd a vision; I would ne'er have striven

As thus with thee in prayer in my sore need.
Oh, lift me as a wave, a leaf, a cloud!

I fall upon the thorns of life! I bleed!

A heavy weight of hours has chain'd and bow'd
One too like thee: tameless, and swift, and proud.

V

Make me thy lyre, even as the forest is:
What if my leaves are falling like its own!
The tumult of thy mighty harmonies

Will take from both a deep, autumnal tone,
Sweet though in sadness. Be thou, Spirit fierce,
My spirit! Be thou me, impetuous one!

Drive my dead thoughts over the universe
Like wither'd leaves to quicken a new birth!
And, by the incantation of this verse,

Scatter, as from an unextinguish'd hearth
Ashes and sparks, my words among mankind!
Be through my lips to unawaken'd earth

The trumpet of a prophecy! O Wind,
If Winter comes, can Spring be far behind?

OZYMANDIAS

I MET a traveller from an antique land,
Who said—"Two vast and trunkless legs of stone
Stand in the desert . . . Near them, on the sand,
Half sunk a shattered visage lies, whose frown,
And wrinkled lip, and sneer of cold command,
Tell that its sculptor well those passions read
Which yet survive, stamped on these lifeless things,
The hand that mocked them, and the heart that fed;
And on the pedestal, these words appear:
My name is Ozymandias, King of Kings;
Look on my Works, ye Mighty, and despair!

Nothing beside remains. Round the decay
Of that colossal Wreck, boundless and bare
The lone and level sands stretch far away."

From
PROMETHEUS UNBOUND

SCENE.—A Ravine of Icy Rocks in the Indian Caucasus. Prometheus is discovered bound to the Precipice. Panthea and Ione are seated at his feet. Time, night. During the Scene, morning slowly breaks.

Prometheus:

> MONARCH OF Gods and Dæmons, and all Spirits
> But One, who throng those bright and rolling worlds
> Which Thou and I alone of living things
> Behold with sleepless eyes! regard this Earth
> Made multitudinous with thy slaves, whom thou
> Requitest for knee-worship, prayer, and praise,
> And toil, and hecatombs of broken hearts,
> With fear and self-contempt and barren hope.
> Whilst me, who am thy foe, eyeless in hate,
> Hast thou made reign and triumph, to thy scorn,
> O'er mine own misery and thy vain revenge.
> Three thousand years of sleep-unsheltered hours,
> And moments aye divided by keen pangs
> Till they seemed years, torture and solitude,
> Scorn and despair,—these are mine empire:—
> More glorious far than that which thou surveyest
> From thine unenvied throne, O Mighty God!
> Almighty, had I deigned to share the shame
> Of thine ill tyranny, and hung not here
> Nailed to this wall of eagle-baffling mountain,
> Black, wintry, dead, unmeasured; without herb,
> Insect, or beast, or shape or sound of life.

Ah me! alas, pain, pain ever, for ever!

    No change, no pause, no hope! Yet I endure.
I ask the Earth, have not the mountains felt?
I ask yon Heaven, the all-beholding Sun,
Has it not seen? The Sea, in storm or calm,
Heaven's ever-changing Shadow, spread below,
Have its deaf waves not heard my agony?
Ah me! alas, pain, pain ever, for ever!

    The crawling glaciers pierce me with the spears
Of their moon-freezing crystals, the bright chains
Eat with their burning cold into my bones.
Heaven's wingèd hound, polluting from thy lips
His beak in poison not his own, tears up
My heart; and shapeless sights come wandering by,
The ghastly people of the realm of dream,
Mocking me: and the Earthquake-fiends are charged
To wrench the rivets from my quivering wounds
When the rocks split and close again behind:
While from their loud abysses howling throng
The genii of the storm, urging the rage
Of whirlwind, and afflict me with keen hail.
And yet to me welcome is day and night,
Whether one breaks the hoar frost of the morn,
Or starry, dim, and slow, the other climbs
The leaden-coloured east; for then they lead
The wingless, crawling hours, one among whom
—As some dark Priest hales the reluctant victim—
Shall drag thee, cruel King, to kiss the blood
From these pale feet, which then might trample thee
If they disdained not such a prostrate slave.
Disdain! Ah no! I pity thee. What ruin
Will hunt thee undefended through wide Heaven!
How will thy soul, cloven to its depth with terror,
Gape like a hell within! I speak in grief,
Not exultation, for I hate no more,
As then ere misery made me wise. The curse

Once breathed on thee I would recall. Ye Mountains,
Whose many-voicèd Echoes, through the mist
Of cataracts, flung the thunder of that spell!
Ye icy Springs, stagnant with wrinkling frost,
Which vibrated to hear me, and then crept
Shuddering through India! Thou serenest Air,
Through which the Sun walks burning without beams!
And ye swift Whirlwinds, who on poisèd wings
Hung mute and moveless o'er yon hushed abyss,
As thunder, louder than your own, made rock
The orbèd world! If then my words had power,
Though I am changed so that aught evil wish
Is dead within; although no memory be
Of what is hate, let them not lose it now!
What was that curse? for ye all heard me speak.

TO A SKYLARK

Hail to thee, blithe Spirit!
Bird thou never wert,
That from Heaven, or near it,
Pourest thy full heart
In profuse strains of unpremeditated art.

Higher still and higher
From the earth thou springest
Like a cloud of fire;
The blue deep thou wingest,
And singing still dost soar, and soaring ever singest.

In the golden lightning
Of the sunken sun,
O'er which clouds are bright'ning,
Thou dost float and run;
Like an unbodied joy whose race is just begun.

The pale purple even

Melts around thy flight;
Like a star of Heaven,
In the broad day-light
Thou art unseen, but yet I hear thy shrill delight,

Keen as are the arrows
Of that silver sphere,
Whose intense lamp narrows
In the white dawn clear
Until we hardly see, we feel that it is there.

All the earth and air
With thy voice is loud,
As, when night is bare,
From one lonely cloud
The moon rains out her beams, and Heaven is overflow'd.

What thou art we know not;
What is most like thee?
From rainbow clouds there flow not
Drops so bright to see
As from thy presence showers a rain of melody.

Like a Poet hidden
In the light of thought,
Singing hymns unbidden,
Till the world is wrought
To sympathy with hopes and fears it heeded not:

Like a high-born maiden
In a palace-tower,
Soothing her love-laden
Soul in secret hour
With music sweet as love, which overflows her bower:

Like a glow-worm golden
In a dell of dew,
Scattering unbeholden
Its aëreal hue

Among the flowers and grass, which screen it from the view:

Like a rose embower'd
In its own green leaves,
By warm winds deflower'd,
Till the scent it gives
Makes faint with too much sweet those heavy-winged thieves:

Sound of vernal showers
On the twinkling grass,
Rain-awaken'd flowers,
All that ever was
Joyous, and clear, and fresh, thy music doth surpass.

Teach us, Sprite or Bird,
What sweet thoughts are thine:
I have never heard
Praise of love or wine
That panted forth a flood of rapture so divine.

Chorus Hymeneal,
Or triumphal chant,
Match'd with thine would be all
But an empty vaunt,
A thing wherein we feel there is some hidden want.

What objects are the fountains
Of thy happy strain?
What fields, or waves, or mountains?
What shapes of sky or plain?
What love of thine own kind? what ignorance of pain?

With thy clear keen joyance
Languor cannot be:
Shadow of annoyance
Never came near thee:
Thou lovest: but ne'er knew love's sad satiety.

Waking or asleep,
Thou of death must deem

Things more true and deep
Than we mortals dream,
Or how could thy notes flow in such a crystal stream?

We look before and after,
And pine for what is not:
Our sincerest laughter
With some pain is fraught;
Our sweetest songs are those that tell of saddest thought.

Yet if we could scorn
Hate, and pride, and fear;
If we were things born
Not to shed a tear,
I know not how thy joy we ever should come near.

Better than all measures
Of delightful sound,
Better than all treasures
That in books are found,
Thy skill to poet were, thou scorner of the ground!

Teach me half the gladness
That thy brain must know,
Such harmonious madness
From my lips would flow
The world should listen then, as I am listening now.

John Clare

AUTUMN

The THISTLEDOWN's flying, though the winds are all still,
On the green grass now lying, now mounting the hill,
The spring from the fountain now boils like a pot;
Through stones past the counting it bubbles red-hot.

The ground parched and cracked is like overbaked bread,

The greensward all wracked is, bents dried up and dead.
The fallow fields glitter like water indeed,
And gossamers twitter, flung from weed unto weed.

Hill-tops like hot iron glitter bright in the sun,
And the rivers we're eying burn to gold as they run;
Burning hot is the ground, liquid gold is the air;
Whoever looks round sees Eternity there.

FIRST LOVE

I ne'er was struck before that hour
    With love so sudden and so sweet,
Her face it bloomed like a sweet flower
    And stole my heart away complete.
My face turned pale as deadly pale,
    My legs refused to walk away,
And when she looked, what could I ail?
    My life and all seemed turned to clay.

And then my blood rushed to my face
    And took my eyesight quite away,
The trees and bushes round the place
    Seemed midnight at noonday.
I could not see a single thing,
    Words from my eyes did start—
They spoke as chords do from the string,
    And blood burnt round my heart.

Are flowers the winter's choice?
    Is love's bed always snow?
She seemed to hear my silent voice,
    Not love's appeals to know.
I never saw so sweet a face
    As that I stood before.
My heart has left its dwelling-place
    And can return no more.

John Keats

LA BELLE DAME SANS MERCI

O WHAT can ail thee, knight-at-arms,
    Alone and palely loitering?
The sedge has withered from the lake,
    And no birds sing.

O what can ail thee, knight-at-arms,
    So haggard and so woe-begone?
The squirrel's granary is full,
    And the harvest's done.

I see a lily on thy brow,
    With anguish moist and fever-dew,
And on thy cheeks a fading rose
    Fast withereth too.

I met a lady in the meads,
    Full beautiful—a faery's child,
Her hair was long, her foot was light,
    And her eyes were wild.

I made a garland for her head,
    And bracelets too, and fragrant zone;
She looked at me as she did love,
    And made sweet moan.

I set her on my pacing steed,
    And nothing else saw all day long,
For sidelong would she bend, and sing
    A faery's song.

She found me roots of relish sweet,
    And honey wild, and manna-dew,
And sure in language strange she said—
    'I love thee true'.

She took me to her Elfin grot,
    And there she wept and sighed full sore,
And there I shut her wild wild eyes
    With kisses four.

And there she lullèd me asleep,
    And there I dreamed—Ah! woe betide!—
The latest dream I ever dreamt
    On the cold hill side.

I saw pale kings and princes too,
    Pale warriors, death-pale were they all;
They cried—'La Belle Dame sans Merci
    Thee hath in thrall!'

I saw their starved lips in the gloam,
    With horrid warning gapèd wide,
And I awoke and found me here,
    On the cold hill's side.

And this is why I sojourn here,
    Alone and palely loitering,
Though the sedge is withered from the lake,
    And no birds sing.

ODE ON A GRECIAN URN

THOU STILL unravish'd bride of quietness,
    Thou foster-child of silence and slow time,
Sylvan historian, who canst thus express
    A flowery tale more sweetly than our rhyme:
What leaf-fring'd legend haunts about thy shape
    Of deities or mortals, or of both,
        In Tempe or the dales of Arcady?
    What men or gods are these? What maidens loth?
What mad pursuit? What struggle to escape?
        What pipes and timbrels? What wild ecstasy?

Heard melodies are sweet, but those unheard

Are sweeter; therefore, ye soft pipes, play on;
　Not to the sensual ear, but, more endear'd,
　　Pipe to the spirit ditties of no tone:
Fair youth, beneath the trees, thou canst not leave
　　Thy song, nor ever can those trees be bare;
　　　　Bold Lover, never, never canst thou kiss,
Though winning near the goal yet, do not grieve;
　　She cannot fade, though thou hast not thy bliss,
　　　　For ever wilt thou love, and she be fair!

Ah, happy, happy boughs! that cannot shed
　　Your leaves, nor ever bid the Spring adieu;
And, happy melodist, unwearied,
　　For ever piping songs for ever new;
More happy love! more happy, happy love!
　　For ever warm and still to be enjoy'd,
　　　　For ever panting, and for ever young;
All breathing human passion far above,
　　That leaves a heart high-sorrowful and cloy'd,
　　　　A burning forehead, and a parching tongue.

Who are these coming to the sacrifice?
　　To what green altar, O mysterious priest,
Lead'st thou that heifer lowing at the skies,
　　And all her silken flanks with garlands drest?
What little town by river or sea shore,
　　Or mountain-built with peaceful citadel,
　　　　Is emptied of this folk, this pious morn?
And, little town, thy streets for evermore
　　Will silent be; and not a soul to tell
　　　　Why thou art desolate, can e'er return.

O Attic shape! Fair attitude! with brede
　　Of marble men and maidens overwrought,
With forest branches and the trodden weed;
　　Thou, silent form, dost tease us out of thought
As doth eternity: Cold Pastoral!
　　When old age shall this generation waste,

    Thou shalt remain, in midst of other woe
Than ours, a friend to man, to whom thou say'st,
    "Beauty is truth, truth beauty,—that is all
        Ye know on earth, and all ye need to know."

ODE TO A NIGHTINGALE

MY HEART aches, and a drowsy numbness pains
   My sense, as though of hemlock I had drunk,
Or emptied some dull opiate to the drains
   One minute past, and Lethe-wards had sunk:
'Tis not through envy of thy happy lot,
   But being too happy in thine happiness,—
      That thou, light-winged Dryad of the trees
        In some melodious plot
   Of beechen green, and shadows numberless,
      Singest of summer in full-throated ease.

O, for a draught of vintage! that hath been
   Cool'd a long age in the deep-delved earth,
Tasting of Flora and the country green,
   Dance, and Provençal song, and sunburnt mirth!
O for a beaker full of the warm South,
   Full of the true, the blushful Hippocrene,
      With beaded bubbles winking at the brim,
        And purple-stained mouth;
   That I might drink, and leave the world unseen,
      And with thee fade away into the forest dim:

Fade far away, dissolve, and quite forget
   What thou among the leaves hast never known,
The weariness, the fever, and the fret
   Here, where men sit and hear each other groan;
Where palsy shakes a few, sad, last gray hairs,
   Where youth grows pale, and spectre-thin, and dies;
      Where but to think is to be full of sorrow

        And leaden-eyed despairs,
    Where Beauty cannot keep her lustrous eyes,
        Or new Love pine at them beyond to-morrow.

Away! away! for I will fly to thee,
    Not charioted by Bacchus and his pards,
But on the viewless wings of Poesy,
    Though the dull brain perplexes and retards:
Already with thee! tender is the night,
    And haply the Queen-Moon is on her throne,
        Cluster'd around by all her starry Fays;
            But here there is no light,
    Save what from heaven is with the breezes blown
        Through verdurous glooms and winding mossy ways.

I cannot see what flowers are at my feet,
    Nor what soft incense hangs upon the boughs,
But, in embalmed darkness, guess each sweet
    Wherewith the seasonable month endows
The grass, the thicket, and the fruit-tree wild;
    White hawthorn, and the pastoral eglantine;
        Fast fading violets cover'd up in leaves;
            And mid-May's eldest child,
    The coming musk-rose, full of dewy wine,
        The murmurous haunt of flies on summer eves.

Darkling I listen; and, for many a time
    I have been half in love with easeful Death,
Call'd him soft names in many a mused rhyme,
    To take into the air my quiet breath;
        Now more than ever seems it rich to die,
    To cease upon the midnight with no pain,
        While thou art pouring forth thy soul abroad
            In such an ecstasy!
    Still wouldst thou sing, and I have ears in vain—
        To thy high requiem become a sod.

Thou wast not born for death, immortal Bird!
    No hungry generations tread thee down;

The voice I hear this passing night was heard
   In ancient days by emperor and clown:
Perhaps the self-same song that found a path
     Through the sad heart of Ruth, when, sick for home,
         She stood in tears amid the alien corn;
            The same that oft-times hath
    Charm'd magic casements, opening on the foam
       Of perilous seas, in faery lands forlorn.

Forlorn! the very word is like a bell
   To toll me back from thee to my sole self!
Adieu! the fancy cannot cheat so well
   As she is fam'd to do, deceiving elf.
Adieu! adieu! thy plaintive anthem fades
    Past the near meadows, over the still stream,
        Up the hill-side; and now 'tis buried deep
          In the next valley-glades:
   Was it a vision, or a waking dream?
       Fled is that music:—Do I wake or sleep?

ON FIRST LOOKING INTO CHAPMAN'S HOMER

MUCH HAVE I travell'd in the realms of gold,
And many goodly states and kingdoms seen;
Round many western islands have I been
Which bards in fealty to Apollo hold.
Oft of one wide expanse had I been told
That deep-brow'd Homer ruled as his demesne;
Yet did I never breathe its pure serene
Till I heard Chapman speak out loud and bold:
Then felt I like some watcher of the skies
When a new planet swims into his ken;
Or like stout Cortez when with eagle eyes
He star'd at the Pacific—and all his men
Look'd at each other with a wild surmise—

Silent, upon a peak in Darien.

Thomas Babington Macaulay

HORATIUS AT THE BRIDGE

A Lay Made About the Year of the City CCCLX.

I

Lars Porsena of Clusium
   By the Nine Gods he swore
That the great house of Tarquin
   Should suffer wrong no more.
By the Nine Gods he swore it,
   And named a trysting day,
And bade his messengers ride forth
East and west and south and north.
   To summon his array.

II

East and west and south and north
   The messengers ride fast.
And tower and town and cottage
   Have heard the trumpet's blast.
Shame on the false Etruscan
   Who lingers in his home.
When Porsena of Clusium
   Is on the march for Rome.

III

The horsemen and the footmen
   Are pouring in amain
From many a stately market-place;
   From many a fruitful plain;

From many a lonely hamlet,
    Which, hid by beech and pine.
Like an eagle's nest, hangs on the crest
    Of purple Apennine;

IV

From lordly Volaterræ
    Where scowls the far-famed hold
Piled by the hands of giants
    For godlike kings of old;
From seagirt Populonia,
    Whose sentinels descry
Sardinia's snowy mountain-tops
    Fringing the southern sky;

V

From the proud mart of Pisæ
    Queen of the western waves.
Where ride Massilia's triremes
    Heavy with fair-haired slaves;
From where sweet Clanis wanders
    Through corn and vines and flowers;
From where Cortona lifts to heaven
    Her diadem of towers.

VI

Tall are the oaks whose acorns
    Drop in dark Auser's rill;
Fat are the stags that champ the boughs
    Of the Ciminian hill;
Beyond all streams Clitumnus
    Is to the herdsman dear;
Best of all pools the fowler loves
    The great Volsinian mere.

VII

But now no stroke of woodman
   Is heard by Auser's rill;
No hunter tracks the stag's green path
   Up the Ciminian hill;
Unwatched along Clitumnus
   Grazes the milk-white steer;
Unharmed the waterfowl may dip
   In the Volsinian mere.

VIII

The harvests of Arretium,
   This year, old men shall reap;
This year, young boys in Umbro
   Shall plunge the struggling sheep;
And in the vats of Luna,
   This year, the must shall foam
Round the white feet of laughing girls
   Whose sires have marched to Rome.

IX

There be thirty chosen prophets,
   The wisest of the land.
Who alway by Lars Porsena
   Both morn and evening stand:
Evening and morn the Thirty
   Have turned the verses o'er,
Traced from the right on linen white
   By mighty seers of yore.

X

And with one voice the Thirty
   Have their glad answer given:
"Go forth, go forth, Lars Porsena;

Go forth, beloved of Heaven:
Go, and return in glory
    To Clusium's royal dome;
And hang round Nurscia's altars
    The golden shields of Rome."

XI

And now hath every city
    Sent up her tale of men:
The foot are fourscore thousand.
    The horse are thousands ten.
Before the gates of Sutrium
    Is met the great array.
A proud man was Lars Porsena
    Upon the trysting day.

XII

For all the Etruscan armies
    Were ranged beneath his eye,
And many a banished Roman,
    And many a stout ally;
And with a mighty following
    To join the muster came
The Tusculan Mamilius,
    Prince of the Latian name.

XIII

But by the yellow Tiber
    Was tumult and affright;
From all the spacious champaign
    To Rome men took their flight.
A mile around the city,
    The throng stopped up the ways;
A fearful sight it was to see
    Through two long nights and days.

XIV

For aged folks on crutches,
    And women great with child,
And mothers sobbing over babes
    That clung to them and smiled,
And sick men borne in litters
    High on the necks of slaves
And troops of sunburnt husbandmen
    With reaping-hooks and staves.

XV

And droves of mules and asses
    Laden with skins of wine,
And endless flocks of goats and sheep,
    And endless herds of kine,
And endless trains of wagons
    That creaked beneath the weight
Of corn-sacks and of household goods,
    Choked every roaring gate.

XVI

Now, from the rock Tarpeian,
    Could the wan burghers spy
The line of blazing villages
    Red in the midnight sky.
The Fathers of the City,
    They sat all night and day,
For every hour some horseman came
    With tidings of dismay.

XVII

To eastward and to westward
    Have spread the Tuscan bands;
Nor house nor fence nor dovecote

In Crustumerium stands.
Verbenna down to Ostia
   Hath wasted all the plain;
Astur hath stormed Janiculum,
   And the stout guards are slain.

XVIII

Iwis, in all the Senate,
   There was no heart so bold,
But sore it ached, and fast it beat,
   When that ill news was told.
Forthwith up rose the Consul,
   Up rose the Fathers all;
In haste they girded up their gowns,
   And hied them to the wall.

XIX

They held a council standing
   Before the River-Gate;
Short time was there, ye well may guess,
   For musing or debate.
Out spake the Consul roundly:
   "The bridge must straight go down;
For since Janiculum is lost,
   Naught else can save the town."

XX

Just then, a scout came flying,
   All wild with haste and fear:
"To arms! To arms, Sir Consul:
   Lars Porsena is here!"
On the low hills to westward
   The Consul fixed his eye,
And saw the swarthy storm of dust
   Rise fast along the sky.

XXI

And nearer fast and nearer
  Doth the red whirlwind come;
And louder still and still more loud,
From underneath that whirling cloud,
Is heard the trumpet's war-note proud,
  The trampling and the hum.
And plainly and more plainly
  Now through the gloom appears,
Far to left and far to right,
In broken gleams of dark-blue light,
The long array of helmets bright,
  The long array of spears.

XXII

And plainly and more plainly,
  Above that glimmering line,
Now might ye see the banners
  Of twelve fair cities shine;
But the banner of proud Clusium
  Was highest of them all,
The terror of the Umbrian;
  The terror of the Gaul.

XXIII

And plainly and more plainly
  Now might the burghers know,
By port and vest, by horse and crest,
  Each warlike Lucumo.
There Cilnius of Arretium
  On his fleet roan was seen;
And Astur of the four-fold shield,
Girt with the brand none else may wield,
Tolumnius with the belt of gold,

And dark Verbenna from the hold
   By reedy Thrasymene.

XXIV

Fast by the royal standard,
   O'erlooking all the war,
Lars Porsena of Clusium
   Sat in his ivory car.
By the right wheel rode Mamilius,
   Prince of the Latian name;
And by the left false Sextus,
   That wrought the deed of shame.

XXV

But when the face of Sextus
   Was seen among the foes,
A yell that rent the firmament
   From all the town arose.
On the house-tops was no woman
   But spat toward him and hissed,
No child but screamed out curses,
   And shook its little first.

XXVI

But the Consul's brow was sad,
   And the Consul's speech was low,
And darkly looked he at the wall,
   And darkly at the foe.
"Their van will be upon us
   Before the bridge goes down;
And if they once might win the bridge,
   What hope to save the town?"

XXVII

Then out spoke brave Horatius,
    The Captain of the Gate;
"To every man upon this earth
    Death cometh soon or late.
And how can man die better
    Than facing fearful odds,
For the ashes of his fathers,
    And the temples of his Gods.

XXVIII

"And for the tender mother
    Who dandled him to rest,
And for the wife who nurses
    His baby at her breast,
And for the holy maidens
    Who feed the eternal flame,
To save them from false Sextus
    That wrought the deed of shame?

XXIX

"Hew down the bridge, Sir Consul,
    With all the speed ye may;
I, with two more to help me,
    Will hold the foe in play.
In yon strait path a thousand
    May well be stopped by three.
Now, who will stand on either hand
    And keep the bridge with me?"

XXX

Then out spake Spurius Lartius;
    A Ramnian proud was he:
"Lo, I will stand at thy right hand,

And keep the bridge with thee."
And out spake strong Herminius;
   Of Titian blood was he:
"I will abide on thy left side,
   And keep the bridge with thee."

XXXI

"Horatius," quoth the Consul,
   "As thou sayest, so let it be."
And straight against that great array
   Forth went the dauntless Three.
For Romans in Rome's quarrel
   Spared neither land nor gold,
Nor son nor wife, nor limb nor life,
   In the brave days of old.

XXXII

Then none was for a party;
   Then all were for the state;
Then the great man helped the poor,
   And the poor man loved the great.
Then lands were fairly portioned;
   Then spoils were fairly sold:
The Romans were like brothers
   In the brave days of old.

XXXIII

Now Roman is to Roman
   More hateful than a foe,
And the Tribunes beard the high,
   And the Fathers grind the low.
As we wax hot in faction,
   In battle we wax cold:
Wherefore men fight not as they fought
   In the brave days of old.

XXXIV

Now while the Three were tightening
    Their harness on their backs,
The Consul was the foremost man
    To take in hand an axe:
And Fathers mixed with Commons
    Seized hatchet, bar, and crow,
And smote upon the planks above,
    And loosed the props below.

XXXV

Meanwhile the Tuscan army,
    Right glorious to behold,
Came flashing back the noonday light,
Rank behind rank, like surges bright
    Of a broad sea of gold.
Four hundred trumpets sounded
    A peal of warlike glee,
As that great host, with measured tread,
And spears advanced, and ensigns spread,
Rolled slowly towards the bridge's head,
    Where stood the dauntless Three.

XXXVI

The Three stood calm and silent,
    And looked upon the foes,
And a great shout of laughter
    From all the vanguard rose;
And forth three chiefs came spurring
    Before that deep array;
To earth they sprang, their swords they drew,
And lifted high their shields, and flew
    To win the narrow way.

XXXVII

Aunus from green Tifernum,
    Lord of the Hill of Vines;
And Seius, whose eight hundred slaves
    Sicken in Ilva's mines;
And Picus, long to Clusium
    Vassal in peace and war,
Who led to fight his Umbrian powers
From that grey crag where, girt with towers,
The fortress of Nequinum lowers
    O'er the pale waves of Nar.

XXXVIII

Stout Lartius hurled down Aunus
    Into the stream beneath:
Herminius struck at Seius,
    And clove him to the teeth:
At Picus brave Horatius
    Darted one fiery thrust;
And the proud Umbrian's gilded arms
    Clashed in the bloody dust.

XXXIX

Then Ocnus of Falerii
    Rushed on the Roman Three;
And Lausulus of Urgo,
    The rover of the sea;
    And Aruns of Volsinium,
    Who slew the great wild boar,
The great wild boar that had his den
Amidst the reeds of Cosa's fen,
And wasted fields, and slaughtered men,
    Along Albinia's shore.

XL

Herminius smote down Aruns;
    Lartius laid Ocnus low:
Right to the heart of Lausulus
    Horatius sent a blow.
"Lie there," he cried, "fell pirate!
    No more, aghast and pale,
From Ostia's walls the crowd shall mark
The track of thy destroying bark.
No more Campania's hinds shall fly
To woods and caverns when they spy
    Thy thrice-accursed sail."

XLI

But now no sound of laughter
    Was heard among the foes.
A wild and wrathful clamour
    From all the vanguard rose.
Six spears' lengths from the entrance
    Halted that deep array,
And for a space no man came forth
    To win the narrow way.

XLII

But hark! the cry is Astur:
    And lo! the ranks divide;
And the great Lord of Luna
    Comes with his stately stride.
Upon his ample shoulders
    Clangs loud the fourfold shield,
And in his hand he shakes the brand
    Which none but he can wield.

XLIII

He smiled on those bold Romans
    A smile serene and high;
He eyed the flinching Tuscans,
    And scorn was in his eye.
Quoth he, "The she-wolf's litter
    Stand savagely at bay:
But will ye dare to follow,
    If Astur clears the way?"

XLIV

Then, whirling up his broadsword
    With both hands to the height,
He rushed against Horatius
    And smote with all his might.
With shield and blade Horatius
    Right deftly turned the blow.
The blow, yet turned, came yet too nigh;
It missed his helm, but gashed his thigh:
The Tuscans raised a joyful cry
    To see the red blood flow.

XLV

He reeled, and on Herminius
    He leaned one breathing-space;
Then, like a wild-cat mad with wounds,
    Sprang right at Astur's face.
Through teeth, and skull, and helmet
    So fierce a thrust he sped,
The good sword stood a handbreadth out
    Behind the Tuscan's head.

XLVI

And the great Lord of Luna

Fell at that deadly stroke,
As falls on Mount Alvernus
   A thunder-smitten oak.
Far o'er the crashing forest
   The giant arms lay spread;
And the pale augurs, muttering low,
   Gaze on the blasted head.

XLVII

On Astur's throat Horatius
   Right firmly pressed his heel,
And thrice and four times tugged amain,
   Ere he wrenched out the steel.
"And see," he cried, "the welcome,
   Fair guests, that waits you here!
What noble Lucumo comes next
   To taste our Roman cheer?"

XLVIII

But at his haughty challenge
   A sullen murmur ran,
Mingled of wrath, and shame, and dread,
   Along that glittering van.
There lacked not men of prowess,
   Nor men of lordly race;
For all Etruria's noblest
   Were round the fatal place.

XLIX

But all Etruria's noblest
   Felt their hearts sink to see
On the earth the bloody corpses,
   In their path the dauntless Three;
And, from the ghastly entrance
   Where those bold Romans stood,

All shrank, like boys who unaware,
Ranging the woods to start a hare,
Come to the mouth of a dark lair
Where, growling low, a fierce old bear
    Lies amidst bones and blood.

L

Was none who would be foremost
    To lead such dire attack?
But those behind cried "Forward!"
    And those before cried "Back!"
And backward now and forward
    Wavers the deep array;
And on the tossing sea of steel,
To and fro the standards reel;
And the victorious trumpet-peal
    Dies fitfully away.

LI

Yet one man for one moment
    Stood out before the crowd;
Well known was he to all the Three,
    And they gave him greeting loud.
"Now welcome, welcome, Sextus!
    Now welcome to thy home!
Why dost thou stay, and turn away?
    Here lies the road to Rome."

LII

Thrice looked he at the city;
    Thrice looked he at the dead;
And thrice came on in fury,
    And thrice turned back in dread:
And, white with fear and hatred,
    Scowled at the narrow way

Where, wallowing in a pool of blood,
    The bravest Tuscans lay.

LIII

But meanwhile axe and lever
    Have manfully been plied;
And now the bridge hangs tottering
    Above the boiling tide.
"Come back, come back, Horatius!"
    Loud cried the Fathers all.
"Back, Lartius! Back, Herminius!
    Back, ere the ruin fall!"

LIV

Back darted Spurius Lartius;
    Herminius darted back:
And as they passed, beneath their feet
    They felt the timbers crack.
But when they turned their faces,
    And on the further shore
Saw brave Horatius stand alone,
    They would have crossed once more.

LV

But with a crash like thunder
    Fell every loosened beam,
And, like a dam, the mighty wreck
    Lay right athwart the stream;
And a loud shout of triumph
    Rose from the walls of Rome,
As to the highest turret-tops
    Was splashed the yellow foam.

LVI

And, like a horse unbroken
    When first he feels the rein,
The furious river struggled hard,
    And tossed his tawny mane,
And burst the curb, and bounded,
    Rejoicing to be free,
And whirling down, in fierce career,
Battlement, and plank, and pier
    Rushed headlong to the sea.

LVII

Alone stood brave Horatius,
    But constant still in mind;
Thrice thirty thousand foes before,
    And the broad flood behind.
"Down with him!" cried false Sextus,
    With a smile on his pale face.
"Now yield thee", cried Lars Porsena,
    "Now yield thee to our grace."

LVIII

Round turned he, as not deigning
    Those craven ranks to see;
Nought spake he to Lars Porsena,
    To Sextus nought spake he;
But he saw on Palatinus
    The white porch of his home;
And he spake to the noble river
    That rolls by the towers of Rome.

LIX

"Oh Tiber, father Tiber!
    To whom the Romans pray,

A Roman's life, a Roman's arms,
  Take thou in charge this day!"
So he spake, and speaking sheathed
  The good sword by his side,
And, with his harness on his back,
  Plunged headlong in the tide.

LX

No sound of joy or sorrow
  Was heard from either bank;
But friends and foes in dumb surprise,
With parted lips and straining eyes,
  Stood gazing where he sank;
And when above the surges
  They saw his crest appear,
All Rome sent forth a rapturous cry,
And even the ranks of Tuscany
  Could scarce forbear to cheer.

LXI

But fiercely ran the current,
  Swollen high by months of rain:
And fast his blood was flowing,
  And he was sore in pain,
And heavy with his armour,
  And spent with changing blows:
And oft they thought him sinking,
  But still again he rose.

LXII

Never, I ween, did swimmer,
  In such an evil case,
Struggle through such a raging flood
  Safe to the landing place:
But his limbs were borne up bravely

By the brave heart within,
And our good father Tiber
   Bore bravely up his chin

LXIII

"Curse on him!" quoth false Sextus,
   "Will not the villain drown?
But for this stay, ere close of day
   We would have sacked the town!"
"Heaven help him!" quoth Lars Porsena,
   "And bring him safe to shore;
For such a gallant feat of arms
   Was never seen before."

LXIV

And now he feels the bottom;
   Now on dry earth he stands;
Now round him throng the Fathers
   To press his gory hands;
And now, with shouts and clapping,
   And noise of weeping loud,
He enters through the River-Gate,
   Borne by the joyous crowd.

LXV

They gave him of the corn-land,
   That was of public right,
As much as two strong oxen
   Could plough from morn till night;
And they made a molten image,
   And set it up on high,
And there it stands unto this day
   To witness if I lie.

LXVI

It stands in the Comitium,
    Plain for all folk to see;
Horatius in his harness,
    Halting upon one knee:
And underneath is written,
    In letters all of gold,
How valiantly he kept the bridge
    In the brave days of old.

LXVII

And still his name sounds stirring
    Unto the men of Rome,
As the trumpet-blast that calls to them
    To charge the Volscian home;
And wives still pray to Juno
    For boys with hearts as bold
As his who kept the bridge so well
    In the brave days of old.

LXVIII

And in the nights of winter,
    When the cold north winds blow,
And the long howling of the wolves
    Is heard amidst the snow;
When round the lonely cottage
    Roars loud the tempest's din,
And the good logs of Algidus
    Roar louder yet within;

LXIX

When the oldest cask is opened,
    And the largest lamp is lit;
When the chestnuts glow in the embers,

And the kid turns on the spit;
When young and old in circle
    Around the firebrands close;
When the girls are weaving baskets,
    And the lads are shaping bows;

LXX

When the goodman mends his armour,
    And trims his helmet's plume;
And the goodwife's shuttle merrily
    Goes flashing through the loom,—
With weeping and with laughter
    Still is the story told,
How well Horatius kept the bridge
    In the brave days of old.

Henry Wadsworth Longfellow

A PSALM OF LIFE

What The Heart Of The Young Man Said To The Psalmist.

TELL ME not, in mournful numbers,
    Life is but an empty dream!
For the soul is dead that slumbers,
    And things are not what they seem.

Life is real! Life is earnest!
    And the grave is not its goal;
Dust thou art, to dust returnest,
    Was not spoken of the soul.

Not enjoyment, and not sorrow,
    Is our destined end or way;
But to act, that each to-morrow

Find us farther than to-day.

Art is long, and Time is fleeting,
    And our hearts, though stout and brave,
Still, like muffled drums, are beating
    Funeral marches to the grave.

In the world's broad field of battle,
    In the bivouac of Life,
Be not like dumb, driven cattle!
    Be a hero in the strife!

Trust no Future, howe'er pleasant!
    Let the dead Past bury its dead!
Act,— act in the living Present!
    Heart within, and God o'erhead!

Lives of great men all remind us
    We can make our lives sublime,
And, departing, leave behind us
    Footprints on the sands of time;

Footprints, that perhaps another,
    Sailing o'er life's solemn main,
A forlorn and shipwrecked brother,
    Seeing, shall take heart again.

Let us, then, be up and doing,
    With a heart for any fate;
Still achieving, still pursuing,
    Learn to labor and to wait.

From EVANGELINE, A TALE OF ACADIE

Prelude

This is the forest primeval. The murmuring pines and the hemlocks,
Bearded with moss, and in garments green, indistinct in the twilight,
Stand like Druids of eld, with voices sad and prophetic,
Stand like harpers hoar, with beards that rest on their bosoms.
Loud from its rocky caverns, the deep-voiced neighboring ocean
Speaks, and in accents disconsolate answers the wail of the forest.

This is the forest primeval; but where are the hearts that beneath it
Leaped like the roe, when he hears in the woodland the voice of the
   huntsman.
Where is the thatch-roofed village, the home of Acadian farmers,
Men whose lives glided on like rivers that water the woodlands,
Darkened by shadows of earth, but reflecting an image of heaven?
Waste are those pleasant farms, and the farmers forever departed!
Scattered like dust and leaves, when the mighty blasts of October
Seize them, and whirl them aloft, and sprinkle them far o'er the ocean
Naught but tradition remains of the beautiful village of Grand-Pré.

Ye who believe in affection that hopes, and endures, and is patient,
Ye who believe in the beauty and strength of woman's devotion,

List to the mournful tradition still sung by the pines of the forest;
List to a Tale of Love in Acadie, home of the happy.

Part the First

Canto I

In the Acadian land, on the shores of the Basin of Minas,
Distant, secluded, still, the little village of Grand-Pré
Lay in the fruitful valley. Vast meadows stretched to the eastward,
Giving the village its name, and pasture to flocks without number.
Dikes, that the hands of the farmers had raised with labor incessant,
Shut out the turbulent tides; but at stated seasons the flood-gates
Opened, and welcomed the sea to wander at will o'er the meadows.
West and south there were fields of flax, and orchards and cornfields
Spreading afar and unfenced o'er the plain; and away to the northward
Blomidon rose, and the forests old, and aloft on the mountains
Sea-fogs pitched their tents, and mists from the mighty Atlantic
Looked on the happy valley, but ne'er from their station descended
There, in the midst of its farms, reposed the Acadian village.
Strongly built were the houses, with frames of oak and of hemlock,
Such as the peasants of Normandy built in the reign of the Henries.
Thatched were the roofs, with dormer-windows; and gables projecting
Over the basement below protected and shaded the doorway.
There in the tranquil evenings of summer, when brightly the sunset

Lighted the village street and gilded the vanes on the chimneys,
Matrons and maidens sat in snow-white caps and in kirtles
Scarlet and blue and green, with distaffs spinning the golden
Flax for the gossiping looms, whose noisy shuttles within doors
Mingled their sound with the whir of the wheels and the songs of the
maidens,
Solemnly down the street came the parish priest, and the children
Paused in their play to kiss the hand he extended to bless them.
Reverend walked he among them; and up rose matrons and maidens,
Hailing his slow approach with words of affectionate welcome.
Then came the laborers home from the field, and serenely the sun sank
Down to his rest, and twilight prevailed. Anon from the belfry
Softly the Angelus sounded, and over the roofs of the village
Columns of pale blue smoke, like clouds of incense ascending,
Rose from a hundred hearths, the homes of peace and contentment.
Thus dwelt together in love these simple Acadian farmers,—
Dwelt in the love of God and of man. Alike were they free from
Fear, that reigns with the tyrant, and envy, the vice of republics.
Neither locks had they to their doors, nor bars to their windows;
But their dwellings were open as day and the hearts of their owners;
There the richest was poor, and the poorest lived in abundance.

Somewhat apart from the village, and nearer the Basin of Minas,
Benedict Bellefontaine, the wealthiest farmer of Grand-Pré,

Dwelt on his goodly acres: and with him, directing his household,
Gentle Evangeline lived, his child, and the pride of the village.
Stalworth and stately in form was the man of seventy winters;
Hearty and hale was he, an oak that is covered with snow-flakes;
White as the snow were his locks, and his cheeks as brown as the oak-leaves.
Fair was she to behold, that maiden of seventeen summers.
Black were her eyes as the berry that grows on the thorn by the wayside,
Black, yet how softly they gleamed beneath the brown shade of her tresses!
Sweet was her breath as the breath of kine that feed in the meadows.
When in the harvest heat she bore to the reapers at noontide
Flagons of home-brewed ale, ah! fair in sooth was the maiden,
Fairer was she when, on Sunday morn, while the bell from its turret
Sprinkled with holy sounds the air, as the priest with his hyssop
Sprinkles the congregation, and scatters blessings upon them,
Down the long street she passed, with her chaplet of beads and her missal,
Wearing her Norman cap and her kirtle of blue, and the ear-rings,
Brought in the olden time from France, and since, as an heirloom,
Handed down from mother to child, through long generations.
But a celestial brightness—a more ethereal beauty—
Shone on her face and encircled her form, when, after confession,
Homeward serenely she walked with God's benediction upon her.

When she had passed, it seemed like the ceasing of exquisite music.

Firmly built with rafters of oak, the house of the farmer
Stood on the side of a hill commanding the sea; and a shady
Sycamore grew by the door, with a woodbine wreathing around it.
Rudely carved was the porch, with seats beneath; and a footpath
Led through an orchard wide, and disappeared in the meadow.
Under the Sycamore-tree were hives overhung by a penthouse,
Such as the traveller sees in regions remote by the roadside,
Built o'er a box for the poor, or the blessed image of Mary.
Farther down, on the slope of the hill, was the well with its moss-grown
Bucket, fastened with iron, and near it a trough for the horses.
Shielding the house from storms, on the north, were the barns and the
   farm-yard,
There stood the broad-wheeled wains and the antique ploughs and the
   harrows;
There were the folds for the sheep; and there, in his feathered seraglio,
Strutted the lordly turkey, and crowed the cock, with the selfsame
Voice that in ages of old had startled the penitent Peter.
Bursting with hay were the barns, themselves a village. In each one
Far o'er the gable projected a roof of thatch; and a staircase,
Under the sheltering eaves, led up to the odorous corn-loft.
There too the dove-cot stood, with its meek and innocent inmates
Murmuring ever of love; while above in the variant breezes
Numberless noisy weathercocks rattled and sang of mutation.

Thus, at peace with God and the world, the farmer of Grand-Pré

Lived on his sunny farm, and Evangeline governed his
  household.
Many a youth, as he knelt in the church and opened his
  missal,
Fixed his eyes upon her as the saint of his deepest devotion;
Happy was he who might touch her hand or the hem of her
  garment!
Many a suitor came to her door, by the darkness befriended,
And, as he knocked and waited to hear the sound of her
  footsteps,
Knew not which beat the louder, his heart or the knocker of
  iron;
Or at the joyous feast of the Patron Saint of the village,
Bolder grew, and pressed her hand in the dance as he
  whispered
Hurried words of love, that seemed a part of the music.
But, among all who came, young Gabriel only was welcome;
Gabriel Lajeunesse, the son of Basil the blacksmith,
Who was a mighty man in the village, and honored of all
  men;
For, since the birth of time, throughout all ages and nations,
Has the craft of the smith been held in repute by the people.
Basil was Benedict's friend. Their children from earliest
  childhood
Grew up together as brother and sister; and Father Felician,
Priest and pedagogue both in the village, had taught them
  their letters
Out of the selfsame book, with the hymns of the church and
  the plain-
    song.
But when the hymn was sung, and the daily lesson completed,
Swiftly they hurried away to the forge of Basil the blacksmith.
There at the door they stood, with wondering eyes to behold
  him
Take in his leathern lap the hoof of the horse as a plaything,
Nailing the shoe in its place; while near him the tire of the
  cart-wheel
Lay like a fiery snake, coiled round in a circle of cinders.

Oft on autumnal eves, when without in the gathering darkness
Bursting with light seemed the smithy, through every cranny and crevice,
Warm by the forge within they watched the laboring bellows,
And as its panting ceased, and the sparks expired in the ashes,
Merrily laughed, and said they were nuns going into the chapel.
Oft on sledges in winter, as swift as the swoop of the eagle,
Down the hillside hounding, they glided away o'er the meadow.
Oft in the barns they climbed to the populous nests on the rafters,
Seeking with eager eyes that wondrous stone, which the swallow
Brings from the shore of the sea to restore the sight of its fledglings;
Lucky was he who found that stone in the nest of the swallow!
Thus passed a few swift years, and they no longer were children.
He was a valiant youth, and his face, like the face of the morning,
Gladdened the earth with its light, and ripened thought into action.
She was a woman now, with the heart and hopes of a woman.
"Sunshine of Saint Eulalie" was she called; for that was the sunshine
Which, as the farmers believed, would load their orchards with apples
She, too, would bring to her husband's house delight and abundance,
Filling it full of love and the ruddy faces of children.

THE LANDLORD'S TALE: PAUL REVERE'S RIDE

LISTEN, my children, and you shall hear
Of the midnight ride of Paul Revere,
On the eighteenth of April, in Seventy-five;
Hardly a man is now alive
Who remembers that famous day and year.

He said to his friend, "If the British march
By land or sea from the town to-night,
Hang a lantern aloft in the belfry arch
Of the North Church tower as a signal light,—
One, if by land, and two, if by sea;
And I on the opposite shore will be,
Ready to ride and spread the alarm
Through every Middlesex village and farm,
For the country folk to be up and to arm."
Then he said, "Good night!" and with muffled oar
Silently rowed to the Charlestown shore,
Just as the moon rose over the bay,
Where swinging wide at her moorings lay
The Somerset, British man-of-war;
A phantom ship, with each mast and spar
Across the moon like a prison bar,
And a huge black hulk, that was magnified
By its own reflection in the tide.

Meanwhile, his friend, through alley and street,
Wanders and watches with eager ears,
Till in the silence around him he hears
The muster of men at the barrack door,
The sound of arms, and the tramp of feet,
And the measured tread of the grenadiers,
Marching down to their boats on the shore.

Then he climbed the tower of the Old North Church,
By the wooden stairs, with stealthy tread,

To the belfry-chamber overhead,
And startled the pigeons from their perch
On the sombre rafters, that round him made
Masses and moving shapes of shade, —
By the trembling ladder, steep and tall,
To the highest window in the wall,
Where he paused to listen and look down
A moment on the roofs of the town,
And the moonlight flowing over all.
Beneath, in the churchyard, lay the dead,
In their night-encampment on the hill,
Wrapped in silence so deep and still
That he could hear, like a sentinel's tread,
The watchful night-wind, as it went
Creeping along from tent to tent,
And seeming to whisper, "All is well!"
A moment only he feels the spell
Of the place and the hour, and the secret dread
Of the lonely belfry and the dead;
For suddenly all his thoughts are bent
On a shadowy something far away,
Where the river widens to meet the bay, —
A line of black that bends and floats
On the rising tide, like a bridge of boats.

Meanwhile, impatient to mount and ride,
Booted and spurred, with a heavy stride
On the opposite shore walked Paul Revere.
Now he patted his horse's side,
Now gazed at the landscape far and near,
Then, impetuous, stamped the earth,
And turned and tightened his saddle girth;
But mostly he watched with eager search
The belfry-tower of the Old North Church,
As it rose above the graves on the hill,
Lonely and spectral and sombre and still.
And lo! as he looks, on the belfry's height

A glimmer, and then a gleam of light!
He springs to the saddle, the bridle he turns,
But lingers and gazes, till full on his sight
A second lamp in the belfry burns!
A hurry of hoofs in a village street,
A shape in the moonlight, a bulk in the dark,
And beneath, from the pebbles, in passing, a spark
Struck out by a steed flying fearless and fleet:
That was all! And yet, through the gloom and the light,
The fate of a nation was riding that night;
And the spark struck out by that steed, in his flight,
Kindled the land into flame with its heat.
He has left the village and mounted the steep,
And beneath him, tranquil and broad and deep,
Is the Mystic, meeting the ocean tides;
And under the alders, that skirt its edge,
Now soft on the sand, now loud on the ledge,
Is heard the tramp of his steed as he rides.

It was twelve by the village clock,
When he crossed the bridge into Medford town.
He heard the crowing of the cock,
And the barking of the farmer's dog,
And felt the damp of the river fog,
That rises after the sun goes down.

It was one by the village clock,
When he galloped into Lexington.
He saw the gilded weathercock
Swim in the moonlight as he passed,
And the meeting-house windows, blank and bare,
Gaze at him with a spectral glare,
As if they already stood aghast
At the bloody work they would look upon.

It was two by the village clock,
When he came to the bridge in Concord town.
He heard the bleating of the flock,

And the twitter of birds among the trees,
And felt the breath of the morning breeze
Blowing over the meadows brown.
And one was safe and asleep in his bed
Who at the bridge would be first to fall,
Who that day would be lying dead,
Pierced by a British musket-ball.

You know the rest. In the books you have read,
How the British Regulars fired and fled, —
How the farmers gave them ball for ball,
From behind each fence and farm-yard wall,
Chasing the red-coats down the lane,
Then crossing the fields to emerge again
Under the trees at the turn of the road,
And only pausing to fire and load.

So through the night rode Paul Revere;
And so through the night went his cry of alarm
To every Middlesex village and farm, —
A cry of defiance and not of fear,
A voice in the darkness, a knock at the door,
And a word that shall echo forevermore!
For, borne on the night-wind of the Past,
Through all our history, to the last,
In the hour of darkness and peril and need,
The people will waken and listen to hear
The hurrying hoof-beats of that steed,
And the midnight message of Paul Revere.

Edgar Allen Poe

ANNABEL LEE

It was many and many a year ago,
    In a kingdom by the sea,
That a maiden there lived whom you may know
    By the name of Annabel Lee;
And this maiden she lived with no other thought
    Than to love and be loved by me.

I was a child and *she* was a child,
    In this kingdom by the sea,
But we loved with a love that was more than love—
    I and my Annabel Lee—
With a love that the wingèd seraphs of Heaven
    Coveted her and me.

And this was the reason that, long ago,
    In this kingdom by the sea,
A wind blew out of a cloud, chilling
    My beautiful Annabel Lee;
So that her highborn kinsmen came
    And bore her away from me,
To shut her up in a sepulchre
    In this kingdom by the sea.

The angels, not half so happy in Heaven,
    Went envying her and me—
Yes!—that was the reason (as all men know,
    In this kingdom by the sea)
That the wind came out of the cloud by night,
    Chilling and killing my Annabel Lee.

But our love it was stronger by far than the love
    Of those who were older than we—
    Of many far wiser than we—
And neither the angels in Heaven above
    Nor the demons down under the sea

Can ever dissever my soul from the soul
  Of the beautiful Annabel Lee;

For the moon never beams, without bringing me dreams
  Of the beautiful Annabel Lee;
And the stars never rise, but I feel the bright eyes
  Of the beautiful Annabel Lee;
And so, all the night-tide, I lie down by the side
  Of my darling—my darling—my life and my bride,
    In her sepulchre there by the sea—
    In her tomb by the sounding sea.

ELDORADO

Gaily bedight,
  A gallant knight,
In sunshine and in shadow,
  Had journeyed long,
  Singing a song,
In search of Eldorado.

  But he grew old—
  This knight so bold—
And o'er his heart a shadow—
  Fell as he found
  No spot of ground
That looked like Eldorado.

  And, as his strength
  Failed him at length,
He met a pilgrim shadow—
  'Shadow,' said he,
  'Where can it be—
This land of Eldorado?'

  'Over the Mountains
  Of the Moon,
Down the Valley of the Shadow,

Ride, boldly ride,'
The shade replied,—
'If you seek for Eldorado!'

THE RAVEN

ONCE UPON a midnight dreary, while I pondered, weak and weary,
Over many a quaint and curious volume of forgotten lore—
　While I nodded, nearly napping, suddenly there came a tapping,
As of some one gently rapping, rapping at my chamber door.
"'Tis some visitor," I muttered, "tapping at my chamber door—
　　Only this and nothing more."

Ah, distinctly I remember it was in the bleak December;
And each separate dying ember wrought its ghost upon the floor.
　Eagerly I wished the morrow;—vainly I had sought to borrow
　From my books surcease of sorrow—sorrow for the lost Lenore—
For the rare and radiant maiden whom the angels name Lenore—
　　Nameless *here* for evermore.

And the silken, sad, uncertain rustling of each purple curtain
Thrilled me—filled me with fantastic terrors never felt before;
　So that now, to still the beating of my heart, I stood repeating
　"'Tis some visitor entreating entrance at my chamber door—
Some late visitor entreating entrance at my chamber door;—
　　This it is and nothing more."

Presently my soul grew stronger; hesitating then no longer,

"Sir," said I, "or Madam, truly your forgiveness I implore;
> But the fact is I was napping, and so gently you came rapping,
> And so faintly you came tapping, tapping at my chamber door,
That I scarce was sure I heard you"—here I opened wide the door;—
> Darkness there and nothing more.

Deep into that darkness peering, long I stood there wondering, fearing,
Doubting, dreaming dreams no mortal ever dared to dream before;
> But the silence was unbroken, and the stillness gave no token,
> And the only word there spoken was the whispered word, "Lenore?"
This I whispered, and an echo murmured back the word, "Lenore!"—
> Merely this and nothing more.

Back into the chamber turning, all my soul within me burning,
Soon again I heard a tapping somewhat louder than before.
> "Surely," said I, "surely that is something at my window lattice;
> Let me see, then, what thereat is, and this mystery explore—
Let my heart be still a moment and this mystery explore;—
> 'Tis the wind and nothing more!"

Open here I flung the shutter, when, with many a flirt and flutter,
In there stepped a stately Raven of the saintly days of yore;
> Not the least obeisance made he; not a minute stopped or stayed he;
> But, with mien of lord or lady, perched above my chamber door—
Perched upon a bust of Pallas just above my chamber door—

Perched, and sat, and nothing more.

Then this ebony bird beguiling my sad fancy into smiling,
By the grave and stern decorum of the countenance it wore,
"Though thy crest be shorn and shaven, thou," I said, "art sure no craven,
Ghastly grim and ancient Raven wandering from the Nightly shore—
Tell me what thy lordly name is on the Night's Plutonian shore!"
    Quoth the Raven "Nevermore."

Much I marvelled this ungainly fowl to hear discourse so plainly,
Though its answer little meaning—little relevancy bore;
  For we cannot help agreeing that no living human being
  Ever yet was blessed with seeing bird above his chamber door—
Bird or beast upon the sculptured bust above his chamber door,
    With such name as "Nevermore."

But the Raven, sitting lonely on the placid bust, spoke only
That one word, as if his soul in that one word he did outpour.
  Nothing farther then he uttered—not a feather then he fluttered—
  Till I scarcely more than muttered "Other friends have flown before—
On the morrow *he* will leave me, as my Hopes have flown before."
    Then the bird said "Nevermore."

Startled at the stillness broken by reply so aptly spoken,
"Doubtless," said I, "what it utters is its only stock and store
  Caught from some unhappy master whom unmerciful Disaster
  Followed fast and followed faster till his songs one burden bore—
Till the dirges of his Hope that melancholy burden bore

Of 'Never—nevermore'."

But the Raven still beguiling all my fancy into smiling,
Straight I wheeled a cushioned seat in front of bird, and bust and door;
Then, upon the velvet sinking, I betook myself to linking
Fancy unto fancy, thinking what this ominous bird of yore—
What this grim, ungainly, ghastly, gaunt, and ominous bird of yore
Meant in croaking "Nevermore."

This I sat engaged in guessing, but no syllable expressing
To the fowl whose fiery eyes now burned into my bosom's core;
This and more I sat divining, with my head at ease reclining
On the cushion's velvet lining that the lamp-light gloated o'er,
But whose velvet-violet lining with the lamp-light gloating o'er,
She shall press, ah, nevermore!

Then, methought, the air grew denser, perfumed from an unseen censer
Swung by Seraphim whose foot-falls tinkled on the tufted floor.
"Wretch," I cried, "thy God hath lent thee—by these angels he hath sent thee
Respite—respite and nepenthe from thy memories of Lenore;
Quaff, oh quaff this kind nepenthe and forget this lost Lenore!"
Quoth the Raven "Nevermore."

"Prophet!" said I, "thing of evil!—prophet still, if bird or devil!—
Whether Tempter sent, or whether tempest tossed thee here ashore,
Desolate yet all undaunted, on this desert land enchanted—

> On this home by Horror haunted—tell me truly, I implore—
Is there—*is* there balm in Gilead?—tell me—tell me, I implore!"
> > Quoth the Raven "Nevermore."

> "Prophet!" said I, "thing of evil!—prophet still, if bird or devil!
By that Heaven that bends above us—by that God we both adore—
> > Tell this soul with sorrow laden if, within the distant Aidenn,
> > It shall clasp a sainted maiden whom the angels name Lenore—
Clasp a rare and radiant maiden whom the angels name Lenore."
> > Quoth the Raven "Nevermore."

> "Be that word our sign of parting, bird or fiend!" I shrieked, upstarting—
"Get thee back into the tempest and the Night's Plutonian shore!
> > Leave no black plume as a token of that lie thy soul hath spoken!
> > Leave my loneliness unbroken!—quit the bust above my door!
Take thy beak from out my heart, and take thy form from off my door!"
> > Quoth the Raven "Nevermore."

> And the Raven, never flitting, still is sitting, *still* is sitting
On the pallid bust of Pallas just above my chamber door;
> > And his eyes have all the seeming of a demon's that is dreaming,
> > And the lamp-light o'er him streaming throws his shadow on the floor;
And my soul from out that shadow that lies floating on the floor
> > Shall be lifted—nevermore!

Alfred, Lord Tennyson

BREAK, BREAK, BREAK

Break, break, break,
   On thy cold gray stones, O Sea!
And I would that my tongue could utter
   The thoughts that arise in me.

O, well for the fisherman's boy,
   That he shouts with his sister at play!
O, well for the sailor lad,
   That he sings in his boat on the bay!

And the stately ships go on
   To their haven under the hill;
But O for the touch of a vanish'd hand,
   And the sound of a voice that is still!

Break, break, break
   At the foot of thy crags, O Sea!
But the tender grace of a day that is dead
   Will never come back to me.

From IN MEMORIAM A. H. H.

XXIII

Now, sometimes in my sorrow shut,
   Or breaking into song by fits,
   Alone, alone, to where he sits,
The Shadow cloak'd from head to foot,

Who keeps the keys of all the creeds,
   I wander, often falling lame,
   And looking back to whence I came,
Or on to where the pathway leads;

And crying, How changed from where it ran
    Thro' lands where not a leaf was dumb;
    But all the lavish hills would hum
The murmur of a happy Pan:

When each by turns was guide to each,
    And Fancy light from Fancy caught,
    And Thought leapt out to wed with Thought
Ere Thought could wed itself with Speech;

And all we met was fair and good,
    And all was good that Time could bring,
    And all the secret of the Spring
Moved in the chambers of the blood;

And many an old philosophy
    On Argive heights divinely sang,
    And round us all the thicket rang
To many a flute of Arcady.

XXIV

And was the day of my delight
    As pure and perfect as I say?
    The very source and fount of Day
Is dash'd with wandering isles of night.

If all was good and fair we met,
    This earth had been the Paradise
    It never look'd to human eyes
Since our first Sun arose and set.

And is it that the haze of grief
    Makes former gladness loom so great?
    The lowness of the present state,
That sets the past in this relief?

Or that the past will always win
    A glory from its being far;
    And orb into the perfect star
We saw not, when we moved therein?

XXV

I know that this was Life,—the track
    Whereon with equal feet we fared;
    And then, as now, the day prepared
The daily burden for the back.

But this it was that made me move
    As light as carrier-birds in air;
    I loved the weight I had to bear,
Because it needed help of Love:

Nor could I weary, heart or limb,
    When mighty Love would cleave in twain
    The lading of a single pain,
And part it, giving half to him.

XXVI

Still onward winds the dreary way;
    I with it; for I long to prove
    No lapse of moons can canker Love,
Whatever fickle tongues may say.

And if that eye which watches guilt
    And goodness, and hath power to see
    Within the green the moulder'd tree,
And towers fall'n as soon as built—

Oh, if indeed that eye foresee
    Or see (in Him is no before)
    In more of life true life no more
And Love the indifference to be,

Then might I find, ere yet the morn
    Breaks hither over Indian seas,
    That Shadow waiting with the keys,
To shroud me from my proper scorn.

XXVII

I envy not in any moods
    The captive void of noble rage,
    The linnet born within the cage,
That never knew the summer woods:

I envy not the beast that takes
    His license in the field of time,
    Unfetter'd by the sense of crime,
To whom a conscience never wakes;

Nor, what may count itself as blest,
    The heart that never plighted troth
    But stagnates in the weeds of sloth;
Nor any want-begotten rest.

I hold it true, whate'er befall;
    I feel it, when I sorrow most;
    'Tis better to have loved and lost
Than never to have loved at all.

THE CHARGE OF THE LIGHT BRIGADE

Half a league, half a league,
Half a league onward,
All in the valley of Death
Rode the six hundred.
"Forward, the Light Brigade!
Charge for the guns!" he said:
Into the valley of Death
Rode the six hundred.

"Forward, the Light Brigade!"
Was there a man dismay'd?
Not tho' the soldier knew

Some one had blunder'd:
Theirs not to make reply,
Theirs not to reason why,
Theirs but to do and die:
Into the valley of Death
Rode the six hundred.

Cannon to right of them,
Cannon to left of them,
Cannon in front of them
Volley'd and thunder'd;
Storm'd at with shot and shell,
Boldly they rode and well,
Into the jaws of Death,
Into the mouth of Hell
Rode the six hundred.

Flash'd all their sabres bare,
Flash'd as they turn'd in air
Sabring the gunners there,
Charging an army, while
All the world wonder'd:
Plunged in the battery-smoke
Right thro' the line they broke;
Cossack and Russian
Reel'd from the sabre-stroke
Shatter'd and sunder'd.
Then they rode back, but not
Not the six hundred.

Cannon to right of them,
Cannon to left of them,
Cannon behind them
Volley'd and thunder'd;
Storm'd at with shot and shell,
While horse and hero fell,
They that had fought so well
Came thro' the jaws of Death,

Back from the mouth of Hell,
All that was left of them,
Left of six hundred.

When can their glory fade?
O the wild charge they made!
All the world wonder'd.
Honor the charge they made!
Honor the Light Brigade,
Noble six hundred!

THE LADY OF SHALOTT

I

ON EITHER side the river lie
Long fields of barley and of rye,
That clothe the wold and meet the sky;
And thro' the field the road runs by
    To many-tower'd Camelot;
And up and down the people go,
Gazing where the lilies blow
Round an island there below,
    The island of Shalott.

Willows whiten, aspens quiver,
Little breezes dusk and shiver
Thro' the wave that runs for ever
By the island in the river
    Flowing down to Camelot.
Four gray walls, and four gray towers,
Overlook a space of flowers,
And the silent isle imbowers
    The Lady of Shalott.

By the margin, willow veil'd,
Slide the heavy barges trail'd
By slow horses; and unhail'd

The shallop flitteth silken-sail'd
    Skimming down to Camelot:
But who hath seen her wave her hand?
Or at the casement seen her stand?
Or is she known in all the land,
    The Lady of Shalott?

Only reapers, reaping early
In among the bearded barley,
Hear a song that echoes cheerly
From the river winding clearly,
    Down to tower'd Camelot:
And by the moon the reaper weary,
Piling sheaves in uplands airy,
Listening, whispers "'Tis the fairy
    Lady of Shalott."

II

There she weaves by night and day
A magic web with colours gay.
She has heard a whisper say,
A curse is on her if she stay
    To look down to Camelot.
She knows not what the curse may be,
And so she weaveth steadily,
And little other care hath she,
    The Lady of Shalott.

And moving thro' a mirror clear
That hangs before her all the year,
Shadows of the world appear.
There she sees the highway near
    Winding down to Camelot:
There the river eddy whirls,
And there the surly village-churls,
And the red cloaks of market girls,
    Pass onward from Shalott.

Sometimes a troop of damsels glad,
An abbot on an ambling pad,
Sometimes a curly shepherd-lad,
Or long-hair'd page in crimson clad,
    Goes by to tower'd Camelot;
And sometimes thro' the mirror blue
The knights come riding two and two:
She hath no loyal knight and true,
    The Lady of Shalott.

But in her web she still delights
To weave the mirror's magic sights,
For often thro' the silent nights
A funeral, with plumes and lights
    And music, went to Camelot:
Or when the moon was overhead,
Came two young lovers lately wed:
"I am half sick of shadows," said
    The Lady of Shalott.

III

A bow-shot from her bower-eaves,
He rode between the barley-sheaves,
The sun came dazzling thro' the leaves,
And flamed upon the brazen greaves
    Of bold Sir Lancelot.
A red-cross knight for ever kneel'd
To a lady in his shield,
That sparkled on the yellow field,
    Beside remote Shalott.

The gemmy bridle glitter'd free,
Like to some branch of stars we see
Hung in the golden Galaxy.
The bridle bells rang merrily
    As he rode down to Camelot:
And from his blazon'd baldric slung

A mighty silver bugle hung,
And as he rode his armour rung,
   Beside remote Shalott.

All in the blue unclouded weather
Thick-jewell'd shone the saddle-leather,
The helmet and the helmet-feather
Burn'd like one burning flame together,
   As he rode down to Camelot.
As often thro' the purple night,
Below the starry clusters bright,
Some bearded meteor, trailing light,
   Moves over still Shalott.

His broad clear brow in sunlight glow'd;
On burnish'd hooves his war-horse trode;
From underneath his helmet flow'd
His coal-black curls as on he rode,
   As he rode down to Camelot.
From the bank and from the river
He flash'd into the crystal mirror,
"Tirra lirra," by the river
   Sang Sir Lancelot.

She left the web, she left the loom,
She made three paces thro' the room,
She saw the water-lily bloom,
She saw the helmet and the plume,
   She look'd down to Camelot.
Out flew the web and floated wide;
The mirror crack'd from side to side;
"The curse is come upon me," cried
   The Lady of Shalott.

IV

In the stormy east-wind straining,
The pale yellow woods were waning,
The broad stream in his banks complaining,

Heavily the low sky raining
    Over tower'd Camelot;
Down she came and found a boat
Beneath a willow left afloat,
And round about the prow she wrote
    The Lady of Shalott.

And down the river's dim expanse
Like some bold seër in a trance,
Seeing all his own mischance—
With a glassy countenance
    Did she look to Camelot.
And at the closing of the day
She loosed the chain, and down she lay;
The broad stream bore her far away,
    The Lady of Shalott.

Lying, robed in snowy white
That loosely flew to left and right—
The leaves upon her falling light—
Thro' the noises of the night
    She floated down to Camelot:
And as the boat-head wound along
The willowy hills and fields among,
They heard her singing her last song,
    The Lady of Shalott.

Heard a carol, mournful, holy,
Chanted loudly, chanted lowly,
Till her blood was frozen slowly,
And her eyes were darken'd wholly,
    Turn'd to tower'd Camelot.
For ere she reach'd upon the tide
The first house by the water-side,
Singing in her song she died,
    The Lady of Shalott.

Under tower and balcony,
By garden-wall and gallery,

A gleaming shape she floated by,
Dead-pale between the houses high,
    Silent into Camelot.
Out upon the wharfs they came,
Knight and burgher, lord and dame,
And round the prow they read her name,
    The Lady of Shalott.

Who is this? and what is here?
And in the lighted palace near
Died the sound of royal cheer;
And they cross'd themselves for fear,
    All the knights at Camelot:
But Lancelot mused a little space;
He said, "She has a lovely face;
God in his mercy lend her grace,
    The Lady of Shalott."

ULYSSES

It little profits that an idle king,
By this still hearth, among these barren crags,
Match'd with an aged wife, I mete and dole
Unequal laws unto a savage race,
That hoard, and sleep, and feed, and know not me.
I cannot rest from travel: I will drink
Life to the lees: All times I have enjoy'd
Greatly, have suffer'd greatly, both with those
That loved me, and alone, on shore, and when
Thro' scudding drifts the rainy Hyades
Vext the dim sea: I am become a name;
For always roaming with a hungry heart
Much have I seen and known; cities of men
And manners, climates, councils, governments,
Myself not least, but honour'd of them all;
And drunk delight of battle with my peers,

Far on the ringing plains of windy Troy.
I am a part of all that I have met;
Yet all experience is an arch wherethro'
Gleams that untravell'd world whose margin fades
For ever and forever when I move.
How dull it is to pause, to make an end,
To rust unburnish'd, not to shine in use!
As tho' to breathe were life! Life piled on life
Were all too little, and of one to me
Little remains: but every hour is saved
From that eternal silence, something more,
A bringer of new things; and vile it were
For some three suns to store and hoard myself,
And this gray spirit yearning in desire
To follow knowledge like a sinking star,
Beyond the utmost bound of human thought.

   This is my son, mine own Telemachus,
To whom I leave the sceptre and the isle,—
Well-loved of me, discerning to fulfil
This labour, by slow prudence to make mild
A rugged people, and thro' soft degrees
Subdue them to the useful and the good.
Most blameless is he, centred in the sphere
Of common duties, decent not to fail
In offices of tenderness, and pay
Meet adoration to my household gods,
When I am gone. He works his work, I mine.

   There lies the port; the vessel puffs her sail:
There gloom the dark, broad seas. My mariners,
Souls that have toil'd, and wrought, and thought with me—
That ever with a frolic welcome took
The thunder and the sunshine, and opposed
Free hearts, free foreheads—you and I are old;
Old age hath yet his honour and his toil;
Death closes all: but something ere the end,
Some work of noble note, may yet be done,

Not unbecoming men that strove with Gods.
The lights begin to twinkle from the rocks:
The long day wanes: the slow moon climbs: the deep
Moans round with many voices. Come, my friends,
'T is not too late to seek a newer world.
Push off, and sitting well in order smite
The sounding furrows; for my purpose holds
To sail beyond the sunset, and the baths
Of all the western stars, until I die.
It may be that the gulfs will wash us down:
It may be we shall touch the Happy Isles,
And see the great Achilles, whom we knew.
Tho' much is taken, much abides; and tho'
We are not now that strength which in old days
Moved earth and heaven, that which we are, we are;
One equal temper of heroic hearts,
Made weak by time and fate, but strong in will
To strive, to seek, to find, and not to yield.

Robert Browning

CHILDE ROLAND TO THE DARK TOWER CAME

I

My first thought was, he lied in every word,
    That hoary cripple, with malicious eye
    Askance to watch the working of his lie
On mine, and mouth scarce able to afford
Suppression of the glee, that pursed and scored
    Its edge, at one more victim gained thereby.

II

What else should he be set for, with his staff?
    What, save to waylay with his lies, ensnare

All travellers who might find him posted there,
And ask the road? I guessed what skull-like laugh
Would break, what crutch 'gin write my epitaph
   For pastime in the dusty thoroughfare,

III

If at his counsel I should turn aside
   Into that ominous tract which, all agree,
   Hides the Dark Tower. Yet acquiescingly
I did turn as he pointed: neither pride
Nor hope rekindling at the end descried,
   So much as gladness that some end might be.

IV

For, what with my whole world-wide wandering,
   What with my search drawn out through years, my hope
   Dwindled into a ghost not fit to cope
With that obstreperous joy success would bring, —
I hardly tried now to rebuke the spring
   My heart made, finding failure in its scope.

V

As when a sick man very near to death
   Seems dead indeed, and feels begin and end
   The tears and takes the farewell of each friend,
And hears one bid the other go, draw breath
Freelier outside, ('since all is o'er,' he saith,
   'And the blow fallen no grieving can amend';)

VI

While some discuss if near the other graves
   Be room enough for this, and when a day
   Suits best for carrying the corpse away,
With care about the banners, scarves and staves:
And still the man hears all, and only craves

He may not shame such tender love and stay.

VII

Thus, I had so long suffered in this quest,
    Heard failure prophesied so oft, been writ
    So many times among 'The Band'—to wit,
The knights who to the Dark Tower's search addressed
Their steps—that just to fail as they, seemed best,
    And all the doubt was now—should I be fit?

VIII

So, quiet as despair, I turned from him,
    That hateful cripple, out of his highway
    Into the path he pointed. All the day
Had been a dreary one at best, and dim
Was settling to its close, yet shot one grim
    Red leer to see the plain catch its estray.

IX

For mark! no sooner was I fairly found
    Pledged to the plain, after a pace or two,
    Than, pausing to throw backward a last view
O'er the safe road, 'twas gone; grey plain all round:
Nothing but plain to the horizon's bound.
    I might go on; nought else remained to do.

X

So, on I went. I think I never saw
    Such starved ignoble nature; nothing throve:
    For flowers—as well expect a cedar grove!
But cockle, spurge, according to their law
Might propagate their kind, with none to awe,
    You'd think; a burr had been a treasure-trove.

XI

No! penury, inertness and grimace,
    In some strange sort, were the land's portion. 'See
      Or shut your eyes,' said nature peevishly,
'It nothing skills: I cannot help my case:
'Tis the Last judgment's fire must cure this place,
    Calcine its clods and set my prisoners free.'

XII

If there pushed any ragged thistle-stalk
    Above its mates, the head was chopped; the bents
      Were jealous else. What made those holes and rents
In the dock's harsh swarth leaves, bruised as to baulk
All hope of greenness? 'tis a brute must walk
    Pashing their life out, with a brute's intents.

XIII

As for the grass, it grew as scant as hair
    In leprosy; thin dry blades pricked the mud
      Which underneath looked kneaded up with blood.
One stiff blind horse, his every bone a-stare,
Stood stupefied, however he came there:
    Thrust out past service from the devil's stud!

XIV

Alive? he might be dead for aught I know,
    With that red gaunt and colloped neck a-strain,
      And shut eyes underneath the rusty mane;
Seldom went such grotesqueness with such woe;
I never saw a brute I hated so;
    He must be wicked to deserve such pain.

XV

I shut my eyes and turned them on my heart.
  As a man calls for wine before he fights,
  I asked one draught of earlier, happier sights,
Ere fitly I could hope to play my part.
Think first, fight afterwards—-the soldier's art:
  One taste of the old time sets all to rights.

XVI

Not it! I fancied Cuthbert's reddening face
  Beneath its garniture of curly gold,
  Dear fellow, till I almost felt him fold
An arm in mine to fix me to the place,
That way he used. Alas, one night's disgrace!
  Out went my heart's new fire and left it cold.

XVII

Giles then, the soul of honour—there he stands
  Frank as ten years ago when knighted first.
  What honest man should dare (he said) he durst.
Good—but the scene shifts—faugh! what hangman-hands
Pin to his breast a parchment? His own bands
  Read it. Poor traitor, spit upon and curst!

XVIII

Better this present than a past like that;
  Back therefore to my darkening path again!
  No sound, no sight as far as eye could strain.
Will the night send a howlet or a bat?
I asked: when something on the dismal flat
  Came to arrest my thoughts and change their train.

XIX

A sudden little river crossed my path
    As unexpected as a serpent comes.
    No sluggish tide congenial to the glooms;
This, as it frothed by, might have been a bath
For the fiend's glowing hoof—to see the wrath
    Of its black eddy bespate with flakes and spumes.

XX

So petty yet so spiteful! All along,
    Low scrubby alders kneeled down over it;
    Drenched willows flung them headlong in a fit
Of route despair, a suicidal throng:
The river which had done them all the wrong,
    Whate'er that was, rolled by, deterred no whit.

XXI

Which, while I forded, —good saints, how I feared
    To set my foot upon a dead man's cheek,
    Each step, or feel the spear I thrust to seek
For hollows, tangled in his hair or beard!
—It may have been a water-rat I speared,
    But, ugh! it sounded like a baby's shriek.

XXII

Glad was I when I reached the other bank.
    Now for a better country. Vain presage!
    Who were the strugglers, what war did they wage,
Whose savage trample thus could pad the dank
Soil to a plash? Toads in a poisoned tank,
    Or wild cats in a red-hot iron cage—

XXIII

The fight must so have seemed in that fell cirque.
    What penned them there, with all the plain to choose?
    No foot-print leading to that horrid mews,
None out of it. Mad brewage set to work
Their brains, no doubt, like galley-slaves the Turk
    Pits for his pastime, Christians against Jews.

XXIV

And more than that—a furlong on—why, there!
    What bad use was that engine for, that wheel,
    Or brake, not wheel—that harrow fit to reel
Men's bodies out like silk? with all the air
Of Tophet's tool, on earth left unaware,
    Or brought to sharpen its rusty teeth of steel.

XXV

Then came a bit of stubbed ground, once a wood,
    Next a marsh, it would seem, and now mere earth
    Desperate and done with; (so a fool finds mirth,
Makes a thing and then mars it, till his mood
Changes and off he goes!) within a rood—
    Bog, clay and rubble, sand and stark black dearth.

XXVI

Now blotches rankling, coloured gay and grim,
    Now patches where some leanness of the soil's
    Broke into moss or substances like boils;
Then came some palsied oak, a cleft in him
Like a distorted mouth that splits its rim
    Gaping at death, and dies while it recoils.

XXVII

And just as far as ever from the end!
    Nought in the distance but the evening, naught
    To point my footstep further! At the thought,
A great black bird, Apollyon's bosom-friend,
Sailed past, nor beat his wide wing dragon-penned
    That brushed my cap—perchance the guide I sought.

XXVIII

For, looking up, aware I somehow grew,
    'Spite of the dusk, the plain had given place
    All round to mountains—with such name to grace
Mere ugly heights and heaps now stolen in view.
How thus they had surprised me, —solve it, you!
    How to get from them was no clearer case.

XXIX

Yet half I seemed to recognize some trick
    Of mischief happened to me, God knows when—
    In a bad dream perhaps. Here ended, then,
Progress this way. When, in the very nick
Of giving up, one time more, came a click
    As when a trap shuts—you're inside the den!

XXX

Burningly it came on me all at once,
    This was the place! those two hills on the right,
    Crouched like two bulls locked horn in horn in fight;
While to the left, a tall scalped mountain . . . Dunce,
Dotard, a-dozing at the very nonce,
    After a life spent training for the sight!

XXXI

What in the midst lay but the Tower itself?
    The round squat turret, blind as the fool's heart,
    Built of brown stone, without a counter-part
In the whole world. The tempest's mocking elf
Points to the shipman thus the unseen shelf
    He strikes on, only when the timbers start.

XXXII

Not see? because of night perhaps? —why, day
    Came back again for that! before it left,
    The dying sunset kindled through a cleft:
The hills, like giants at a hunting, lay,
Chin upon hand, to see the game at bay,—-
    'Now stab and end the creature—-to the heft!'

XXXIII

Not hear? when noise was everywhere! it tolled
    Increasing like a bell. Names in my ears
    Of all the lost adventurers my peers, —
How such a one was strong, and such was bold,
And such was fortunate, yet, each of old
    Lost, lost! one moment knelled the woe of years.

XXXIV

There they stood, ranged along the hill-sides, met
    To view the last of me, a living frame
    For one more picture! in a sheet of flame
I saw them and I knew them all. And yet
Dauntless the slug-horn to my lips I set,
    And blew. '*Childe Roland to the Dark Tower came.*'

MY LAST DUCHESS

Ferrara

That's my last Duchess painted on the wall,
Looking as if she were alive. I call
That piece a wonder, now; Fra Pandolf's hands
Worked busily a day, and there she stands.
Will't please you sit and look at her? I said
'Fra Pandolf' by design, for never read
Strangers like you that pictured countenance,
The depth and passion of its earnest glance,
But to myself they turned (since none puts by
The curtain I have drawn for you, but I)
And seemed as they would ask me, if they durst,
How such a glance came there; so, not the first
Are you to turn and ask thus. Sir, 'twas not
Her husband's presence only, called that spot
Of joy into the Duchess' cheek; perhaps
Fra Pandolf chanced to say, 'Her mantle laps
Over my lady's wrist too much,' or 'Paint
Must never hope to reproduce the faint
Half-flush that dies along her throat.' Such stuff
Was courtesy, she thought, and cause enough
For calling up that spot of joy. She had
A heart—how shall I say?—too soon made glad,
Too easily impressed; she liked whate'er
She looked on, and her looks went everywhere.
Sir, 'twas all one! My favour at her breast,
The dropping of the daylight in the West,
The bough of cherries some officious fool
Broke in the orchard for her, the white mule
She rode with round the terrace—all and each
Would draw from her alike the approving speech,
Or blush, at least. She thanked men—good! but thanked
Somehow—I know not how—as if she ranked
My gift of a nine-hundred-years-old name

With anybody's gift. Who'd stoop to blame
This sort of trifling? Even had you skill
In speech—which I have not—to make your will
Quite clear to such an one, and say, 'Just this
Or that in you disgusts me; here you miss,
Or there exceed the mark'—and if she let
Herself be lessoned so, nor plainly set
Her wits to yours, forsooth, and made excuse—
E'en then would be some stooping; and I choose
Never to stoop. Oh, sir, she smiled, no doubt,
Whene'er I passed her; but who passed without
Much the same smile? This grew; I gave commands;
Then all smiles stopped together. There she stands
As if alive. Will't please you rise? We'll meet
The company below, then. I repeat,
The Count your master's known munificence
Is ample warrant that no just pretense
Of mine for dowry will be disallowed;
Though his fair daughter's self, as I avowed
At starting, is my object. Nay, we'll go
Together down, sir. Notice Neptune, though,
Taming a sea-horse, thought a rarity,
Which Claus of Innsbruck cast in bronze for me!

Walt Whitman

O CAPTAIN! MY CAPTAIN!

O Captain! my Captain! our fearful trip is done,
The ship has weather'd every rack, the prize we sought is won,
The port is near, the bells I hear, the people all exulting,
While follow eyes the steady keel, the vessel grim and daring;
    But O heart! heart! heart!
        O the bleeding drops of red,
            Where on the deck my Captain lies,

                Fallen cold and dead.

O Captain! my Captain! rise up and hear the bells;
Rise up—for you the flag is flung—for you the bugle trills,
For you bouquets and ribbon'd wreaths—for you the shores a-crowding,
For you they call, the swaying mass, their eager faces turning;
    Here Captain! dear father!
        This arm beneath your head!
           It is some dream that on the deck,
              You've fallen cold and dead.

My Captain does not answer, his lips are pale and still,
My father does not feel my arm, he has no pulse nor will,
The ship is anchor'd safe and sound, its voyage closed and done,
From fearful trip the victor ship comes in with object won;
    Exult O shores, and ring O bells!
        But I with mournful tread,
           Walk the deck my Captain lies,
              Fallen cold and dead.

THE DALLIANCE OF THE EAGLES

SKIRTING THE river road, (my forenoon walk, my rest,)
Skyward in air a sudden muffled sound, the dalliance of the eagles,
The rushing amorous contact high in space together,
The clinching interlocking claws, a living, fierce, gyrating wheel,
Four beating wings, two beaks, a swirling mass tight grappling,
In tumbling turning clustering loops, straight downward falling,
Till o'er the river pois'd, the twain yet one, a moment's lull,
A motionless still balance in the air, then parting, talons loosing,

Upward again on slow-firm pinions slanting, their separate diverse
   flight,
She hers, he his, pursuing.

Emily Dickinson

BECAUSE I COULD NOT STOP FOR DEATH

BECAUSE I could not stop for Death –
He kindly stopped for me –
The Carriage held but just Ourselves –
And Immortality.

We slowly drove – He knew no haste
And I had put away
My labor and my leisure too,
For His Civility –

We passed the School, where Children strove
At Recess – in the Ring –
We passed the Fields of Gazing Grain –
We passed the Setting Sun –

Or rather – He passed Us –
The Dews drew quivering and Chill –
For only Gossamer, my Gown –
My Tippet – only Tulle –

We paused before a House that seemed
A Swelling of the Ground –
The Roof was scarcely visible –
The Cornice – in the Ground –

Since then – 'tis Centuries – and yet
Feels shorter than the Day
I first surmised the Horses' Heads

Were toward Eternity –

TELL ALL THE TRUTH BUT TELL IT SLANT

Tell all the truth but tell it slant —
Success in Circuit lies
Too bright for our infirm Delight
The Truth's superb surprise
As Lightning to the Children eased
With explanation kind
The Truth must dazzle gradually
Or every man be blind —

THERE'S A CERTAIN SLANT OF LIGHT

There's a certain Slant of light,
Winter Afternoons –
That oppresses, like the Heft
Of Cathedral Tunes –

Heavenly Hurt, it gives us –
We can find no scar,
But internal difference –
Where the Meanings, are –

None may teach it – Any –
'Tis the seal Despair –
An imperial affliction
Sent us of the Air –

When it comes, the Landscape listens –
Shadows – hold their breath –
When it goes, 'tis like the Distance
On the look of Death –

Lewis Carroll

JABBERWOCKY

'Twas brillig, and the slithy toves
    Did gyre and gimble in the wabe:
All mimsy were the borogoves,
    And the mome raths outgrabe.

"Beware the Jabberwock, my son!
    The jaws that bite, the claws that catch!
Beware the Jubjub bird, and shun
    The frumious Bandersnatch!"

He took his vorpal sword in hand;
    Long time the manxome foe he sought—
So rested he by the Tumtum tree
    And stood awhile in thought.

And, as in uffish thought he stood,
    The Jabberwock, with eyes of flame,
Came whiffling through the tulgey wood,
    And burbled as it came!

One, two! One, two! And through and through
    The vorpal blade went snicker-snack!
He left it dead, and with its head
    He went galumphing back.

"And hast thou slain the Jabberwock?
    Come to my arms, my beamish boy!
O frabjous day! Callooh! Callay!"
    He chortled in his joy.

'Twas brillig, and the slithy toves
    Did gyre and gimble in the wabe:
All mimsy were the borogoves,
    And the mome raths outgrabe.

THE WALRUS AND THE CARPENTER

"The sun was shining on the sea,
   Shining with all his might:
He did his very best to make
   The billows smooth and bright —
And this was odd, because it was
   The middle of the night.

The moon was shining sulkily,
   Because she thought the sun
Had got no business to be there
   After the day was done —
"It's very rude of him," she said,
   "To come and spoil the fun."

The sea was wet as wet could be,
   The sands were dry as dry.
You could not see a cloud, because
   No cloud was in the sky:
No birds were flying overhead —
   There were no birds to fly.

The Walrus and the Carpenter
   Were walking close at hand;
They wept like anything to see
   Such quantities of sand:
If this were only cleared away,'
   They said, it would be grand!'

If seven maids with seven mops
   Swept it for half a year,
Do you suppose,' the Walrus said,
   That they could get it clear?'
I doubt it,' said the Carpenter,
   And shed a bitter tear.

O Oysters, come and walk with us!'

The Walrus did beseech.
'A pleasant walk, a pleasant talk,
   Along the briny beach:
We cannot do with more than four,
   To give a hand to each.'

The eldest Oyster looked at him,
   But never a word he said:
The eldest Oyster winked his eye,
   And shook his heavy head —
Meaning to say he did not choose
   To leave the oyster-bed.

But four young Oysters hurried up,
   All eager for the treat:
Their coats were brushed, their faces washed,
   Their shoes were clean and neat —
And this was odd, because, you know,
   They hadn't any feet.

Four other Oysters followed them,
   And yet another four;
And thick and fast they came at last,
   And more, and more, and more —
All hopping through the frothy waves,
   And scrambling to the shore.

The Walrus and the Carpenter
   Walked on a mile or so,
And then they rested on a rock
   Conveniently low:
And all the little Oysters stood
   And waited in a row.

'The time has come,' the Walrus said,
   'To talk of many things:
Of shoes — and ships — and sealing-wax —
   Of cabbages — and kings —
And why the sea is boiling hot —

And whether pigs have wings.'

But wait a bit,' the Oysters cried,
   Before we have our chat;
For some of us are out of breath,
   And all of us are fat!'
No hurry!' said the Carpenter.
   They thanked him much for that.

A loaf of bread,' the Walrus said,
   Is what we chiefly need:
Pepper and vinegar besides
   Are very good indeed —
Now if you're ready, Oysters dear,
   We can begin to feed.'

But not on us!' the Oysters cried,
   Turning a little blue.
After such kindness, that would be
   A dismal thing to do!'
The night is fine,' the Walrus said.
   Do you admire the view?

It was so kind of you to come!
   And you are very nice!'
The Carpenter said nothing but
   Cut us another slice:
I wish you were not quite so deaf —
   I've had to ask you twice!'

It seems a shame,' the Walrus said,
   To play them such a trick,
After we've brought them out so far,
   And made them trot so quick!'
The Carpenter said nothing but
   The butter's spread too thick!'

I weep for you,' the Walrus said:
   I deeply sympathize.'
With sobs and tears he sorted out

    Those of the largest size,
Holding his pocket-handkerchief
    Before his streaming eyes.

O Oysters,' said the Carpenter,
    You've had a pleasant run!
Shall we be trotting home again?'
    But answer came there none —
And this was scarcely odd, because
    They'd eaten every one."

Thomas Hardy

A BROKEN APPOINTMENT

You DID not come,
And marching Time drew on, and wore me numb,—
Yet less for loss of your dear presence there
Than that I thus found lacking in your make
That high compassion which can overbear
Reluctance for pure lovingkindness' sake
Grieved I, when, as the hope-hour stroked its sum,
You did not come.

You love not me,
And love alone can lend you loyalty;
—I know and knew it. But, unto the store
Of human deeds divine in all but name,
Was it not worth a little hour or more
To add yet this: Once you, a woman, came
To soothe a time-torn man; even though it be
You love not me?

IN TIME OF 'THE BREAKING OF NATIONS'

I

Only a man harrowing clods
   In a slow silent walk
With an old horse that stumbles and nods
   Half asleep as they stalk.

II

Only thin smoke without flame
   From the heaps of couch-grass;
Yet this will go onward the same
   Though Dynasties pass.

III

Yonder a maid and her wight
   Come whispering by:
War's annals will cloud into night
   Ere their story die.

THE DARKLING THRUSH

I leant upon a coppice gate
   When Frost was spectre-grey,
And Winter's dregs made desolate
   The weakening eye of day.
The tangled bine-stems scored the sky
   Like strings of broken lyres,
And all mankind that haunted nigh
   Had sought their household fires.

The land's sharp features seemed to be
   The Century's corpse outleant,
His crypt the cloudy canopy,
   The wind his death-lament.

The ancient pulse of germ and birth
    Was shrunken hard and dry,
And every spirit upon earth
    Seemed fervourless as I.

At once a voice arose among
    The bleak twigs overhead
In a full-hearted evensong
    Of joy illimited;
An aged thrush, frail, gaunt, and small,
    In blast-beruffled plume,
Had chosen thus to fling his soul
    Upon the growing gloom.

So little cause for carolings
    Of such ecstatic sound
Was written on terrestrial things
    Afar or nigh around,
That I could think there trembled through
    His happy good-night air
Some blessed Hope, whereof he knew
    And I was unaware.

WESSEX HEIGHTS

THERE ARE some heights in Wessex, shaped as if by a kindly hand
For thinking, dreaming, dying on, and at crises when I stand,
Say, on Ingpen Beacon eastward, or on Wylls-Neck westwardly,
I seem where I was before my birth, and after death may be.

In the lowlands I have no comrade, not even the lone man's friend—
Her who suffereth long and is kind; accepts what he is too weak
    to mend:
Down there they are dubious and askance; there nobody

thinks as I,
But mind-chains do not clank where one's next neighbour is the sky.

In the towns I am tracked by phantoms having weird detective ways—
Shadows of beings who fellowed with myself of earlier days:
They hang about at places, and they say harsh heavy things—
Men with a wintry sneer, and women with tart disparagings.

Down there I seem to be false to myself, my simple self that was,
And is not now, and I see him watching, wondering what crass cause
Can have merged him into such a strange continuator as this,
Who yet has something in common with himself, my chrysalis.

I cannot go to the great grey Plain; there's a figure against the moon,
Nobody sees it but I, and it makes my breast beat out of tune;
I cannot go to the tall-spired town, being barred by the forms now passed
For everybody but me, in whose long vision they stand there fast.

There's a ghost at Yell'ham Bottom chiding loud at the fall of the night,
There's a ghost in Froom-side Vale, thin-lipped and vague, in a shroud of white,
There is one in the railway train whenever I do not want it near,
I see its profile against the pane, saying what I would not hear.

As for one rare fair woman, I am now but a thought of hers,
I enter her mind and another thought succeeds me that she prefers;
Yet my love for her in its fulness she herself even did not know;

Well, time cures hearts of tenderness, and now I can let her
   go.
So I am found on Ingpen Beacon, or on Wylls-Neck to the
   west,
Or else on homely Bulbarrow, or little Pilsdon Crest,
Where men have never cared to haunt, nor women have
   walked
      with me,
And ghosts then keep their distance; and I know some liberty.

Gerard Manley Hopkins

BINSEY POPLARS

Felled 1879

MY ASPENS dear, whose airy cages quelled,
   Quelled or quenched in leaves the leaping sun,
      All felled, are all felled;
         Of a fresh and following folded rank
            Not spared, not one
            That dandled a sandalled
            Shadow that swam or sank
On meadow & river & wind-wandering weed-winding bank.

O if we but knew what we do
         When we delve or hew—
      Hack and rack the growing green!
         Since country is so tender
      To touch, her being só slender,
      That, like this sleep and seeing ball
      That, like this sleep and seeing ball
      But a prick will make no eye at all,
      Where we, even where we mean
            To mend her we end her,
         When we hew or delve:
After-comers cannot guess the beauty been.

Ten or twelve, only ten or twelve
    Strokes of havoc unselve
        The sweet especial scene,
  Rural scene, a rural scene,
  Sweet especial rural scene.

GOD'S GRANDEUR

THE WORLD is charged with the grandeur of God.
  It will flame out, like shining from shook foil;
  It gathers to a greatness, like the ooze of oil
Crushed. Why do men then now not reck his rod?
Generations have trod, have trod, have trod;
  And all is seared with trade; bleared, smeared with toil;
  And wears man's smudge and shares man's smell: the soil
Is bare now, nor can foot feel, being shod.

And for all this, nature is never spent;
  There lives the dearest freshness deep down things;
And though the last lights off the black West went
  Oh, morning, at the brown brink eastward, springs—
Because the Holy Ghost over the bent
  World broods with warm breast and with ah! bright wings.

PIED BEAUTY

GLORY BE to God for dappled things—
  For skies of couple-colour as a brinded cow;
      For rose-moles all in stipple upon trout that swim;
Fresh-firecoal chestnut-falls; finches' wings;
  Landscape plotted and pieced—fold, fallow, and plough;
      And áll trádes, their gear and tackle and trim.

All things counter, original, spare, strange;
  Whatever is fickle, freckled (who knows how?)
      With swift, slow; sweet, sour; adazzle, dim;

He fathers-forth whose beauty is past change:
>> Praise him.

THE WINDHOVER

I CAUGHT this morning morning's minion, king-
>> dom of daylight's dauphin, dapple-dawn-drawn Falcon, in
>> his riding
> Of the rolling level underneath him steady air, and striding
High there, how he run upon the rein of a wimpling wing
In his ecstasy! then off, off forth on swing,
>> As a skate's heel sweeps smooth on a bow-bend: the hurl
>> and gliding
> Rebuffed the big wind. My heart in hiding
Stirred for a bird, —the achieve of; the mastery of the thing!

&Brute beauty and valour and act, oh, air, pride, plume, here
>> Buckle! AND the fire that breaks from thee then, a billion
Times told lovelier, more dangerous, O my chevalier!

> No wonder of it: shéer plód makes plough down sillion
Shine, and blue-bleak embers, ah my dear,
Fall, gall themselves, and gash gold-vermillion

WRECK OF
THE DEUTSCHLAND

To the happy memory of five Franciscan Nuns, exiles by the Falk Laws, drowned between midnight and morning of Dec. 7th, 1875

I

THOU MASTERING me
God! giver of breath and bread;
World's strand, sway of the sea;
Lord of living and dead;

Thou hast bound bones & veins in me, fastened me flesh,
And after it almost unmade, what with dread,
Thy doing: and dost thou touch me afresh?
Over again I feel thy finger and find thee.

I did say yes
O at lightning and lashed rod;
Thou heardst me truer than tongue confess
Thy terror, O Christ, O God;
Thou knowest the walls, altar and hour and night:
The swoon of a heart that the sweep and the hurl of thee trod
Hard down with a horror of height:
And the midriff astrain with leaning of, laced with fire of
  stress.

The frown of his face
Before me, the hurtle of hell
Behind, where, where was a, where was a place?
I whirled out wings that spell
And fled with a fling of the heart to the heart of the Host.
My heart, but you were dovewinged, I can tell,
Carrier-witted, I am bold to boast,
To flash from the flame to the flame then, tower from the
  grace to the grace.

I am soft sift
In an hourglass—at the wall
Fast, but mined with a motion, a drift,
And it crowds and it combs to the fall;
I steady as a water in a well, to a poise, to a pane,
But roped with, always, all the way down from the tall
Fells or flanks of the voel, a vein
Of the gospel proffer, a pressure, a principle, Christ's gift.

I kiss my hand
To the stars, lovely-asunder
Starlight, wafting him out of it; and
Glow, glory in thunder;
Kiss my hand to the dappled-with-damson west:

Since, tho' he is under the world's splendour and wonder,
His mystery must be instressed, stressed;
For I greet him the days I meet him, and bless when I understand.

Not out of his bliss
Springs the stress felt
Nor first from heaven (and few know this)
Swings the stroke dealt—
Stroke and a stress that stars and storms deliver,
That guilt is hushed by, hearts are flushed by and melt—
But it rides time like riding a river
(And here the faithful waver, the faithless fable and miss).

It dates from day
Of his going in Galilee;
Warm-laid grave of a womb-life grey;
Manger, maiden's knee;
The dense and the driven Passion, and frightful sweat;
Thence the discharge of it, there its swelling to be,
Though felt before, though in high flood yet—
What none would have known of it, only the heart, being hard at bay,

Is out with it! Oh,
We lash with the best or worst
Word last! How a lush-kept plush-capped sloe
Will, mouthed to flesh-burst,
Gush!—flush the man, the being with it, sour or sweet,
Brim, in a flash, full!—Hither then, last or first,
To hero of Calvary, Christ,'s feet—
Never ask if meaning it, wanting it, warned of it—men go.

Be adored among men,
God, three-numberéd form;
Wring thy rebel, dogged in den,
Man's malice, with wrecking and storm.
Beyond saying sweet, past telling of tongue,
Thou art lightning and love, I found it, a winter and warm;

Father and fondler of heart thou hast wrung:
Hast thy dark descending and most art merciful then.

With an anvil-ding
And with fire in him forge thy will
Or rather, rather then, stealing as Spring
Through him, melt him but master him still:
Whether at once, as once at a crash Paul,
Or as Austin, a lingering-out swéet skíll,
Make mercy in all of us, out of us all
Mastery, but be adored, but be adored King.

II

"Some find me a sword; some
The flange and the rail; flame,
Fang, or flood" goes Death on drum,
And storms bugle his fame.
But wé dréam we are rooted in earth—Dust!
Flesh falls within sight of us, we, though our flower the same,
Wave with the meadow, forget that there must
The sour scythe cringe, and the blear share come.

On Saturday sailed from Bremen,
American-outward-bound,
Take settler and seamen, tell men with women,
Two hundred souls in the round—
O Father, not under thy feathers nor ever as guessing
The goal was a shoal, of a fourth the doom to be drowned;
Yet did the dark side of the bay of thy blessing
Not vault them, the million of rounds of thy mercy not reeve even them in?

Into the snows she sweeps,
Hurling the haven behind,
The Deutschland, on Sunday; and so the sky keeps,
For the infinite air is unkind,
And the sea flint-flake, black-backed in the regular blow,
Sitting Eastnortheast, in cursed quarter, the wind;

Wiry and white-fiery and whirlwind-swivellèd snow
Spins to the widow-making unchilding unfathering deeps.

She drove in the dark to leeward,
She struck—not a reef or a rock
But the combs of a smother of sand: night drew her
Dead to the Kentish Knock;
And she beat the bank down with her bows and the ride of
    her keel:
The breakers rolled on her beam with ruinous shock;
And canvass and compass, the whorl and the wheel
Idle for ever to waft her or wind her with, these she endured.

Hope had grown grey hairs,
Hope had mourning on,
Trenched with tears, carved with cares,
Hope was twelve hours gone;
And frightful a nightfall folded rueful a day
Nor rescue, only rocket and lightship, shone,
And lives at last were washing away:
To the shrouds they took,—they shook in the hurling and
    horrible airs.

One stirred from the rigging to save
The wild woman-kind below,
With a rope's end round the man, handy and brave—
He was pitched to his death at a blow,
For all his dreadnought breast and braids of thew:
They could tell him for hours, dandled the to and fro
Through the cobbled foam-fleece, what could he do
With the burl of the fountains of air, buck and the flood of
    the wave?

They fought with God's cold—
And they could not and fell to the deck
(Crushed them) or water (and drowned them) or rolled
With the sea-romp over the wreck.
Night roared, with the heart-break hearing a heart-broke
    rabble,

The woman's wailing, the crying of child without check—
Till a lioness arose breasting the babble,
A prophetess towered in the tumult, a virginal tongue told.

Ah, touched in your bower of bone
Are you! turned for an exquisite smart,
Have you! make words break from me here all alone,
Do you!—mother of being in me, heart.
O unteachably after evil, but uttering truth,
Why, tears! is it? tears; such a melting, a madrigal start!
Never-eldering revel and river of youth,
What can it be, this glee? the good you have there of your own?

Sister, a sister calling
A master, her master and mine!—
And the inboard seas run swirling and hawling;
The rash smart sloggering brine
Blinds her; but she that weather sees one thing, one;
Has one fetch in her: she rears herself to divine
Ears, and the call of the tall nun
To the men in the tops and the tackle rode over the storm's brawling.

She was first of a five and came
Of a coifèd sisterhood.
(O Deutschland, double a desperate name!
O world wide of its good!
But Gertrude, lily, and Luther, are two of a town,
Christ's lily and beast of the waste wood:
From life's dawn it is drawn down,
Abel is Cain's brother and breasts they have sucked the same.)

Loathed for a love men knew in them,
Banned by the land of their birth,
Rhine refused them, Thames would ruin them;
Surf, snow, river and earth
Gnashed: but thou art above, thou Orion of light;
Thy unchancelling poising palms were weighing the worth,

Thou martyr-master: in thy sight
Storm flakes were scroll-leaved flowers, lily showers—sweet heaven was astrew in them.

Five! the finding and sake
And cipher of suffering Christ.
Mark, the mark is of man's make
And the word of it Sacrificed.
But he scores it in scarlet himself on his own bespoken,
Before-time-taken, dearest prizèd and pricèd—
Stigma, signal, cinquefoil token
For lettering of the lamb's fleece, ruddying of the rose-flake.

Joy fall to thee, father Francis,
Drawn to the Life that died;
With the gnarls of the nails in thee, niche of the lance, his Lovescape crucified
And seal of his seraph-arrival! and these thy daughters
And five-livèd and leavèd favour and pride,
Are sisterly sealed in wild waters,
To bathe in his fall-gold mercies, to breathe in his all-fire glances.

Away in the loveable west,
On a pastoral forehead of Wales,
I was under a roof here, I was at rest,
And they the prey of the gales;
She to the black-about air, to the breaker, the thickly
Falling flakes, to the throng that catches and quails
Was calling "O Christ, Christ, come quickly":
The cross to her she calls Christ to her, christens her wildworst Best.

The majesty! what did she mean?
Breathe, arch and original Breath.
Is it love in her of the being as her lover had been?
Breathe, body of lovely Death.
They were else-minded then, altogether, the men

Woke thee with a we are perishing in the weather of
   Gennesareth.
Or ís it that she cried for the crown then,
The keener to come at the comfort for feeling the combating
   keen?

For how to the heart's cheering
The down-dugged ground-hugged grey
Hovers off, the jay-blue heavens appearing
Of pied and peeled May!
Blue-beating and hoary-glow height; or night, still higher,
With belled fire and the moth-soft Milky way,
What by your measure is the heaven of desire,
The treasure never eyesight got, nor was ever guessed what for
   the hearing?

No, but it was not these.
The jading and jar of the cart,
Time's tasking, it is fathers that asking for ease
Of the sodden-with-its-sorrowing heart,
Not danger, electrical horror; then further it finds
The appealing of the Passion is tenderer in prayer apart:
Other, I gather, in measure her mind's
Burden, in wind's burly and beat of endragonèd seas.

But how shall I ... make me room there:
Reach me a ... Fancy, come faster—
Strike you the sight of it? look at it loom there,
Thing that she ... there then! the Master,
Ipse, the only one, Christ, King, Head:
He was to cure the extremity where he had cast her;
Do, deal, lord it with living and dead;
Let him ride, her pride, in his triumph, despatch and have
   done with his doom there.

Ah! there was a heart right
There was single eye!
Read the unshapeable shock night
And knew the who and the why;

Wording it how but by him that present and past,
Heaven and earth are word of, worded by?—
The Simon Peter of a soul! to the blast
Tarpeian-fast, but a blown beacon of light.

Jesu, heart's light,
Jesu, maid's son,
What was the feast followed the night
Thou hadst glory of this nun?—
Feast of the one woman without stain.
For so conceivèd, so to conceive thee is done;
But here was heart-throe, birth of a brain,
Word, that heard and kept thee and uttered thee outright.

Well, she has thee for the pain, for the
Patience; but pity of the rest of them!
Heart, go and bleed at a bitterer vein for the
Comfortless unconfessed of them—
No not uncomforted: lovely-felicitous Providence
Finger of a tender of, O of a feathery delicacy, the breast of
  the
Maiden could obey so, be a bell to, ring of it, and
Startle the poor sheep back! is the shipwrack then a harvest,
  does tempest carry the grain for thee?

I admire thee, master of the tides,
Of the Yore-flood, of the year's fall;
The recurb and the recovery of the gulf's sides,
The girth of it and the wharf of it and the wall;
Staunching, quenching ocean of a motionable mind;
Ground of being, and granite of it: past all
Grasp God, throned behind
Death with a sovereignty that heeds but hides, bodes but
  abides;

With a mercy that outrides
The all of water, an ark
For the listener; for the lingerer with a love glides
Lower than death and the dark;

A vein for the visiting of the past-prayer, pent in prison,
The-last-breath penitent spirits—the uttermost mark
Our passion-plungèd giant risen,
The Christ of the Father compassionate, fetched in the storm of his strides.

Now burn, new born to the world,
Doubled-naturèd name,
The heaven-flung, heart-fleshed, maiden-furled
Miracle-in-Mary-of-flame,
Mid-numbered he in three of the thunder-throne!
Not a dooms-day dazzle in his coming nor dark as he came;
Kind, but royally reclaiming his own;
A released shower, let flash to the shire, not a lightning of fire hard-hurled.

Dame, at our door
Drowned, and among our shoals,
Remember us in the roads, the heaven-haven of the Reward:
Our Kíng back, Oh, upon énglish sóuls!
Let him easter in us, be a dayspring to the dimness of us, be a crimson-cresseted east,
More brightening her, rare-dear Britain, as his reign rolls,
Pride, rose, prince, hero of us, high-priest,
Our hearts' charity's hearth's fire, our thoughts' chivalry's throng's Lord.

William Ernest Henley

INVICTUS

OUT OF the night that covers me,
   Black as the pit from pole to pole,
I thank whatever gods may be
   For my unconquerable soul.

In the fell clutch of circumstance
   I have not winced nor cried aloud.

Under the bludgeonings of chance
  My head is bloody, but unbowed.

Beyond this place of wrath and tears
  Looms but the Horror of the shade,
And yet the menace of the years
  Finds and shall find me unafraid.

It matters not how strait the gate,
  How charged with punishments the scroll,
I am the master of my fate,
  I am the captain of my soul.

A. E. Housman

A SHROPSHIRE LAD, VIII

'FAREWELL TO barn and stack and tree,
  Farewell to Severn shore.
Terence, look your last at me,
  For I come home no more.

'The sun burns on the half-mown hill,
  By now the blood is dried;
And Maurice amongst the hay lies still
  And my knife is in his side.

'My mother thinks us long away;
  'Tis time the field were mown.
She had two sons at rising day,
  To-night she'll be alone.

'And here's a bloody hand to shake,
  And oh, man, here's good-bye;
We'll sweat no more on scythe and rake,
  My bloody hands and I.

'I wish you strength to bring you pride,
  And a love to keep you clean,

And I wish you luck, come Lammastide,
    At racing on the green.

'Long for me the rick will wait,
    And long will wait the fold,
And long will stand the empty plate,
    And dinner will be cold.'

A SHROPSHIRE LAD, XL

INTO my heart an air that kills
    From yon far country blows:
What are those blue remembered hills,
    What spires, what farms are those?

That is the land of lost content,
    I see it shining plain,
The happy highways where I went
    And cannot come again.

Rudyard Kipling

GUNGA DIN

YOU MAY talk o' gin and beer
When you're quartered safe out 'ere,
An' you're sent to penny-fights an' Aldershot it;
But when it comes to slaughter
You will do your work on water,
An' you'll lick the bloomin' boots of 'im that's got it.
Now in Injia's sunny clime,
Where I used to spend my time
A-servin' of 'Er Majesty the Queen,
Of all them blackfaced crew
The finest man I knew
Was our regimental bhisti, Gunga Din,

> He was 'Din! Din! Din!
> 'You limpin' lump o' brick-dust, Gunga Din!
> 'Hi! Slippy *hitherao*
> 'Water, get it! *Panee lao*,
> 'You squidgy-nosed old idol, Gunga Din.'

The uniform 'e wore
Was nothin' much before,
An' rather less than 'arf o' that be'ind,
For a piece o' twisty rag
An' a goatskin water-bag
Was all the field-equipment 'e could find.
When the sweatin' troop-train lay
In a sidin' through the day,
Where the 'eat would make your bloomin' eyebrows crawl,
We shouted 'Harry By!'
Till our throats were bricky-dry,
Then we wopped 'im 'cause 'e couldn't serve us all.
> It was 'Din! Din! Din!
> 'You 'eathen, where the mischief 'ave you been?
> 'You put some *juldee* in it
> 'Or I'll *marrow* you this minute
> 'If you don't fill up my helmet, Gunga Din!'

'E would dot an' carry one
Till the longest day was done;
An' 'e didn't seem to know the use o' fear.
If we charged or broke or cut,
You could bet your bloomin' nut,
'E'd be waitin' fifty paces right flank rear.
With 'is mussick on 'is back,
'E would skip with our attack,
An' watch us till the bugles made 'Retire,'
An' for all 'is dirty 'ide
'E was white, clear white, inside
When 'e went to tend the wounded under fire!
> It was 'Din! Din! Din!'
> With the bullets kickin' dust-spots on the green.

>   When the cartridges ran out,
>   You could hear the front-ranks shout,
>   'Hi! ammunition-mules an' Gunga Din!'

I shan't forgit the night
When I dropped be'ind the fight
With a bullet where my belt-plate should 'a' been.
I was chokin' mad with thirst,
An' the man that spied me first
Was our good old grinnin', gruntin' Gunga Din.
'E lifted up my 'ead,
An' he plugged me where I bled,
An' 'e guv me 'arf-a-pint o' water green.
It was crawlin' and it stunk,
But of all the drinks I've drunk,
I'm gratefullest to one from Gunga Din.
>   It was 'Din! Din! Din!
>   "Ere's a beggar with a bullet through 'is spleen;
>   "E's chawin' up the ground,
>   'An' 'e's kickin' all around:
>   'For Gawd's sake git the water, Gunga Din!'

'E carried me away
To where a dooli lay,
An' a bullet come an' drilled the beggar clean.
'E put me safe inside,
An' just before 'e died,
'I 'ope you liked your drink,' sez Gunga Din.
So I'll meet 'im later on
At the place where 'e is gone—
Where it's always double drill and no canteen.
'E'll be squattin' on the coals
Givin' drink to poor damned souls,
An' I'll get a swig in hell from Gunga Din!
>   Yes, Din! Din! Din!
>   You Lazarushian-leather Gunga Din!
>   Though I've belted you and flayed you,
>   By the livin' Gawd that made you,

You're a better man than I am, Gunga Din!

IF—

('Brother Square-Toes'—Rewards and Fairies)

IF YOU can keep your head when all about you
    Are losing theirs and blaming it on you,
If you can trust yourself when all men doubt you,
    But make allowance for their doubting too;
If you can wait and not be tired by waiting,
    Or being lied about, don't deal in lies,
Or being hated, don't give way to hating,
    And yet don't look too good, nor talk too wise:

If you can dream—and not make dreams your master;
    If you can think—and not make thoughts your aim;
If you can meet with Triumph and Disaster
    And treat those two impostors just the same;
If you can bear to hear the truth you've spoken
    Twisted by knaves to make a trap for fools,
Or watch the things you gave your life to, broken,
    And stoop and build 'em up with worn-out tools:

If you can make one heap of all your winnings
    And risk it on one turn of pitch-and-toss,
And lose, and start again at your beginnings
    And never breathe a word about your loss;
If you can force your heart and nerve and sinew
    To serve your turn long after they are gone,
And so hold on when there is nothing in you
    Except the Will which says to them: 'Hold on!'

If you can talk with crowds and keep your virtue,
    Or walk with Kings—nor lose the common touch,
If neither foes nor loving friends can hurt you,
    If all men count with you, but none too much;
If you can fill the unforgiving minute

With sixty seconds' worth of distance run,
Yours is the Earth and everything that's in it,
    And—which is more—you'll be a Man, my son!

THE BEGINNINGS

It was not part of their blood,
It came to them very late
With long arrears to make good,
When the English began to hate.

They were not easily moved,
They were icy-willing to wait
Till every count should be proved,
Ere the English began to hate.

Their voices were even and low,
Their eyes were level and straight.
There was neither sign nor show,
When the English began to hate.

It was not preached to the crowd,
It was not taught by the State.
No man spoke it aloud,
When the English began to hate.

It was not suddenly bred,
It will not swiftly abate,
Through the chill years ahead,
When Time shall count from the date
That the English began to hate.

THE GODS OF
THE COPYBOOK HEADINGS

As I pass through my incarnations in every age and race,
I make my proper prostrations to the Gods of the Market Place.
Peering through reverent fingers I watch them flourish and fall,
And the Gods of the Copybook Headings, I notice, outlast them all.

We were living in trees when they met us. They showed us each in turn
That Water would certainly wet us, as Fire would certainly burn:
But we found them lacking in Uplift, Vision and Breadth of Mind,
So we left them to teach the Gorillas while we followed the March of Mankind.

We moved as the Spirit listed. They never altered their pace,
Being neither cloud nor wind-borne like the Gods of the Market Place,
But they always caught up with our progress, and presently word would come
That a tribe had been wiped off its icefield, or the lights had gone out in Rome.

With the Hopes that our World is built on they were utterly out of touch,
They denied that the Moon was Stilton; they denied she was even Dutch;
They denied that Wishes were Horses; they denied that a Pig had Wings;
So we worshipped the Gods of the Market Who promised these beautiful things.

When the Cambrian measures were forming, They promised perpetual peace.

They swore, if we gave them our weapons, that the wars of
   the tribes would cease.
But when we disarmed They sold us and delivered us bound
   to our foe,
And the Gods of the Copybook Headings said: "Stick to the
   Devil you know."

On the first Feminian Sandstones we were promised the Fuller
   Life
(Which started by loving our neighbour and ended by loving
   his wife)
Till our women had no more children and the men lost
   reason and faith,
And the Gods of the Copybook Headings said: "The Wages
   of Sin is Death."

In the Carboniferous Epoch we were promised abundance for
   all,
By robbing selected Peter to pay for collective Paul;
But, though we had plenty of money, there was nothing our
   money could buy,
And the Gods of the Copybook Headings said: "If you don't
   work you die."

Then the Gods of the Market tumbled, and their smooth-
   tongued wizards withdrew
And the hearts of the meanest were humbled and began to
   believe it was true
That All is not Gold that Glitters, and Two and Two make
   Four
And the Gods of the Copybook Headings limped up to
   explain it once more.

As it will be in the future, it was at the birth of Man
There are only four things certain since Social Progress began.
That the Dog returns to his Vomit and the Sow returns to her
   Mire,
And the burnt Fool's bandaged finger goes wabbling back to
   the Fire;

And that after this is accomplished, and the brave new world begins
When all men are paid for existing and no man must pay for his sins,
As surely as Water will wet us, as surely as Fire will burn,
The Gods of the Copybook Headings with terror and slaughter return!

W. B. Yeats

AN IRISH AIRMAN FORESEES HIS DEATH

I KNOW that I shall meet my fate
Somewhere among the clouds above;
Those that I fight I do not hate,
Those that I guard I do not love;
My country is Kiltartan Cross,
My countrymen Kiltartan's poor,
No likely end could bring them loss
Or leave them happier than before.
Nor law, nor duty bade me fight,
Nor public men, nor cheering crowds,
A lonely impulse of delight
Drove to this tumult in the clouds;
I balanced all, brought all to mind,
The years to come seemed waste of breath,
A waste of breath the years behind
In balance with this life, this death.

LEDA AND THE SWAN

A SUDDEN blow: the great wings beating still
Above the staggering girl, her thighs caressed
By the dark webs, her nape caught in his bill,
He holds her helpless breast upon his breast.

How can those terrified vague fingers push
The feathered glory from her loosening thighs?
And how can body, laid in that white rush,
But feel the strange heart beating where it lies?

A shudder in the loins engenders there
The broken wall, the burning roof and tower
And Agamemnon dead.
          Being so caught up,
So mastered by the brute blood of the air,
Did she put on his knowledge with his power
Before the indifferent beak could let her drop?

SAILING TO BYZANTIUM

I

THAT IS no country for old men. The young
In one another's arms, birds in the trees,
—Those dying generations—at their song,
The salmon-falls, the mackerel-crowded seas,
Fish, flesh, or fowl, commend all summer long
Whatever is begotten, born, and dies.
Caught in that sensual music all neglect
Monuments of unageing intellect.

II

An aged man is but a paltry thing,
A tattered coat upon a stick, unless
Soul clap its hands and sing, and louder sing

For every tatter in its mortal dress,
Nor is there singing school but studying
Monuments of its own magnificence;
And therefore I have sailed the seas and come
To the holy city of Byzantium.

III

O sages standing in God's holy fire
As in the gold mosaic of a wall,
Come from the holy fire, perne in a gyre,
And be the singing-masters of my soul.
Consume my heart away; sick with desire
And fastened to a dying animal
It knows not what it is; and gather me
Into the artifice of eternity.

IV

Once out of nature I shall never take
My bodily form from any natural thing,
But such a form as Grecian goldsmiths make
Of hammered gold and gold enamelling
To keep a drowsy Emperor awake;
Or set upon a golden bough to sing
To lords and ladies of Byzantium
Of what is past, or passing, or to come.

THE LAKE ISLE OF INNISFREE

I will arise and go now, and go to Innisfree,
And a small cabin build there, of clay and wattles made;
Nine bean-rows will I have there, a hive for the honey-bee,
And live alone in the bee-loud glade.

And I shall have some peace there, for peace comes dropping slow,

Dropping from the veils of the morning to where the cricket sings;
There midnight's all a glimmer, and noon a purple glow,
And evening full of the linnet's wings.

I will arise and go now, for always night and day
I hear lake water lapping with low sounds by the shore;
While I stand on the roadway, or on the pavements grey,
I hear it in the deep heart's core.

Hilaire Belloc

THE REBEL

THERE IS a wall of which the stones
Are lies and bribes and dead men's bones.
And wrongfully this evil wall
Denies what all men made for all,
And shamelessly this wall surrounds
Our homesteads and our native grounds.

But I will gather and I will ride,
And I will summon a countryside,
And many a man shall hear my halloa
Who never had thought the horn to follow;
And many a man shall ride with me
Who never had thought on earth to see
High Justice in her armoury.

When we find them where they stand,
A mile of men on either hand,
I mean to charge from right away
And force the flanks of their array,
And press them inward from the plains,
And drive them clamouring down the lanes,
And gallop and harry and have them down,
And carry the gates and hold the town.

Then shall I rest me from my ride
With my great anger satisfied.

Only, before I eat and drink,
When I have killed them all, I think
That I will batter their carven names,
And slit the pictures in their frames,
And burn for scent their cedar door,
And melt the gold their women wore,
And hack their horses at the knees,
And hew to death their timber trees,
And plough their gardens deep and through—
And all these things I mean to do
For fear perhaps my little son
Should break his hands, as I have done.

Stephen Crane

A MAN SAID TO THE UNIVERSE

A MAN said to the universe:
"Sir, I exist!"
"However," replied the universe,
"The fact has not created in me
A sense of obligation."

IN THE DESERT

IN THE desert
I saw a creature, naked, bestial,
Who, squatting upon the ground,
Held his heart in his hands,
And ate of it.
I said, "Is it good, friend?"

"It is bitter—bitter," he answered;

"But I like it
"Because it is bitter,
"And because it is my heart."

G. K. Chesterton

ELEGY IN A COUNTRY CHURCHYARD

THE MEN that worked for England
They have their graves at home:
And bees and birds of England
About the cross can roam.

But they that fought for England,
Following a falling star,
Alas, alas for England
They have their graves afar.

And they that rule in England,
In stately conclave met,
Alas, alas for England,
They have no graves as yet.

From THE BALLAD OF THE WHITE HORSE

I

THE VISION OF THE KING

BEFORE THE gods that made the gods
Had seen their sunrise pass,
The White Horse of the White Horse Vale
Was cut out of the grass.

Before the gods that made the gods
Had drunk at dawn their fill,
The White Horse of the White Horse Vale
Was hoary on the hill.

Age beyond age on British land,
Aeons on aeons gone,
Was peace and war in western hills,
And the White Horse looked on.

For the White Horse knew England
When there was none to know;
He saw the first oar break or bend,
He saw heaven fall and the world end,
O God, how long ago.

For the end of the world was long ago,
And all we dwell to-day
As children of some second birth,
Like a strange people left on earth
After a judgment day.

For the end of the world was long ago,
When the ends of the world waxed free,
When Rome was sunk in a waste of slaves,
And the sun drowned in the sea.

When Caesar's sun fell out of the sky
And whoso hearkened right
Could only hear the plunging
Of the nations in the night.

When the ends of the earth came marching in
To torch and cresset gleam.
And the roads of the world that lead to Rome
Were filled with faces that moved like foam,
Like faces in a dream.

And men rode out of the eastern lands,
Broad river and burning plain;

Trees that are Titan flowers to see,
And tiger skies, striped horribly,
With tints of tropic rain.

Where Ind's enamelled peaks arise
Around that inmost one,
Where ancient eagles on its brink,
Vast as archangels, gather and drink
The sacrament of the sun.

And men brake out of the northern lands,
Enormous lands alone,
Where a spell is laid upon life and lust
And the rain is changed to a silver dust
And the sea to a great green stone.

And a Shape that moveth murkily
In mirrors of ice and night,
Hath blanched with fear all beasts and birds,
As death and a shock of evil words
Blast a man's hair with white.

And the cry of the palms and the purple moons,
Or the cry of the frost and foam,
Swept ever around an inmost place,
And the din of distant race on race
Cried and replied round Rome.

And there was death on the Emperor
And night upon the Pope:
And Alfred, hiding in deep grass,
Hardened his heart with hope.

A sea-folk blinder than the sea
Broke all about his land,
But Alfred up against them bare
And gripped the ground and grasped the air,
Staggered, and strove to stand.

He bent them back with spear and spade,

With desperate dyke and wall,
With foemen leaning on his shield
And roaring on him when he reeled;
And no help came at all.

He broke them with a broken sword
A little towards the sea,
And for one hour of panting peace,
Ringed with a roar that would not cease,
With golden crown and girded fleece
Made laws under a tree.
The Northmen came about our land
A Christless chivalry:
Who knew not of the arch or pen,
Great, beautiful half-witted men
From the sunrise and the sea.

Misshapen ships stood on the deep
Full of strange gold and fire,
And hairy men, as huge as sin
With horned heads, came wading in
Through the long, low sea-mire.

Our towns were shaken of tall kings
With scarlet beards like blood:
The world turned empty where they trod,
They took the kindly cross of God
And cut it up for wood.

Their souls were drifting as the sea,
And all good towns and lands
They only saw with heavy eyes,
And broke with heavy hands,

Their gods were sadder than the sea,
Gods of a wandering will,
Who cried for blood like beasts at night,
Sadly, from hill to hill.

They seemed as trees walking the earth,

As witless and as tall,
Yet they took hold upon the heavens
And no help came at all.

They bred like birds in English woods,
They rooted like the rose,
When Alfred came to Athelney
To hide him from their bows

There was not English armour left,
Nor any English thing,
When Alfred came to Athelney
To be an English king.

For earthquake swallowing earthquake
Uprent the Wessex tree;
The whirlpool of the pagan sway
Had swirled his sires as sticks away
When a flood smites the sea.

And the great kings of Wessex
Wearied and sank in gore,
And even their ghosts in that great stress
Grew greyer and greyer, less and less,
With the lords that died in Lyonesse
And the king that comes no more.

And the God of the Golden Dragon
Was dumb upon his throne,
And the lord of the Golden Dragon
Ran in the woods alone.

And if ever he climbed the crest of luck
And set the flag before,
Returning as a wheel returns,
Came ruin and the rain that burns,
And all began once more.

And naught was left King Alfred
But shameful tears of rage,

In the island in the river
In the end of all his age.

In the island in the river
He was broken to his knee:
And he read, writ with an iron pen,
That God had wearied of Wessex men
And given their country, field and fen,
To the devils of the sea.

And he saw in a little picture,
Tiny and far away,
His mother sitting in Egbert's hall,
And a book she showed him, very small,
Where a sapphire Mary sat in stall
With a golden Christ at play.

It was wrought in the monk's slow manner,
From silver and sanguine shell,
Where the scenes are little and terrible,
Keyholes of heaven and hell.

In the river island of Athelney,
With the river running past,
In colours of such simple creed
All things sprang at him, sun and weed,
Till the grass grew to be grass indeed
And the tree was a tree at last.

Fearfully plain the flowers grew,
Like the child's book to read,
Or like a friend's face seen in a glass;
He looked; and there Our Lady was,
She stood and stroked the tall live grass
As a man strokes his steed.

Her face was like an open word
When brave men speak and choose,
The very colours of her coat

Were better than good news.

She spoke not, nor turned not,
Nor any sign she cast,
Only she stood up straight and free,
Between the flowers in Athelney,
And the river running past.

One dim ancestral jewel hung
On his ruined armour grey,
He rent and cast it at her feet:
Where, after centuries, with slow feet,
Men came from hall and school and street
And found it where it lay.

"Mother of God," the wanderer said,
"I am but a common king,
Nor will I ask what saints may ask,
To see a secret thing.

"The gates of heaven are fearful gates
Worse than the gates of hell;
Not I would break the splendours barred
Or seek to know the thing they guard,
Which is too good to tell.

"But for this earth most pitiful,
This little land I know,
If that which is for ever is,
Or if our hearts shall break with bliss,
Seeing the stranger go?

"When our last bow is broken, Queen,
And our last javelin cast,
Under some sad, green evening sky,
Holding a ruined cross on high,
Under warm westland grass to lie,
Shall we come home at last?"

And a voice came human but high up,

Like a cottage climbed among
The clouds; or a serf of hut and croft
That sits by his hovel fire as oft,
But hears on his old bare roof aloft
A belfry burst in song.

"The gates of heaven are lightly locked,
We do not guard our gain,
The heaviest hind may easily
Come silently and suddenly
Upon me in a lane.

"And any little maid that walks
In good thoughts apart,
May break the guard of the Three Kings
And see the dear and dreadful things
I hid within my heart.

"The meanest man in grey fields gone
Behind the set of sun,
Heareth between star and other star,
Through the door of the darkness fallen ajar,
The council, eldest of things that are,
The talk of the Three in One.

"The gates of heaven are lightly locked,
We do not guard our gold,
Men may uproot where worlds begin,
Or read the name of the nameless sin;
But if he fail or if he win
To no good man is told.

"The men of the East may spell the stars,
And times and triumphs mark,
But the men signed of the cross of Christ
Go gaily in the dark.

"The men of the East may search the scrolls
For sure fates and fame,
But the men that drink the blood of God

Go singing to their shame.

"The wise men know what wicked things
Are written on the sky,
They trim sad lamps, they touch sad strings,
Hearing the heavy purple wings,
Where the forgotten seraph kings
Still plot how God shall die.

"The wise men know all evil things
Under the twisted trees,
Where the perverse in pleasure pine
And men are weary of green wine
And sick of crimson seas.

"But you and all the kind of Christ
Are ignorant and brave,
And you have wars you hardly win
And souls you hardly save.

"I tell you naught for your comfort,
Yea, naught for your desire,
Save that the sky grows darker yet
And the sea rises higher.

"Night shall be thrice night over you,
And heaven an iron cope.
Do you have joy without a cause,
Yea, faith without a hope?"

Even as she spoke she was not,
Nor any word said he,
He only heard, still as he stood
Under the old night's nodding hood,
The sea-folk breaking down the wood
Like a high tide from sea.

He only heard the heathen men,
Whose eyes are blue and bleak,
Singing about some cruel thing

Done by a great and smiling king
In daylight on a deck.

He only heard the heathen men,
Whose eyes are blue and blind,
Singing what shameful things are done
Between the sunlit sea and the sun
When the land is left behind.

V
ETHANDUNE: THE FIRST STROKE

King Guthrum was a dread king,
Like death out of the north;
Shrines without name or number
He rent and rolled as lumber,
From Chester to the Humber
He drove his foemen forth.

The Roman villas heard him
In the valley of the Thames,
Come over the hills roaring
Above their roofs, and pouring
On spire and stair and flooring
Brimstone and pitch and flames.

Sheer o'er the great chalk uplands
And the hill of the Horse went he,
Till high on Hampshire beacons
He saw the southern sea.

High on the heights of Wessex
He saw the southern brine,
And turned him to a conquered land,
And where the northern thornwoods stand,
And the road parts on either hand,
There came to him a sign.

King Guthrum was a war-chief,
A wise man in the field,

And though he prospered well, and knew
How Alfred's folk were sad and few,
Not less with weighty care he drew
Long lines for pike and shield.

King Guthrum lay on the upper land,
On a single road at gaze,
And his foe must come with lean array,
Up the left arm of the cloven way,
To the meeting of the ways.

And long ere the noise of armour,
An hour ere the break of light,
The woods awoke with crash and cry,
And the birds sprang clamouring harsh and high,
And the rabbits ran like an elves' army
Ere Alfred came in sight.

The live wood came at Guthrum,
On foot and claw and wing,
The nests were noisy overhead,
For Alfred and the star of red,
All life went forth, and the forest fled
Before the face of the King.

But halted in the woodways
Christ's few were grim and grey,
And each with a small, far, bird-like sight
Saw the high folly of the fight;
And though strange joys had grown in the night,
Despair grew with the day.

And when white dawn crawled through the wood,
Like cold foam of a flood,
Then weakened every warrior's mood,
In hope, though not in hardihood;
And each man sorrowed as he stood
In the fashion of his blood.

For the Saxon Franklin sorrowed

For the things that had been fair;
For the dear dead woman, crimson-clad,
And the great feasts and the friends he had;
But the Celtic prince's soul was sad
For the things that never were.

In the eyes Italian all things
But a black laughter died;
And Alfred flung his shield to earth
And smote his breast and cried—

"I wronged a man to his slaying,
And a woman to her shame,
And once I looked on a sworn maid
That was wed to the Holy Name.

"And once I took my neighbour's wife,
That was bound to an eastland man,
In the starkness of my evil youth,
Before my griefs began.

"People, if you have any prayers,
Say prayers for me:
And lay me under a Christian stone
In that lost land I thought my own,
To wait till the holy horn is blown,
And all poor men are free."

Then Eldred of the idle farm
Leaned on his ancient sword,
As fell his heavy words and few;
And his eyes were of such alien blue
As gleams where the Northman saileth new
Into an unknown fiord.

"I was a fool and wasted ale—
My slaves found it sweet;
I was a fool and wasted bread,
And the birds had bread to eat.

"The kings go up and the kings go down,
And who knows who shall rule;
Next night a king may starve or sleep,
But men and birds and beasts shall weep
At the burial of a fool.

"O, drunkards in my cellar,
Boys in my apple tree,
The world grows stern and strange and new,
And wise men shall govern you,
And you shall weep for me.

"But yoke me my own oxen,
Down to my own farm;
My own dog will whine for me,
My own friends will bend the knee,
And the foes I slew openly
Have never wished me harm."

And all were moved a little,
But Colan stood apart,
Having first pity, and after
Hearing, like rat in rafter,
That little worm of laughter
That eats the Irish heart.

And his grey-green eyes were cruel,
And the smile of his mouth waxed hard,
And he said, "And when did Britain
Become your burying-yard?

"Before the Romans lit the land,
When schools and monks were none,
We reared such stones to the sun-god
As might put out the sun.

"The tall trees of Britain
We worshipped and were wise,
But you shall raid the whole land through
And never a tree shall talk to you,

Though every leaf is a tongue taught true
And the forest is full of eyes.

"On one round hill to the seaward
The trees grow tall and grey
And the trees talk together
When all men are away.

"O'er a few round hills forgotten
The trees grow tall in rings,
And the trees talk together
Of many pagan things.

"Yet I could lie and listen
With a cross upon my clay,
And hear unhurt for ever
What the trees of Britain say."

A proud man was the Roman,
His speech a single one,
But his eyes were like an eagle's eyes
That is staring at the sun.

"Dig for me where I die," he said,
"If first or last I fall—
Dead on the fell at the first charge,
Or dead by Wantage wall;

"Lift not my head from bloody ground,
Bear not my body home,
For all the earth is Roman earth
And I shall die in Rome."

Then Alfred, King of England,
Bade blow the horns of war,
And fling the Golden Dragon out,
With crackle and acclaim and shout,
Scrolled and aflame and far.

And under the Golden Dragon
Went Wessex all along,

Past the sharp point of the cloven ways,
Out from the black wood into the blaze
Of sun and steel and song.

And when they came to the open land
They wheeled, deployed and stood;
Midmost were Marcus and the King,
And Eldred on the right-hand wing,
And leftwards Colan darkling,
In the last shade of the wood.

But the Earls of the Great Army
Lay like a long half moon,
Ten poles before their palisades,
With wide-winged helms and runic blades
Red giants of an age of raids,
In the thornland of Ethandune.

Midmost the saddles rose and swayed,
And a stir of horses' manes,
Where Guthrum and a few rode high
On horses seized in victory;
But Ogier went on foot to die,
In the old way of the Danes.

Far to the King's left Elf the bard
Led on the eastern wing
With songs and spells that change the blood;
And on the King's right Harold stood,
The kinsman of the King.

Young Harold, coarse, with colours gay,
Smoking with oil and musk,
And the pleasant violence of the young,
Pushed through his people, giving tongue
Foewards, where, grey as cobwebs hung,
The banners of the Usk.

But as he came before his line
A little space along,

His beardless face broke into mirth,
And he cried: "What broken bits of earth
Are here? For what their clothes are worth
I would sell them for a song."

For Colan was hung with raiment
Tattered like autumn leaves,
And his men were all as thin as saints,
And all as poor as thieves.

No bows nor slings nor bolts they bore,
But bills and pikes ill-made;
And none but Colan bore a sword,
And rusty was its blade.

And Colan's eyes with mystery
And iron laughter stirred,
And he spoke aloud, but lightly
Not labouring to be heard.

"Oh, truly we be broken hearts,
For that cause, it is said,
We light our candles to that Lord
That broke Himself for bread.

"But though we hold but bitterly
What land the Saxon leaves,
Though Ireland be but a land of saints,
And Wales a land of thieves,

"I say you yet shall weary
Of the working of your word,
That stricken spirits never strike
Nor lean hands hold a sword.

"And if ever ye ride in Ireland,
The jest may yet be said,
There is the land of broken hearts,
And the land of broken heads."

Not less barbarian laughter

Choked Harold like a flood,
"And shall I fight with scarecrows
That am of Guthrum's blood?

"Meeting may be of war-men,
Where the best war-man wins;
But all this carrion a man shoots
Before the fight begins."

And stopping in his onward strides,
He snatched a bow in scorn
From some mean slave, and bent it on
Colan, whose doom grew dark; and shone
Stars evil over Caerleon,
In the place where he was born.

For Colan had not bow nor sling,
On a lonely sword leaned he,
Like Arthur on Excalibur
In the battle by the sea.

To his great gold ear-ring Harold
Tugged back the feathered tail,
And swift had sprung the arrow,
But swifter sprang the Gael.

Whirling the one sword round his head,
A great wheel in the sun,
He sent it splendid through the sky,
Flying before the shaft could fly—
It smote Earl Harold over the eye,
And blood began to run.

Colan stood bare and weaponless,
Earl Harold, as in pain,
Strove for a smile, put hand to head,
Stumbled and suddenly fell dead;
And the small white daisies all waxed red
With blood out of his brain.

And all at that marvel of the sword,
Cast like a stone to slay,
Cried out. Said Alfred: "Who would see
Signs, must give all things. Verily
Man shall not taste of victory
Till he throws his sword away."

Then Alfred, prince of England,
And all the Christian earls,
Unhooked their swords and held them up,
Each offered to Colan, like a cup
Of chrysolite and pearls.

And the King said, "Do thou take my sword
Who have done this deed of fire,
For this is the manner of Christian men,
Whether of steel or priestly pen,
That they cast their hearts out of their ken
To get their heart's desire.

"And whether ye swear a hive of monks,
Or one fair wife to friend,
This is the manner of Christian men,
That their oath endures the end.

"For love, our Lord, at the end of the world,
Sits a red horse like a throne,
With a brazen helm and an iron bow,
But one arrow alone.

"Love with the shield of the Broken Heart
Ever his bow doth bend,
With a single shaft for a single prize,
And the ultimate bolt that parts and flies
Comes with a thunder of split skies,
And a sound of souls that rend.

"So shall you earn a king's sword,
Who cast your sword away."
And the King took, with a random eye,

A rude axe from a hind hard by
And turned him to the fray.

For the swords of the Earls of Daneland
Flamed round the fallen lord.
The first blood woke the trumpet-tune,
As in monk's rhyme or wizard's rune,
Beginneth the battle of Ethandune
With the throwing of the sword.

THE DONKEY

When fishes flew and forests walked
    And figs grew upon thorn,
Some moment when the moon was blood
    Then surely I was born.

With monstrous head and sickening cry
    And ears like errant wings,
The devil's walking parody
    On all four-footed things.

The tattered outlaw of the earth,
    Of ancient crooked will;
Starve, scourge, deride me: I am dumb,
    I keep my secret still.

Fools! For I also had my hour;
    One far fierce hour and sweet:
There was a shout about my ears,
    And palms before my feet.

THE ROLLING ENGLISH ROAD

Before the Roman came to Rye or out to Severn strode,
The rolling English drunkard made the rolling English road.
A reeling road, a rolling road, that rambles round the shire,
And after him the parson ran, the sexton and the squire;
A merry road, a mazy road, and such as we did tread
The night we went to Birmingham by way of Beachy Head.

I knew no harm of Bonaparte and plenty of the Squire,
And for to fight the Frenchman I did not much desire;
But I did bash their baggonets because they came arrayed
To straighten out the crooked road an English drunkard made,
Where you and I went down the lane with ale-mugs in our hands,
The night we went to Glastonbury by way of Goodwin Sands.

His sins they were forgiven him; or why do flowers run
Behind him; and the hedges all strengthening in the sun?
The wild thing went from left to right and knew not which was which,
But the wild rose was above him when they found him in the ditch.
God pardon us, nor harden us; we did not see so clear
The night we went to Bannockburn by way of Brighton Pier.

My friends, we will not go again or ape an ancient rage,
Or stretch the folly of our youth to be the shame of age,
But walk with clearer eyes and ears this path that wandereth,
And see undrugged in evening light the decent inn of death;
For there is good news yet to hear and fine things to be seen,
Before we go to Paradise by way of Kensal Green.

Robert Frost

STOPPING BY WOODS ON A SNOWY EVENING

Whose woods these are I think I know.
His house is in the village though;
He will not see me stopping here
To watch his woods fill up with snow.

My little horse must think it queer
To stop without a farmhouse near
Between the woods and frozen lake
The darkest evening of the year.

He gives his harness bells a shake
To ask if there is some mistake.
The only other sound's the sweep
Of easy wind and downy flake.

The woods are lovely, dark and deep,
But I have promises to keep,
And miles to go before I sleep,
And miles to go before I sleep.

THE ROAD NOT TAKEN

Two roads diverged in a yellow wood,
And sorry I could not travel both
And be one traveler, long I stood
And looked down one as far as I could
To where it bent in the undergrowth;

Then took the other, as just as fair,
And having perhaps the better claim,
Because it was grassy and wanted wear;
Though as for that the passing there

Had worn them really about the same,

And both that morning equally lay
In leaves no step had trodden black.
Oh, I kept the first for another day!
Yet knowing how way leads on to way,
I doubted if I should ever come back.

I shall be telling this with a sigh
Somewhere ages and ages hence:
Two roads diverged in a wood, and I—
I took the one less traveled by,
And that has made all the difference.

Edward Thomas

ADLESTROP

Yes. I remember Adlestrop—
The name, because one afternoon
Of heat the express-train drew up there
Unwontedly. It was late June.

The steam hissed. Someone cleared his throat.
No one left and no one came
On the bare platform. What I saw
Was Adlestrop—only the name

And willows, willow-herb, and grass,
And meadowsweet, and haycocks dry,
No whit less still and lonely fair
Than the high cloudlets in the sky.

And for that minute a blackbird sang
Close by, and round him, mistier,
Farther and farther, all the birds
Of Oxfordshire and Gloucestershire.

GONE, GONE AGAIN

Gone, gone again,
May, June, July,
And August gone,
Again gone by,

Not memorable
Save that I saw them go,
As past the empty quays
The rivers flow.

And now again,
In the harvest rain,
The Blenheim oranges
Fall grubby from the trees,

As when I was young—
And when the lost one was here—
And when the war began
To turn young men to dung.

Look at the old house,
Outmoded, dignified,
Dark and untenanted,
With grass growing instead

Of the footsteps of life,
The friendliness, the strife;
In its beds have lain
Youth, love, age, and pain:

I am something like that;
Only I am not dead,
Still breathing and interested
In the house that is not dark:—

I am something like that:
Not one pane to reflect the sun,
For the schoolboys to throw at—
They have broken every one.

THE CHILD ON THE CLIFFS

MOTHER, the root of this little yellow flower
Among the stones has the taste of quinine.
Things are strange to-day on the cliff. The sun shines so bright,
And the grasshopper works at his sewing-machine
So hard. Here's one on my hand, mother, look;
I lie so still. There's one on your book.

But I have something to tell more strange. So leave
Your book to the grasshopper, mother dear,—
Like a green knight in a dazzling market-place,—
And listen now. Can you hear what I hear
Far out? Now and then the foam there curls
And stretches a white arm out like a girl's.

Fishes and gulls ring no bells. There cannot be
A chapel or church between here and Devon,
With fishes or gulls ringing its bell,—hark!—
Somewhere under the sea or up in heaven.
"It's the bell, my son, out in the bay
On the buoy. It does sound sweet to-day."

Sweeter I never heard, mother, no, not in all Wales.
I should like to be lying under that foam,
Dead, but able to hear the sound of the bell,
And certain that you would often come
And rest, listening happily.
I should be happy if that could be.

Wallace Stevens

SUNDAY MORNING

I

Complacencies of the peignoir, and late
Coffee and oranges in a sunny chair,
And the green freedom of a cockatoo
Upon a rug mingle to dissipate
The holy hush of ancient sacrifice.
She dreams a little, and she feels the dark
Encroachment of that old catastrophe,
As a calm darkens among water-lights.
The pungent oranges and bright, green wings
Seem things in some procession of the dead,
Winding across wide water, without sound.
The day is like wide water, without sound,
Stilled for the passing of her dreaming feet
Over the seas, to silent Palestine,
Dominion of the blood and sepulchre.

II

Why should she give her bounty to the dead?
What is divinity if it can come
Only in silent shadows and in dreams?
Shall she not find in comforts of the sun,
In pungent fruit and bright, green wings, or else
In any balm or beauty of the earth,
Things to be cherished like the thought of heaven?
Divinity must live within herself:
Passions of rain, or moods in falling snow;
Grievings in loneliness, or unsubdued
Elations when the forest blooms; gusty
Emotions on wet roads on autumn nights;
All pleasures and all pains, remembering
The bough of summer and the winter branch.

These are the measures destined for her soul.

III

Jove in the clouds had his inhuman birth.
No mother suckled him, no sweet land gave
Large-mannered motions to his mythy mind.
He moved among us, as a muttering king,
Magnificent, would move among his hinds,
Until our blood, commingling, virginal,
With heaven, brought such requital to desire
The very hinds discerned it, in a star.
Shall our blood fail? Or shall it come to be
The blood of paradise? And shall the earth
Seem all of paradise that we shall know?
The sky will be much friendlier then than now,
A part of labor and a part of pain,
And next in glory to enduring love,
Not this dividing and indifferent blue.

IV

She says, "I am content when wakened birds,
Before they fly, test the reality
Of misty fields, by their sweet questionings;
But when the birds are gone, and their warm fields
Return no more, where, then, is paradise?"
There is not any haunt of prophecy,
Nor any old chimera of the grave,
Neither the golden underground, nor isle
Melodious, where spirits gat them home,
Nor visionary south, nor cloudy palm
Remote on heaven's hill, that has endured
As April's green endures; or will endure
Like her remembrance of awakened birds,
Or her desire for June and evening, tipped
By the consummation of the swallow's wings.

V

She says, "But in contentment I still feel
The need of some imperishable bliss."
Death is the mother of beauty; hence from her,
Alone, shall come fulfilment to our dreams
And our desires. Although she strews the leaves
Of sure obliteration on our paths,
The path sick sorrow took, the many paths
Where triumph rang its brassy phrase, or love
Whispered a little out of tenderness,
She makes the willow shiver in the sun
For maidens who were wont to sit and gaze
Upon the grass, relinquished to their feet.
She causes boys to pile new plums and pears
On disregarded plate. The maidens taste
And stray impassioned in the littering leaves.

VI

Is there no change of death in paradise?
Does ripe fruit never fall? Or do the boughs
Hang always heavy in that perfect sky,
Unchanging, yet so like our perishing earth,
With rivers like our own that seek for seas
They never find, the same receding shores
That never touch with inarticulate pang?
Why set the pear upon those river-banks
Or spice the shores with odors of the plum?
Alas, that they should wear our colors there,
The silken weavings of our afternoons,
And pick the strings of our insipid lutes!
Death is the mother of beauty, mystical,
Within whose burning bosom we devise
Our earthly mothers waiting, sleeplessly.

VII

Supple and turbulent, a ring of men
Shall chant in orgy on a summer morn
Their boisterous devotion to the sun,
Not as a god, but as a god might be,
Naked among them, like a savage source.
Their chant shall be a chant of paradise,
Out of their blood, returning to the sky;
And in their chant shall enter, voice by voice,
The windy lake wherein their lord delights,
The trees, like serafin, and echoing hills,
That choir among themselves long afterward.
They shall know well the heavenly fellowship
Of men that perish and of summer morn.
And whence they came and whither they shall go
The dew upon their feet shall manifest.

VIII

She hears, upon that water without sound,
A voice that cries, "The tomb in Palestine
Is not the porch of spirits lingering.
It is the grave of Jesus, where he lay."
We live in an old chaos of the sun,
Or old dependency of day and night,
Or island solitude, unsponsored, free,
Of that wide water, inescapable.
Deer walk upon our mountains, and the quail
Whistle about us their spontaneous cries;
Sweet berries ripen in the wilderness;
And, in the isolation of the sky,
At evening, casual flocks of pigeons make
Ambiguous undulations as they sink,
Downward to darkness, on extended wings.

THE SNOW MAN

ONE MUST have a mind of winter
To regard the frost and the boughs
Of the pine-trees crusted with snow;

And have been cold a long time
To behold the junipers shagged with ice,
The spruces rough in the distant glitter

Of the January sun; and not to think
Of any misery in the sound of the wind,
In the sound of a few leaves,

Which is the sound of the land
Full of the same wind
That is blowing in the same bare place

For the listener, who listens in the snow,
And, nothing himself, beholds
Nothing that is not there and the nothing that is.

Alfred Noyes

THE BARREL-ORGAN

THERE'S A barrel-organ carolling across a golden street
    In the City as the sun sinks low;
And the music's not immortal; but the world has made it sweet
    And fulfilled it with the sunset glow;
And it pulses through the pleasures of the City and the pain
    That surround the singing organ like a large eternal light;
And they've given it a glory and a part to play again
    In the Symphony that rules the day and night.

And now it's marching onward through the realms of old romance
    And trolling out a fond familiar tune,

And now it's roaring cannon down to fight the King of France,
    And now it's prattling softly to the moon,
And all around the organ there's a sea without a shore
    Of human joys and wonders and regrets;
To remember and to recompense the music evermore
    For what the cold machinery forgets . . .

> Yes; as the music changes,
>   Like a prismatic glass,
> It takes the light and ranges
>   Through all the moods that pass;
> Dissects the common carnival
>   Of passions and regrets,
> And gives the world a glimpse of all
>   The colours it forgets.
>
> And there *La Traviata* sighs
>   Another sadder song;
> And there *Il Trovatore* cries
>   A tale of deeper wrong;
> And bolder knights to battle go
>   With sword and shield and lance,
> Than ever here on earth below
>   Have whirled into—*a dance!*—

Go down to Kew in lilac-time, in lilac-time, in lilac-time;
    Go down to Kew in lilac-time (it isn't far from London!)
And you shall wander hand in hand with love in summer's wonderland;
    Go down to Kew in lilac-time (it isn't far from London!)

The cherry-trees are seas of bloom and soft perfume and sweet perfume,
    The cherry-trees are seas of bloom (and oh, so near to London!)
And there they say, when dawn is high and all the world's a blaze of sky

   The cuckoo, though he's very shy, will sing a song for
     London.

The Dorian nightingale is rare and yet they say you'll hear
  him there
    At Kew, at Kew in lilac-time (and oh, so near to London!)
The linnet and the throstle, too, and after dark the long halloo
    And golden-eyed *tu-whit, tu-whoo,* of owls that ogle
      London.

For Noah hardly knew a bird of any kind that isn't heard
    At Kew, at Kew in lilac-time (and oh, so near to London!)
And when the rose begins to pout and all the chestnut spires
  are out
    You'll hear the rest without a doubt, all chorussing for
      London:—

Come down to Kew in lilac-time, in lilac-time, in lilac-time;
   Come down to Kew in lilac-time (it isn't far from London!)
And you shall wander hand in hand with love in summer's
wonderland;
   Come down to Kew in lilac-time (it isn't far from London!)

And then the troubadour begins to thrill the golden street,
    In the City as the sun sinks low;
And in all the gaudy busses there are scores of weary feet
Making time, sweet time, with a dull mechanic beat,
And a thousand hearts are plunging to a love they'll never
  meet,
Through the meadows of the sunset, through the poppies and
  the wheat,
    In the land where the dead dreams go.

Verdi, Verdi, when you wrote *Il Trovatore* did you dream
    Of the city when the sun sinks low,
Of the organ and the monkey and the many-coloured stream
On the Picadilly pavement, of the myriad eyes that seem
To be litten for a moment with a wild Italian gleam
As *A che la morte* parodies the world's eternal theme
    And pulses with the sunset-glow.

There's a thief, perhaps, that listens with a face of frozen stone
    In the City as the sun sinks low;
There's a portly man of business with a balance of his own,
There's a clerk and there's a butcher of a soft reposeful tone.
And they're all of them returning to the heavens they have known:
They are crammed and jammed in busses and—they're each of them alone
    In the land where the dead dreams go.

There's a very modish woman and her smile is very bland
    In the City as the sun sinks low;
And her hansom jingles onward, but her little jewelled hand
Is clenched a little tighter and she cannot understand
What she wants or why she wanders to that undiscovered land,
For the parties there are not at all the sort of thing she planned,
    In the land where the dead dreams go.

There's a rowing man that listens, and his heart is crying out
    In the City as the sun sinks low;
For the barge, the eight, the Isis, and the coach's whoop and shout,
For the minute-gun, the counting and the long dishevelled rout,
For the howl along the tow-path and a fate that's still in doubt,
For a roughened oar to handle and a race to think about
    In the land where the dead dreams go.

There's a labourer that listens to the voices of the dead
    In the City as the sun sinks low;
And his hand begins to tremble and his face to smoulder red,
As he sees a loafer watching him and—there he turns his head
And stares into the sunset where his April love is fled,
For he hears her softly singing, and his lonely soul is led
    Through the land where the dead dreams go.

There's an old and haggard demi-rep, it's ringing in her ears,
   In the City as the sun sinks low;
With the wild and empty sorrow of the love that blights and sears,
Oh, and if she hurries onward, then be sure, be sure she hears,
Hears and bears the bitter burden of the unforgotten years,
And her laugh's a little harsher and her eyes are brimmed with tears
   For the land where the dead dreams go.

There's a barrel-organ carolling across a golden street
   In the City as the sun sinks low;
Though the music's only Verdi there's a world to make it sweet
Just as yonder yellow sunset where the earth and heaven meet
Mellows all the sooty City! Hark, a hundred thousand feet
Are marching on to glory through the poppies and the wheat
   In the land where the dead dreams go.

     So it's Jeremiah, Jeremiah,
        What have you to say
     When you meet the garland girls
        Tripping on their way?

     All around my gala hat
        I wear a wreath of roses
     (A long and lonely year it is
        I've waited for the May!)
     If any one should ask you,
        The reason why I wear it is—
     My own love, my true love,
        Is coming home to-day.

And it's buy a bunch of violets for the lady
   (It's lilac-time in London; It's lilac-time in London!)
Buy a bunch of violets for the lady
   While the sky burns blue above:

On the other side the street you'll find it shady
   (It's lilac-time in London! It's lilac-time in London!)

But buy a bunch of violets for the lady,
    And tell her she's your own true love.

There's a barrel-organ carolling across a golden street
    In the City as the sun sinks glittering and slow;
And the music's not immortal; but the world has made it sweet
And enriched it with the harmonies that make a song complete
In the deeper heavens of music where the night and morning meet,
    As it dies into the sunset-glow;
And it pulses through the pleasures of the City and the pain
    That surround the singing organ like a large eternal light,
And they've given it a glory and a part to play again
    In the Symphony that rules the day and night.

    And there, as the music changes,
        The song runs round again.
    Once more it turns and ranges
        Through all its joy and pain,
    Dissects the common carnival
        Of passions and regrets;
    And the wheeling world remembers all
        The wheeling song forgets.

    Once more *La Traviata* sighs
        Another sadder song:
    Once more *Il Trovatore* cries
        A tale of deeper wrong;
    Once more the knights to battle go
        With sword and shield and lance
    Till once, once more, the shattered foe
        Has whirled into—a dance!

Come down to Kew in lilac-time, in lilac-time, in lilac time;
    Come down to Kew in lilac-time (it isn't far from London!)
And you shall wander hand and hand with love in summer's wonderland;

Come down to Kew in lilac-time (it isn't far from London!)

THE HIGHWAYMAN

I

THE WIND was a torrent of darkness among the gusty trees.
The moon was a ghostly galleon tossed upon cloudy seas.
The road was a ribbon of moonlight over the purple moor,
And the highwayman came riding—
   Riding—riding—
The highwayman came riding, up to the old inn-door.

He'd a French cocked-hat on his forehead, a bunch of lace at his chin,
A coat of the claret velvet, and breeches of brown doe-skin.
They fitted with never a wrinkle. His boots were up to the thigh.
And he rode with a jewelled twinkle,
   His pistol butts a-twinkle,
His rapier hilt a-twinkle, under the jewelled sky.

Over the cobbles he clattered and clashed in the dark inn-yard.
He tapped with his whip on the shutters, but all was locked and barred.
He whistled a tune to the window, and who should be waiting there
But the landlord's black-eyed daughter,
   Bess, the landlord's daughter,
Plaiting a dark red love-knot into her long black hair.

And dark in the dark old inn-yard a stable-wicket creaked
Where Tim the ostler listened. His face was white and peaked.
His eyes were hollows of madness, his hair like mouldy hay,
But he loved the landlord's daughter,
   The landlord's red-lipped daughter.
Dumb as a dog he listened, and he heard the robber say—

"One kiss, my bonny sweetheart, I'm after a prize to-night,
But I shall be back with the yellow gold before the morning light;
Yet, if they press me sharply, and harry me through the day,
Then look for me by moonlight,
    Watch for me by moonlight,
I'll come to thee by moonlight, though hell should bar the way."

He rose upright in the stirrups. He scarce could reach her hand,
But she loosened her hair in the casement. His face burnt like a brand
As the black cascade of perfume came tumbling over his breast;
And he kissed its waves in the moonlight,
    (O, sweet black waves in the moonlight!)
Then he tugged at his rein in the moonlight, and galloped away to the west.

II

He did not come in the dawning. He did not come at noon;
And out of the tawny sunset, before the rise of the moon,
When the road was a gypsy's ribbon, looping the purple moor,
A red-coat troop came marching—
    Marching—marching—
King George's men came marching, up to the old inn-door.

They said no word to the landlord. They drank his ale instead.
But they gagged his daughter, and bound her, to the foot of her narrow bed.
Two of them knelt at her casement, with muskets at their side!
There was death at every window;
    And hell at one dark window;
For Bess could see, through her casement, the road that *he* would ride.

They had tied her up to attention, with many a sniggering
  jest.
They had bound a musket beside her, with the muzzle
  beneath her breast!
"Now, keep good watch!" and they kissed her. She heard the
  doomed man say—
Look for me by moonlight;
  Watch for me by moonlight;
I'll come to thee by moonlight, though hell should bar the way!

She twisted her hands behind her; but all the knots held good!
She writhed her hands till her fingers were wet with sweat or
  blood!
They stretched and strained in the darkness, and the hours
  crawled by like years
Till, now, on the stroke of midnight,
  Cold, on the stroke of midnight,
The tip of one finger touched it! The trigger at least was hers!

The tip of one finger touched it. She strove no more for the
  rest.
Up, she stood up to attention, with the muzzle beneath her
  breast.
She would not risk their hearing; she would not strive again;
For the road lay bare in the moonlight;
  Blank and bare in the moonlight;
And the blood of her veins, in the moonlight, throbbed to her
  love's refrain.

Tlot-tlot; tlot-tlot! Had they heard it? The horsehoofs ringing
  clear;
Tlot-tlot; tlot-tlot, in the distance? Were they deaf that they did
  not hear?
Down the ribbon of moonlight, over the brow of the hill,
The highwayman came riding—
  Riding—riding—
The red coats looked to their priming! She stood up, straight
  and still.

Tlot-tlot, in the frosty silence! *Tlot-tlot*, in the echoing night!

Nearer he came and nearer. Her face was like a light.
Her eyes grew wide for a moment; she drew one last deep breath,
Then her finger moved in the moonlight,
    Her musket shattered the moonlight,
Shattered her breast in the moonlight and warned him—with her death.

He turned. He spurred to the west; he did not know who stood
Bowed, with her head o'er the musket, drenched with her own blood!
Not till the dawn he heard it, and his face grew grey to hear
How Bess, the landlord's daughter,
    The landlord's black-eyed daughter,
Had watched for her love in the moonlight, and died in the darkness there.

Back, he spurred like a madman, shrieking a curse to the sky,
With the white road smoking behind him and his rapier brandished high.
Blood red were his spurs in the golden noon; wine-red was his velvet coat;
When they shot him down on the highway,
    Down like a dog on the highway,
And he lay in his blood on the highway, with a bunch of lace at his throat.

. . .

And still of a winter's night, they say, when the wind is in the trees,
When the moon is a ghostly galleon tossed upon cloudy seas,
When the road is a ribbon of moonlight over the purple moor,
A highwayman comes riding—
    Riding—riding—
A highwayman comes riding, up to the old inn-door.

Over the cobbles he clatters and clangs in the dark inn-yard.
He taps with his whip on the shutters, but all is locked and barred.
He whistles a tune to the window, and who should be waiting there
But the landlord's black-eyed daughter,

> Bess, the landlord's daughter,
> Plaiting a dark red love-knot into her long black hair.

James Elroy Flecker

THE GOLDEN JOURNEY TO SAMARKAND

Prologue

I

We who with songs beguile your pilgrimage
— And swear that Beauty lives though lilies die,
We Poets of a proud old lineage
— Who sing to find your hearts, we know not why, —

What shall we tell you? Tales, marvellous tales
— Of ships and stars and isles where good men rest,
Where nevermore the rose of sunset pales,
— And winds and shadows fall toward the West:

And there the world's first huge white-bearded kings
— In dim glades sleeping, murmur in their sleep,
And closer round their breasts the ivy clings,
— Cutting its pathway slow and red and deep.

II

And how beguile you? Death has no repose
— Warmer and deeper than that Orient sand
Which hides the beauty and bright faith of those
— Who made the Golden Journey to Samarkand.

And now they wait and whiten peaceably,
— Those conquerors, those poets, those so fair:
They know time comes, not only you and I,
— But the whole world shall whiten, here or there;

When those long caravans that cross the plain
— With dauntless feet and sound of silver bells
Put forth no more for glory or for gain,
— Take no more solace from the palm-girt wells.

When the great markets by the sea shut fast
— All that calm Sunday that goes on and on:
When even lovers find their peace at last
— And Earth is but a star, that once had shone.

Epilogue

— At the Gate of the Sun, Bagdad, in olden time.

The Merchants: (together)

> A way, for we are ready to a man!
> — Our camels sniff the evening and are glad.
> Lead on, O Master of the Caravan:
> — Lead on the Merchant-Princes of Bagdad.

The Chief Draper:

> Have we not Indian carpets dark as wine,
> — Turbans and sashes, gowns and bows and veils,
> And broideries of intricate design,
> — And printed hangings in enormous bales?

The Chief Grocer:

> We have rose-candy, we have spikenard,
> — Mastic and terebinth and oil and spice,
> And such sweet jams meticulously jarred
> — As God's own Prophet eats in Paradise.

The Principal Jews:

> And we have manuscripts in peacock styles
> — By Ali of Damascus; we have swords
> Engraved with storks and apes and crocodiles,
> — And heavy beaten necklaces, for Lords.

The Master Of The Caravan:

But you are nothing but a lot of Jews.

The Principal Jews:

Sir, even dogs have daylight, and we pay.

The Master of the Caravan:

But who are ye in rags and rotten shoes,
— You dirty-bearded, blocking up the way?

The Pilgrims:

We are the Pilgrims, master; we shall go
— Always a little further: it may be
Beyond that last blue mountain barred with snow,
— Across that angry or that glimmering sea,

White on a throne or guarded in a cave
— There lives a prophet who can understand
Why men were born: but surely we are brave,
— Who make the Golden Journey to Samarkand.

The Chief Merchant:

We gnaw the nail of hurry. Master, away!

One Of The Women:

— O turn your eyes to where your children stand.
Is not Bagdad the beautiful? O stay!

The Merchants: (in chorus)

— We take the Golden Road to Samarkand.

An Old Man:

Have you not girls and garlands in your homes,
— Eunuchs and Syrian boys at your command?
Seek not excess: God hateth him who roams!

The Merchants: (in chorus)

— We make the Golden Journey to Samarkand.

A Pilgrim With a Beautiful Voice:

Sweet to ride forth at evening from the wells
— When shadows pass gigantic on the sand,
And softly through the silence beat the bells
— Along the Golden Road to Samarkand.

A Merchant:

We travel not for trafficking alone:
— By hotter winds our fiery hearts are fanned:
For lust of knowing what should not be known
— We make the Golden Journey to Samarkand.

The Master of the Caravan:

Open the gate, O watchman of the night!

The Watchman:

— Ho, travellers, I open. For what land
Leave you the dim-moon city of delight?

The Merchants (with a shout):

— We make the Golden Journey to Samarkand.
[The Caravan passes through the gate]

The Watchman (consoling the women):

What would ye, ladies? It was ever thus.
— Men are unwise and curiously planned.

A Woman:

— They have their dreams, and do not think of us.

Voices of the Caravan: (in the distance, singing)

— We make the Golden Journey to Samarkand.

Ezra Pound

CANTO I

AND THEN went down to the ship,
Set keel to breakers, forth on the godly sea, and,
We set up mast and sail on that thwart ship,
Bore sheep aboard her, and our bodies also
Heavy with weeping, and winds from sternward
Bore us out onward with bellying canvas,
Circe's this craft, the trim-coifed goddess.
Then sat we amidships, wind jamming the tiller,
Thus with stretched sail, we went over sea till day's end.
Sun to his slumber, shadows o'er all the ocean,
Came we then to the bounds of deepest water,
To the Kimmerian lands, and peopled cities
Covered with close-webbed mist, unpierced ever
With glitter of sun-rays
Nor with stars stretched, nor looking back from heaven
Swartest night stretched over wretched men there.
The ocean following backward, came we then to the place
Aforesaid by Circe.
Here did they rites, Perimedes and Eurylochus,
And drawing sword from my hip
I dug the ell-square pitkin;
Poured we libations unto each the dead,
First mead and then sweet wine, water mixed with white flour.
Then prayed I many a prayer to the sickly death's-heads;
A set in Ithaca, sterile bulls of the best
For sacrifice, heaping the pyre with goods,
A sheep to Tiresias only, black and a bell-sheep.
Dark blood flowed in the fosse,
Souls out of Erebus, cadaverous dead, of brides
Of youths and of the old who had borne much;
Souls stained with recent tears, girls tender,
Men many, mauled with bronze lance heads,

Battle spoil, bearing yet dreory arms,
These many crowded about me; with shouting,
Pallor upon me, cried to my men for more beasts;
Slaughtered the herds, sheep slain of bronze;
Poured ointment, cried to the gods,
To Pluto the strong, and praised Proserpine;
Unsheathed the narrow sword,
I sat to keep off the impetuous impotent dead,
Till I should hear Tiresias.
But first Elpenor came, our friend Elpenor,
Unburied, cast on the wide earth,
Limbs that we left in the house of Circe,
Unwept, unwrapped in sepulchre, since toils urged other.
Pitiful spirit. And I cried in hurried speech:
"Elpenor, how art thou come to this dark coast?
"Cam'st thou afoot, outstripping seamen?"
And he in heavy speech:
"Ill fat and abundant wine. I slept in Circe's ingle.
"Going down the long ladder unguarded,
"I fell against the buttress,
"Shattered the nape-nerve, the soul sought Avernus.
"But thou, O King, I bid remember me, unwept, unburied,
"Heap up mine arms, be tomb by sea-bord, and inscribed:
"A man of no fortune, and with a name to come.
"And set my oar up, that I swung mid fellows."

And Anticlea came, whom I beat off, and then Tiresias
   Theban,
Holding his golden wand, knew me, and spoke first:
"A second time? why? man of ill star,
"Facing the sunless dead and this joyless region?
"Stand from the fosse, leave me my blood bever
"For soothsay."
And I stepped back,
And he strong with the blood, said then: "Odysseus
"Shalt return through spiteful Neptune, over dark seas,
"Lose all companions." And then Anticlea came.

Lie quiet Divus. I mean, that is Andreas Divus,
In officina Wecheli, 1538, out of Homer.
And he sailed, by Sirens and thence outward and away
And unto Circe
Venerandam,
In the Cretan's phrase, with the golden crown, Aphrodite,
Cypri munomenta sortida est, mirthful, orichalchi, with golden
Girdles and breast bands, thou with dark eyelids
Bearing the golden bough of Argicida. So that:

CANTO XLV

With *Usura*

WITH USURA hath no man a house of good stone
each block cut smooth and well fitting
that design might cover their face,
with usura
hath no man a painted paradise on his church wall
harpes et luz
or where virgin receiveth message
and halo projects from incision,
with usura
seeth no man Gonzaga his heirs and his concubines
no picture is made to endure nor to live with
but it is made to sell and sell quickly
with usura, sin against nature
is thy bread ever more of stale rags
is thy bread dry as paper,
with no mountain wheat, no strong flour
with usura the line grows thick
with usura is no clear demarcation
and no man can find site for his dwelling.
Stonecutter is kept from his stone
weaver is kept from his loom

WITH USURA
wool comes not to market
sheep bringeth no gain with usura
Usura is a murrain, usura
blunteth the needle in the maid's hand
and stopped the spinner's cunning. Pietro Lombardo
came not by usura
Duccio came not by usura
nor Pier della Francesca; Zuan Bellin' not by usura
nor was 'La Calunnia' painted.
Came not by usura Angelico; came not Ambrogio Praedis,
Came no church of cut stone signed: *Adamo me fecit*.
Not by usura St. Trophime
Not by usura Saint Hilaire,
Usura rusteth the chisel
It rusteth the craft and the craftsman
It gnaweth the thread in the loom
None learneth to weave gold in her pattern;
Azure hath a canker by usura; cramoisy is unbroidered
Emerald findeth no Memling
Usura slayeth the child in the womb
It stayeth the young man's courting
It hath brought palsey to bed, lyeth
between the young bride and her bridegroom
   CONTRA NATURAM
They have brought whores for Eleusis
Corpses are set to banquet
at behest of usura.

IN A STATION OF THE METRO

THE APPARITION of these faces in the crowd:
Petals on a wet, black bough.

THE SEAFARER

May I for my own self song's truth reckon,
Journey's jargon, how I in harsh days
Hardship endured oft.
Bitter breast-cares have I abided,
Known on my keel many a care's hold,
And dire sea-surge, and there I oft spent
Narrow nightwatch nigh the ship's head
While she tossed close to cliffs. Coldly afflicted,
My feet were by frost benumbed.
Chill its chains are; chafing sighs
Hew my heart round and hunger begot
Mere-weary mood. Lest man know not
That he on dry land loveliest liveth,
List how I, care-wretched, on ice-cold sea,
Weathered the winter, wretched outcast
Deprived of my kinsmen;
Hung with hard ice-flakes, where hail-scur flew,
There I heard naught save the harsh sea
And ice-cold wave, at whiles the swan cries,
Did for my games the gannet's clamour,
Sea-fowls, loudness was for me laughter,
The mews' singing all my mead-drink.
Storms, on the stone-cliffs beaten, fell on the stern
In icy feathers; full oft the eagle screamed
With spray on his pinion.
Not any protector
May make merry man faring needy.
This he little believes, who aye in winsome life
Abides 'mid burghers some heavy business,
Wealthy and wine-flushed, how I weary oft
Must bide above brine.
Neareth nightshade, snoweth from north,
Frost froze the land, hail fell on earth then
Corn of the coldest. Nathless there knocketh now
The heart's thought that I on high streams

The salt-wavy tumult traverse alone.
Moaneth alway my mind's lust
That I fare forth, that I afar hence
Seek out a foreign fastness.
For this there's no mood-lofty man over earth's midst,
Not though he be given his good, but will have in his youth greed;
Nor his deed to the daring, nor his king to the faithful
But shall have his sorrow for sea-fare
Whatever his lord will.
He hath not heart for harping, nor in ring-having
Nor winsomeness to wife, nor world's delight
Nor any whit else save the wave's slash,
Yet longing comes upon him to fare forth on the water.
Bosque taketh blossom, cometh beauty of berries,
Fields to fairness, land fares brisker,
All this admonisheth man eager of mood,
The heart turns to travel so that he then thinks
On flood-ways to be far departing.
Cuckoo calleth with gloomy crying,
He singeth summerward, bodeth sorrow,
The bitter heart's blood. Burgher knows not —
He the prosperous man — what some perform
Where wandering them widest draweth.
So that but now my heart burst from my breast-lock,
My mood 'mid the mere-flood,
Over the whale's acre, would wander wide.
On earth's shelter cometh oft to me,
Eager and ready, the crying lone-flyer,
Whets for the whale-path the heart irresistibly,
O'er tracks of ocean; seeing that anyhow
My lord deems to me this dead life
On loan and on land, I believe not
That any earth-weal eternal standeth
Save there be somewhat calamitous
That, ere a man's tide go, turn it to twain.
Disease or oldness or sword-hate

Beats out the breath from doom-gripped body.
And for this, every earl whatever, for those speaking after —
Laud of the living, boasteth some last word,
That he will work ere he pass onward,
Frame on the fair earth 'gainst foes his malice,
Daring ado . . .
So that all men shall honour him after
And his laud beyond them remain 'mid the English,
Aye, for ever, a lasting life's-blast,
Delight mid the doughty.
Days little durable,
And all arrogance of earthen riches,
There come now no kings nor Cæsars
Nor gold-giving lords like those gone.
Howe'er in mirth most magnified,
Whoe'er lived in life most lordliest,
Drear all this excellence, delights undurable!
Waneth the watch, but the world holdeth.
Tomb hideth trouble. The blade is layed low.
Earthly glory ageth and seareth.
No man at all going the earth's gait,
But age fares against him, his face paleth,
Grey-haired he groaneth, knows gone companions,
Lordly men are to earth o'ergiven,
Nor may he then the flesh-cover, whose life ceaseth,
Nor eat the sweet nor feel the sorry,
Nor stir hand nor think in mid heart,
And though he strew the grave with gold,
His born brothers, their buried bodies
Be an unlikely treasure hoard.

Rupert Brooke

THE SOLDIER

If I should die, think only this of me:
    That there's some corner of a foreign field
That is for ever England. There shall be
    In that rich earth a richer dust concealed;
A dust whom England bore, shaped, made aware,
    Gave, once, her flowers to love, her ways to roam;
A body of England's, breathing English air,
    Washed by the rivers, blest by suns of home.

And think, this heart, all evil shed away,
    A pulse in the eternal mind, no less
        Gives somewhere back the thoughts by England
           given;
Her sights and sounds; dreams happy as her day;
    And laughter, learnt of friends; and gentleness,
        In hearts at peace, under an English heaven.

Robert E. Howard

A SONG OF THE NAKED LANDS

You lolled in gardens where breezes fanned
    The blossom's shivering shard;
But we were bred in a naked land
    Where life was bitter hard.

You raped the grapes of their purple soul
    For your wine cups brimming high;
We stooped to the dregs of the muddy hole
    That was bitter with alkali.

And you grew flabby and round of limb,
    Short of nerve and breath;

But we grew rugged and lean and grim
    In our naked grip with Death.

Silk was too harsh for your dainty skin,
    Red wine too poor for your drought;
We hunted the holes that the rain stood in,
    And stripped the wolf for our clout.

Round were your bellies, soft your hand,
    Soft with the fat of earth;
Yours was the wealth of a smiling land,
    Ours the desert's dearth.

You sang beneath the locust tree,
    Forgetful of hunger and hate:
"It has always been, it will always be!" –
    Even then we were at your gate.

You lolled by fountain and golden hall
    Until that frenzied morn
When we burst the gates and breached the wall
    And cut you down like corn.

We reaped the yield and we plowed the field
    With red and dripping shares,
And you could not fight and you could not run,
    You could only die like hares.

Grim was the barter, red the trade,
    With dripping swords for coins,
And your women screamed in the trampled sand
    With bruised and bleeding loins.

Skilled was the brain and skilled the hand
    That shaped the stubborn stone,
But the brain spilled on the bloody sand
    When iron split the bone.

The hand that traced the gilded frieze,
    That scrolled the written page,
It could not turn the driven steel,

Backed by the primal rage.

Of what avail the harp and lute,
  Gemmed girdle and purple cloak,
When the dripping axe was smiting home
  In the flame and the blinding smoke?

Blood smeared your satin and silk and lace.
  You heard your children moan,
And you elders howled in the market place
  Where we stripped them skin from bone.

And where your bearded judges sat
  And bade men live or die,
A naked slayer roared and waved
  A bloody scalp on high.

Over the ruins arched and spired
  The billowing smoke cloud waves;
And you who lived when the sword was tired,
  You live but as our slaves.

Our hard hands clutch your golden cups,
  Our rough feet crush your flowers;
We stable our horses in your halls,
  And all your wealth is ours.

We have doffed our wolfskin clouts for silks,
  We wear them clumsily.
Our eyes are bleak, our beards unshorn,
  Our matted locks stream free.

But our sons will trim their beards and hair,
  Don cloaks of crimson hue;
They will take your daughters to their beds,
  Till they grow soft as you.

They will trade their freedom for harps and lutes,
  Discard the bow and the dart;
They will build a prison of satin and gold,
  And call it Culture and Art.

They will lie in the lap of a smiling land,
    Till its rusts unman and rot them,
And they scorn their blood, and the calloused hand,
    And the fathers who begot them.

But our brothers still dwell in the sun-seared waste
    And their sons are hard and lank;
They will hunt the wolf-pack that we chased,
    And drink the water we.

The hungers we knew they too will know,
    The scars of fangs and of briars;
In the rocks where they crouch when the sandstorms blow
    They will find the marks of our fires.

They will know the hungers that once we had,
    While the stream of centuries runs,
Till they burst from the desert, hunger-mad,
    To slaughter our slothful sons.

www.ingramcontent.com/pod-product-compliance
Lightning Source LLC
Chambersburg PA
CBHW020134130526
44590CB00039B/159